JOHN WESLEY AND MODERN RELIGION

JOHN WESLEY
AND
MODERN RELIGION

By

UMPHREY LEE, Ph.D., D.D.

COKESBURY PRESS

NASHVILLE

SET UP, ELECTROTYPED, PRINTED, AND BOUND
BY THE PARTHENON PRESS AT NASHVILLE
TENNESSEE, UNITED STATES OF AMERICA

C

To

UMPHREY LEE, JR.

WITH THE HOPE THAT HE WILL
GROW UP A LOVER OF BOOKS

PREFACE

THE following study of Wesley's religion and theology is offered both as a contribution to the history of modern Christianity and as an evaluation of Wesley's place in present-day religion. It is the author's conviction that the traditional conception of Wesley's experience and thought is in many ways misleading, and that a truer picture may now be presented by use of the richer materials available to the student. These materials concern not only Wesley but also the life and thought of his century; and this volume is an attempt to depict Wesley in the light of his century instead of in the light of nineteenth-century Methodism or of nineteenth-century ideas of the eighteenth century. The notes give not only authority for quotations and statements but also try to indicate some of the literature on the subject.

I am under obligation to many friends who have read parts or all of the manuscript and have helped with their criticism. Among these I must mention Professors N. C. McPherson, Jr., and Robert W. Goodloe of Southern Methodist University. Professor John H. McGinnis of the same institution has wasted no little time with me in discussions of the eighteenth century and the Romantic Movement. It is not his fault if I am yet far from a correct understanding of the dominant trends of the period. The publishers' readers have also helped with pertinent criticisms; and I am under obligation to the publishers themselves and to Mr. Lovick Pierce, in particular, for many courtesies. My wife has helped, not only with the proof-reading and other drudgery, but throughout the preparation of the manuscript.

Permission has been granted by the Epworth Press for quotations from the Standard Edition of the *Journal of John Wesley,* edited by Nehemiah Curnock; the Standard Edition of the *Letters of John Wesley,* edited by John Telford; and also the Standard Edition of *John Wesley's Sermons,* annotated by Dr. E. H. Sugden. The Abingdon Press, New York, are the American agents for these publications and have also given consent to their use in this volume.

U. L.

TABLE OF CONTENTS

Contents

Fall; original sin; Wesley's psychology; restoration of man. Preventing grace. Wesley and Calvinism. Wesley's association of Calvinism with deterministic physics and psychology. Authority in religion: the Bible; the Ante-Nicene Fathers; Reason; Christian experience. The meaning of Christian experience; evidential value; guidance; the experience of others.

Wesley on orthodoxy. A psychological analysis of salvation. The new birth. Instantaneous conversion. "An irreconcilable variability." "Realization" of the love of God. Origins of Wesley's doctrine of faith. Meaning of faith; sources of definition; justifying faith; faith as intuitive knowledge. Assurance; some Christians may not have it. Religion as love; Easter and Good Friday. Outward obedience a substantial part of religion. Salvation by grace. Faith and works. Development of doctrine. Wesley on Luther. Present and final salvation. The *Minutes* of 1770: controversy over them; Fletcher's interpretation. Wesley on faith and works. Union of Catholic and Protestant doctrines.

Perfectibility in the eighteenth century. Relation of Wesley's doctrine of perfection to his experience. Origins and development of his doctrine. What changes were made after 1738. Confusion of conversion and perfection. Original sin and perfection. Sanctification both gradual and instantaneous. Faith. Grace and holiness. Perfection both goal and attainment. Wesley's ethical interest. Religion and morality. Perfection sought in ordinary life. Economic morality.

The distinctive vocation of the Christian man. Perfection a doctrine of development.

Contents

CHAPTER I

THE INTERPRETATION OF WESLEY

In the Great East Window of Liverpool Cathedral, Protestantism's "modern" cathedral *par excellence,* one panel, as is meet in a Te Deum window, is devoted to the Goodly Fellowship of the Prophets. Isaiah and Elijah are there, as are also St. Bernard and St. Francis; and the prophetic succession is continued in Cranmer, Butler, Keble, and Westcott. In this latter group, standing a little back as if doubtful whether the Anglican authorities really meant to include him, is John Wesley, father of the people called Methodists. The visitor in Liverpool who recalls Wesley's struggle with the Church of England in the eighteenth century may ask why the Establishment has now put Wesley among the prophets. Cynics will quote old lines about the cities which claimed Homer dead, but more thoughtful men will take the appraisal seriously and will seek the reasons therefor both in Wesley and in his times.

An obvious reason for setting Wesley in "the goodly fellowship" is that his is one of the most numerous and influential movements inaugurated in Protestantism in modern times. One must, of course, remember, in making such a statement, that "modern times" do not really go back beyond the seventeenth century. While history must not be divided into neat chronological bundles, it was from the seventeenth century

1

that the western world began to manifest the characteristics of the present era. In order to make clear the argument of this book, it will be well to look at this statement a little more closely.

It was in the latter seventeenth century that Western men began to adopt rather generally a modern conception of the physical universe. More and more men began to think of the universe as a mechanism, like Paley's watch, determined by a few simple laws which Newton had discovered. And this mechanical ordering was gradually conceived as characteristic of all things, of all beings, from the lowest organism to the man capable of appreciating the excellencies of the British constitution. It was in this period, too, that the Western world began to take on the appearance which it bears to-day. In the latter eighteenth and in the nineteenth centuries, in England, and later on the Continent and in North America, industrial cities sprang up and the now familiar ugliness of factories began to smirch the landscape. The whole fabric of an industrial civilization was rising. But there was another change which took place, a change in the world-view. Over against the mechanistic theories which characterized the new sciences arose a view which is known as "romantic." The romanticists despised, or pretended to despise, the scientist who would peep and botanize on his mother's grave; they preferred to obtain their knowledge by intuition, communing with daffodils, having intimations of immortality by ruined abbeys. For them the expansive emotions were better than cold reason and denying conscience. And in the face of civilized

2

complexities they exalted the savage, the peasant, and the child.

The point is that the world of science, of the Industrial Revolution, and of the Romantic Movement is the modern world; and John Wesley's life and work lie within the boundaries of this period. That his movement is one of the largest arising in Protestantism in the modern era needs little proof. Statistics of Methodism show this, but they do not tell the whole of Methodist influence. To a large extent, evangelical Christianity has been moved, if not directly by Wesley or Methodism, at least by tendencies which owe much to him. "We are all Methodists now," complains a Protestant Episcopalian expounder of Karl Barth; and for good or evil the fact is undeniable that millions in America and England who care little for the first Methodist have adopted the religious position which is usually associated with his work.

But mere contemporaneousness, although it may explain why Wesley is modern, hardly justifies including him among the prophets. The latter term implies that he had a word for the modern world. And, indeed, the historian has before him the problem of the success of Methodism. Why did Wesley's revival appeal to so large a number of people in the eighteenth and nineteenth centuries? And why did Methodist theology come to be so widely adopted in English-speaking Christendom? These questions can only be answered by a study of the congruities of Methodism and the modern world. That is to say, Methodism cannot be understood merely by a study of its ancestry. Only as the movement is seen in

relation to the temper of the world to which it minis-
tered can the true character of the Wesleyan revival
be discovered. To study Methodism thus is not
simply to sketch in eighteenth-century local color,
as early Renaissance painters used to put in moun-
tains or Greek columns. The most profitable method
is to set Wesley's experience and theology against the
background of great modern movements, those movements which were to give character to the present era.

In no sense does such an approach ignore the essential *religiousness* of Wesley. The student of
Wesley must never forget that Wesley believed in
God, that he trusted in Christ. To him Jesus of
Nazareth was not an incidental figure in the world's
cultural history, but the center of all life, the ground
of all human hope. Nor can Wesley be understood
by those who are ignorant of the Christian tradition.
To know him one must understand the rock from
which he was hewn. But no man can merely revive
a former theology or a past religious movement; and
Wesley did not simply reproduce first-century or
sixteenth-century Christianity. His movement, like
every other, spoke the language of its age and was
influenced by the movements of the time.

Some students have found an affinity between
Wesley's methods and thought and the nascent
scientific ideas of the eighteenth century. It is true
that, in the formulation of his doctrines, in the gath-
ering of data concerning religious experience, Wesley
used a method which approximates that which is
now called experimental. It would be correct to
speak of the empirical character of Methodism, but

scientific is not the word. If one wishes to use the word to indicate the practical-mindedness of eighteenth-century Englishmen, which prepared the way for later scientific advance and for the utilitarianism which furthered mechanical methods and mechanical views, then Wesley, too, may be called scientific. But further than this one may not go.

Some social historians have explained Methodism, to their own satisfaction, as a by-product of the Industrial Revolution.[1] The latter movement with the congestion of population in cities, unsanitary and oppressive conditions in factories, the break-up of the supposedly idyllic cottage manufactories, brought with it misery and unrest. Methodism, so runs the theory, was an emotional escape for the poor, who were caught in a maelstrom which quickly engulfed them; in Lecky's famous phrase, the religious revival saved England from a revolution. To this theory, however, there are some very pertinent objections.

In the first place, there was no such sudden break between the old order and the new as some historians have imagined. So slowly, indeed, did the changes come about that some writers now object to the phrase, "The Industrial Revolution," since "a revolution which continued for 150 years and had been in preparation for another 150 years may well seem to need a new label."[2] There was, it is true, a quickened tempo after 1750. The first changes were in the newer industries of iron, cotton, and pottery; but the factory system developed slowly. And the theory that Methodism was a by-product of the Industrial Revolution, an opiate for an oppressed proletariat,

5

breaks down in collision with the calendar. Historians have sometimes been overly fond of chronology, but one can hardly dispense with it altogether. The facts are that most of the inventions which made modern industrial development possible came after 1763, when Wesley had been carrying on his religious revival for nearly a quarter of a century; and Watt's steam engine came into use, even in a very restricted way, only a few years before Wesley's death.

In the second place, recent study of social conditions in the eighteenth century have led to some revisions of former estimates. It would seem that writers have been inclined to reconstruct conditions in the eighteenth century in accordance with late nineteenth-century and twentieth-century social theories. Poor housing conditions, child labor, long hours of work were undoubtedly evils of the factory system; but these existed before the factories came. And there is now evidence that the protests against them which arose during the period when the factories were developing were signs of an awakening social conscience rather than of entirely new miseries. In other words, Methodism did not arise as an opiate for people suffering from the evils of the new industrial system; and therefore, the theory that Wesley succeeded in sidetracking the emotions of an oppressed proletariat so that they fixed their minds on heaven rather than on justice here, thus averting a revolution, is no longer tenable. The conditions which produced the French Revolution did not exist to the same degree in eighteenth-century England. It is probable that

6

the latter country would not have had a "French Revolution," even if Wesley had never lived.[3]

True, Methodism flourished mainly in the districts which were to be the centers of England's new industrial society. The triangle formed by London, Bristol, and Newcastle-upon-Tyne contains the major territory of the Wesleyan movement in the eighteenth century. But whatever escape Methodists found in the revival was an escape from the untoward conditions of England before power-industry had transformed the country. The exact relations of Wesleyanism and the Industrial Revolution will not be determined until there have been completed adequate biographical studies of the leaders and workers in those movements in the nineteenth century.

It has become almost a commonplace to relate Wesley to the third of the modern movements mentioned—that is, Romanticism. Wesley, it is said, inaugurated a Romantic Movement in Religion. It has become the more common to speak of such a relationship since "Romantic Movement" has been extended to denote a widespread change in standards of value in many areas. "The French Revolution and Napoleon, Shelley and Byron and Beethoven, and the new Houses of Parliament"[4] have all been crowded together as different manifestations of Romanticism. Such verbal hospitality is a bit disconcerting. And it is the more disconcerting when one considers that no two writers seem to agree as to what Romanticism is. To some, Romanticism is a term applicable only in literary or æsthetic theory, designating perhaps a preference for the predominance of imagination over reason and the sense of fact.[5] To others the word stands for one of the fundamental characteristics of humanity, the second member of the series: "Head and Heart; Intellect and Feeling; Reserve and Passion; Selection and Sympathy; Restraint and Enthusiasm; Obedience and Freedom." [6] Yet others conceive Romanticism as the submergence of man in Nature, an emotional naturalism.[7] And so the list runs on: the assertion of the self; a return to the Middle Ages; escape from reality.

If it is difficult to arrive at a definition of Romanticism which will satisfy anyone but the author of the definition, it is nevertheless beyond doubt that the close of the eighteenth and the beginning of the nineteenth centuries saw a change in the world view; and this change has affected wide areas of life down to our own times. It is possible, without insisting upon any definition of Romanticism, to indicate certain aspects of this shift in the world view.

In part, this change was a revolt against the narrow intellectualism of the eighteenth century. While recognizing definite limits of the human understanding, it was assumed that man might by reasoning find out all that could be known of the universe and of life. Professor Whitehead speaks of "the jaunty assurance" of Pope when he writes of the universe as "a mighty maze! but not without a plan." [8] And whether one wrote a poem, planned a garden, or directed a life, reason was the guide. The young Wesley spoke the language of his time when he wrote his mother that faith is "an assent to any truth upon rational grounds." Against this hegemony of the reason certain writers revolted in the name of forgotten aspects of human nature. The heart also has its reasons.

> Thanks to the human heart by which we live,
> Thanks to its tenderness, its joys, and fears,
> To me the meanest flower that blows can give
> Thoughts that do often lie too deep for tears.

And intuition may be the road to deeper reality, to "something interfused."

The "return to Nature," about which so much has been said in discussions of English Romanticism, was not merely preference for landscapes. Neither was it altogether a submergence of man in the flux of nature. In part, at least, this preoccupation with nature, with daffodils and yellow primroses, was an assertion of man's place in the universe as that of more than an observer of the Universal Machine. Modern critics of Newtonian science, with full recognition of the epochal importance of its conceptions, nevertheless point out that it dwarfed man himself. "Wherever was taught as truth the universal formula of gravitation, there was also insinuated as a nimbus of surrounding belief that man is but the puny and local spectator, nay, irrelevant product of an infinite, self-moving engine, which existed eternally before him and will be eternally after him, enshrining the rigour of mathematical relationships while banishing into impotence all ideal imaginations. . . ." [9] The romantic poet's impatience with those who would peep and botanize sprang from a conviction that there are other avenues to truth than analysis and another role for man to play than that of an admiring timekeeper to mechanical Nature.

9

Opposed to the conception of Nature as a complicated mechanism was the idea of Nature as the simple, the spontaneous. Genius is the gift of Nature as grace is the gift of God. This view was carried to the point of idealizing the savage, the peasant and the child. Most is to be expected from those who are unspoiled by the sophistications of the town and its culture; mute, inglorious Miltons are possibly buried in every country churchyard. South Sea Islanders were actually lionized in London society in the middle of the eighteenth century. The "noble savage" was thought of as living in original purity, uncontaminated by civilization. This was "Nature's Simple Plan." [10]

It was to be expected that those who sought for simplicity and spontaneity as opposed to the mechanical in life and thought should look back to more unsophisticated and, presumably, nobler times. Somewhere in the past men had been purer, living nearer to the fountains of unsullied Nature. In England, the cult of the Middle Ages was partly admiration for a period which was thought to have been less hampered by the claims of reason and to have shown the exuberance of unfettered Nature.

For many in Western Europe, thought, belief, the arts, political life, all had been carried on under the principle that "excellence consists in conformity to a standard conceived as universal, static, uncomplicated, uniform for every rational being." [11] The revolt against such a conception was not necessarily a revolt against authority, but against too much regulation. The riches of individual life and growth must

10

not be crushed by mechanical control. It is in this sense that there was a preference for those tendencies which emphasized "a richly diversified development of individuals and groups rather than a mathematical uniformity, and, most significant of all, the genesis and growth of things rather than their mechanical uniformity." [12]

A movement which affected so many areas of life could not leave religion unaffected. It is interesting to note the ways in which historians have found traces of what is called Romanticism in religion. One writer sees its effects in heightened traditionalism. "Alike in art, in literature, in philosophy, in religion, a single impulse had revealed itself. It was the impulse to look backward rather than forward, reverence for the primitive, distrust of 'march of intellect' . . . . a suspicion that science was about to overstep its limits to the eternal undoing of the human spirit, a passionate return to the natural instincts against the artificial contrivances of an arrogant Reason." [13] An earlier writer interpreted fondness of especially Continental Romanticists for the Middle Ages as a preference for the medieval "combination of depth of feeling with rudeness of manners," its myths, tales, legends, enthusiasms, and adventures.[14] Another theologian classes as romantic the theologies which define religion as essentially feeling, which presuppose a religious sense, or emphasize "experience." [15]

There have been only tentative efforts to illuminate the exact relations of Methodism and the changed world view; but the likenesses have been often emphasized. "Methodism," wrote the late President

11

McGiffert, "put an end to the barren rationalism of the eighteenth century; it substituted immediate experience for reasoned demonstration, direct knowledge for indirect in the religious sphere . . . . it brought the feelings once more into repute, and aided the nineteenth-century reaction against the narrow intellectualism of the eighteenth; it gave a new meaning and an independent value to religion; it promoted individualism and emancipation from the bondage of ecclesiasticism." [16]

But President McGiffert's words are the guarded words of a trained scholar. He recognizes the ways in which Methodism "aided" and "promoted" certain tendencies; he does not say that these were Wesley's only interests or intentions. Yet this is precisely what has often been implied by Methodist and non-Methodist scholars alike. To say that Wesley was a romanticist in that he "emphasized the emotional rather than the rational side of human nature, a richly diversified development of the individual and groups rather than a mathematical uniformity, and, most significant of all, the genesis and growth of things rather than their mechanical ordering" is one thing. To say that Wesley depreciated the rational side of human nature; that he cared nothing for uniformity, for rules (saving, of course, moral ones), or for institutions; that he preached a religion of feeling, would be quite another thing.

It is instructive to look for a moment at the traditional picture of Wesley's experience and theology. According to this view he was brought up a High Churchman, devoted to form and order, accepting

12

uniformity in doctrine and discipline as necessary to salvation. In this faith he lived a blameless but unfruitful life at Oxford and in America. But learning from the Moravians the Lutheran—or was it the Calvinist?—doctrine of justification by faith, he struggled with a sense of sin, of unbelief, until he was converted in a little meeting in Aldersgate Street, May 24, 1738. From this time, the spiritual birthday both of Wesley and of Methodism, he preached a radically changed message. Justification is by faith only; man must be converted, and that instantaneously; he must know his sins to be forgiven by the witness of the Holy Spirit; he must be sanctified by a work of grace, also receivable instantaneously by faith. Experience is the great word, for that only is religion which one feels. An emotional, individualistic religion required a voluntary Church composed of converted members. To promote this, Wesley and his helpers organized missions and societies and, finally, a Church. With his conversion Wesley's High Churchmanship disappeared, and a religion of individual experience, colored strongly by emotion, took its place. Methodism became an English Pietism; and individualism, feeling, experience, freedom from ecclesiasticism became the marks of the new movement. Sometimes to this is added the revival of orthodoxy of the Reformation type. Signs of a faith other than this in Wesley's later years are laid to the infirmities of old age. His true message was that of 1738, the year of the conversion.

One hastens to add that this view has, in parts, been challenged by many Methodist and non-Methodist scholars; but it has been so widely held both by apologists and by attackers of Methodism that it may well be called the traditional interpretation. But one cannot avoid the question: "How far does this truly represent Wesley himself?" That it has often been the message of Methodists cannot be denied; and many students of the movement have assumed that Methodism must have represented the teachings of the founder. In America, the exigency of controversy drove the defenders of American Methodism to identify the religion preached during the early nineteenth century with the doctrine of Wesley himself. In England, the necessity of defending a lay ministry, not only against the attacks of the Establishment but also against the criticisms of some of the Methodists themselves, produced a similar appeal to the principles of the "venerable Father." And tradition is strong. Once believed that Methodism is a romantic religious movement deriving its principal doctrines from the "faith-religion" of Luther and Calvin, by way of Moravianism, it is difficult to persuade even historians to revise their opinions. "Look," they say, "at Methodists of the nineteenth century, and see if they are not wearing the many-colored cloak which their father gave them."

He would be a bold man, indeed, who would claim that the followers of Wesley completely misunderstood him. The tradition of Wesley must be allowed to stand as evidence, and good evidence, as to the way in which the nineteenth century and many in the eighteenth century understood him. But it is also fallacious to assume that any institution necessarily

14

reproduces with accuracy the intentions of its founder. Certainly most historians do not now believe that
the Franciscan Order faithfully reproduced the ideals
of St. Francis. And Methodism in nineteenth-century England, to say nothing of Methodism on the
American frontier, faced conditions, participated in
a time-spirit, which must have colored its conception
of religion.

In the case of Wesley another consideration must
be given weight. It is unnecessary, at this late date,
to insist upon his keenness of mind or upon the variety
of his interests. But Wesley was a genius, and sometimes a genius is not best understood by those who
stand closest to him. Frequently it requires the perspective of time for a right appreciation of a great
man's mind. That Wesley was not entirely understood in his own day is evidenced by the opposition
he met from some who, all agree now, were both wise
and good. And even Wesley's closest friends disagreed in their interpretations of his motives. Dr.
John Whitehead, who preached Wesley's funeral
sermon, was sure that Wesley's ordinations were the
acts of an old man overborne by the importunities of
his preachers. Yet the majority of Methodist preachers were equally positive that Wesley deliberately
sought to set up, both in England and America, a
Methodist Church. That such disagreements occurred can be no surprise to those who remember that
Wesley's mind had been open, for more than three-
score years, to more diverse influences than that of
any other Churchman in England. He had, during
a long life, conversed with all sorts and conditions of

men. He had watched men and movements in far-away America, in the Germanies, and in every nook and corner of the British Isles. Nurtured in the traditions of the Church of England, he had associated with some of the leading Nonjurors. He was, for a Church of England clergyman, more than usually well read in the history and doctrine of the Catholic branch of Christianity. And books in almost every conceivable field of learning, so far as they were available to an eighteenth-century man in Western Europe, are noted in his remarkable *Journal*. Of the modern languages, he read German, French, Spanish, and Italian. This is not to claim great scholarship for Wesley, but a wide mental horizon. It would be remarkable if a mind so virile should not have taken on a breadth and depth not easily cramped into simple doctrinal formulas. And it would be still more remarkable if men of less experience, however excellent they may have been in other ways, should have grasped Wesley's thought in all its variety and richness.

It should be possible, therefore, after the lapse of almost one hundred and fifty years, to assess more accurately the traditional picture. In considering Wesley's religion and theology, it is tempting to discuss how far he was a romantic; but the word is too indefinite. It is better to ask how far Wesley was part of the modern movement—call it what one will—toward a preference for emotion, individualism, diversity, and growth, over reason, uniformity, and regulation. This is not merely an academic question. To-day both the defenders of tradition and their

16

opponents are uniting in attack upon what has been called "modern religion." Feeling, they say, has been too much exalted; subjectivism has been reduced to an absurdity; freedom has become anarchy. As in politics, in economics, and in literature, so also in religion there is a demand for reassessment. A re-examination of Wesley's religion and theology is necessary, therefore, for anyone who would hazard an opinion as to his importance for contemporary religion. Only by such a re-examination can one hope to determine whether John Wesley is a stained-glass saint or a living prophet.

CHAPTER II

RELIGION IN EIGHTEENTH-CENTURY ENGLAND

It has been the fashion to paint the religious life of eighteenth-century England in the darkest colors. "Never had religion seemed at so low an ebb," is Green's often-quoted judgment; and endless variations on this theme have included pictures of lifeless churches, worldly clergy, skeptical universities, unchurched masses, political corruption, drunken and debauched areas in the great cities. These accounts are accurate; but they do not tell the whole truth. Dr. Sykes has very pertinently insisted that the Church of England in the eighteenth century must be seen from the vantage point of the seventeenth century. That century bequeathed to its successor a depleted ministry and a bigoted partisanship which ill fitted the Church to deal with the Deists and with practical problems which came with the new century. Seen in the light of the preceding century, the Georgian period "can claim a generous measure of praise for the good which it accomplished, and a more equitable degree of censure for the failings which were to no small extent the result of its peculiar situation." [1]

There is, of course, room for criticism enough. The Church had been subordinated both to nationalistic and to commercial interests. Among the intellectual classes skepticism was the mode, and it has been often remarked that in these circles the Church was smiled at by those who did not deride it. The desire for peace and distrust of everything which might disturb the *status quo* made for sterility in religion, so that there is some truth in the statement that "the typical mental attitude in the early eighteenth century was that of acceptance, as distinct from that of wonder, curiosity or challenge." [2]

But it is easy to exaggerate the darker pigments. If the Church tended to a latitudinarian spirit, it was not insensible to the newer currents of thought and was preparing the way for a fuller appreciation of the new knowledge. If speculative theology suffered, the ethical interests of religion were conserved. Indeed, the accusation of insensibility and of spiritual deadness is too often made from a partial survey of the facts. The literature to which appeal is made is the literature of the town and of a certain class in the town. Just as Professor Trevelyan remarks that a true picture of Britain in the eighteenth century must take account of Clive, of Wolfe, of Captain Cook, of Wesley and of James Watt,[3] so one might insist that a picture of English religion of the period must include Isaac Watts, Philip Doddridge, William Law, Bishop Butler, Bishop Berkeley, and many a country parson as well.

Certainly the best-advertised group of the first half of the century were the Deists. In general, they insisted upon natural religion as distinguished from revealed. God has given in nature what can be discovered by man's reason, and there is no need that he should superadd anything. "Must not their reason," asks Tindal, "antecedently to all external revelation, afford certain tests to distinguish between truth and falsehood, in all religious matters?" And he added: "If it be evident that we cannot discern whether any instituted religion contains everything worthy and nothing unworthy of a divine original; except we can antecedently by our reason discern what is or is not worthy of having God for its author; it necessarily follows, that natural and revealed religion cannot differ." [4] Since natural and revealed religion must be the same, there is no need for a revelation to be added to natural religion discoverable by reason.

And this natural religion is understandable as well as discoverable by all; it is religion reduced to the simplest terms. While revealed religion is for those to whom it is revealed, natural religion is for everybody; and while revealed religion is not the same for all, since those who were living at the time of the revelation have the most certainty, for example, natural religion is the same everywhere for everyone. In general, the Deists reduced the tenets of natural religion to three: the existence of God, of a moral law, and the certainty of future rewards and punishments.

In a penetrating study of the parallel between Deism and Classicism, Professor Lovejoy has shown how the theory of the Deists agrees with that of the neo-classical critics of the Augustan Age. Both are expressions of the world view which seeks excellence in uniformity. "The object of the effort of the religious, moral, or social reformer, as of the literary critic, is therefore to standardize men and their beliefs, their likings, their activities, and their institutions." [5] And Professor Lovejoy indicates the various other characteristics of Deism which follow from this fundamental principle. The individual is free to depend upon his own reason, but this reason, at bottom, is identical with that of other men; or, men may depend upon "common sense," that is, upon the sense common to all men. Such an attitude would, of course, be opposed to originality, to any considerable emphasis upon individual differences. Moreover, what is abstruse or so involved as to be obscure to the majority is either unimportant or untrue.

Deism did not penetrate far beyond the intellectual class. The controversy over it was a battle of books. But a very similar attitude was widespread among the religious of the early eighteenth century. Social conditions called for moderation; the Revolution left both government and trade on uneasy footings, and fanaticism of all kinds was suspected. In this atmosphere flourished a religion of moderation, emphasizing ethical requirements, subordinating all abstruse speculation, and fearing excessive zeal for doctrine or Church. Social good was the test of religion, and the common path was the way:

> For forms of government, let fools contest;
> Whate'er is best administered is best;
> For modes of faith, let graceless zealots fight;
> His can't be wrong, whose life is in the right:
> In faith and hope the world will disagree,
> But all mankind's concern is Charity:
> All must be false that thwart this one great end;
> And all of God, that bless mankind, or mend.

21

Or again:

> Take nature's path, and mad opinion's leave;
> All states can reach it, and all heads conceive;
> Obvious her goods, in no extreme they dwell;
> There needs but thinking right, and meaning well.

Such an attitude was easy for the religiously indifferent of the day. The young clergyman was warned not to fly too high; he was to essay a more modest path, to flee the "pride" of which the Augustan Age was so afraid. But earnest men might also hold such an ideal. Robert Dodsley's *Art of Preaching*, published perhaps about 1738,[6] may be taken as illustrative of this temper so prevalent throughout the greater part of the century among the Established clergy, and also among most of the Dissenters. The very fact that Dodsley's poem on preaching is "in imitation of Horace's Art of Poetry" testifies to the moderating, regulatory mood in which it is written.

The preacher, according to Dodsley, must avoid extremes of orthodoxy or heterodoxy:

> Most Preachers err (except the wiser few)
> Thinking establish'd Doctrines, therefore true:
> Others, too fond of Novelty and Schemes,
> Amuse the World with airy idle Dreams:
> Thus too much Faith, or too presuming Wit,
> Are Rocks where Bigots, or Free-thinkers split.

He must now be guided by something other than the authority which once determined man's beliefs:

> Reason now reigns, and by her Aid we hope
> Truth may revive, and sickening Error droop:
> She the sole Judge, the Rule, the gracious Light
> Kind Heaven has lent to guide our Minds aright.

Of the subjects which grace the pulpit, Dodsley specifies "Truth, moral Virtue, Piety, and Peace"; and, while men have a right to their opinions, yet "sacred ought to be the publick Peace as Private Liberty."

It is necessary that the preacher feel what he preaches, and he should take care to preach virtue with charm and denounce vice with severity. Nevertheless, adds the poet with a sneer:

> With Zeal defend whate'er the Church believes,
> If you expect to thrive, or wear Lawn Sleeves.

To avoid obscure doctrines, and to preach virtue by simple rules, is the preacher's great business. There is a broad tolerance in Dodsley, albeit the tolerance of evasion. "Such Points as these be far too deep for Man."

> Sure 'tis much nobler, and more like Divine,
> T' enlarge the Path to Heaven, than to confine;
> Insist Alone on useful Points, or plain;
> And know, God cannot hate a virtuous Man.
>
> 'Tis yours in useful Sermons to explain,
> Both what we owe to God, and what to Man.
> 'Tis yours the Charms of Liberty to paint,
> His Country's Love in every Breast to plant:
> Yours every social Virtue to improve,
> Justice, Forbearance, Charity, and Love;
> Yours too the private Virtues to augment,
> Of Prudence, Temperance, Modesty, Content.

Reason, morality, public and private peace, the public good, moderation, these are the aims of the preacher. Religion is a restraining, regulatory, mitigating power, designed to make man live according to reason and to preserve social peace and happiness.

But while the *via media* of moral and rational religion was sufficient for some, others sought more earnestly for holiness of heart and life. Purposely, this survey is confined to the earlier part of the century, that it may be evident what streams were freshening English religious life before the Evangelical Revival. And no survey can neglect the moral and spiritual earnestness illustrated by the Religious Societies.[7] In the not very fruitfully religious period of the Restoration, Dr. Anthony Horneck organized a group of young men in London into a religious society, which met once a week to promote holiness of life. This society was composed of members of the Church of England, and they used no prayers but those of the Church, carefully avoiding, since laymen took part, prayers reserved for the minister. The special rules to be observed contained practical admonitions: to love one another; not to revile those who reviled them; to keep close to the Church of England; to pray, if possible, seven times a day; to examine themselves every night.

The high aims of societies regulated in a similar fashion may be seen from the preamble to the rules of the society at St. Giles' Cripplegate. This sets forth, "That the Sole design of this Society, being to promote Real Holiness of heart and Life; it is Absolutely necessary, that the Persons who enter into it do seriously Resolve to apply themselves in good earnest to all means proper to make them wise unto Salvation." [8] This society, like the others, sought to encourage Bible reading, prayer, frequent communion, and daily examination of one's life.

In the societies, members were to avoid discussing politics or worldly matters, and each was to watch over the other; "and if they find any that walks disorderly let him Admonish him privately by himself and if it prove ineffectual let him be reprov'd before one or two more and if this prove ineffectual also, let him be reprov'd before the whole Society and if this reclaims him not let him be Excluded." [9] In short, the societies were to exercise disciplinary care over their members, as they were to encourage each to enter upon a course of guidance and discipline for himself. From the provision that apprentices were not to be received, and from the lists of members of the society at St. Giles', it appears that the membership was among the trades and artisan classes: joiners, leather dressers, tailors, perukemakers, buttonmakers, needlemakers, schoolmasters, are among those listed. [10]

During the years following and well on into the eighteenth century, these societies developed and grew until they had no little effect. They later enjoined tenderness toward Dissenters, but remained Church of England societies, emphasizing attendance upon Church services and frequent communion. In addition, the members were bound to works of charity and to the forwarding of educational work—that is, catechizing—among the poor.

The societies met with opposition from those who saw them as encroachments upon the ministerial office and duties, and they incurred suspicion as political organizations. Moreover, the organization of the Society for the Reformation of Manners, which busied itself with prosecution of offenders against public decency, profane swearers, and the like, gave rise to contention about informers and spying; and the religious societies suffered from public confusion of the two. But the societies left a permanent impression upon the religious life of England. Canon Overton says that the Society for the Promotion of Christian Knowledge was a "daughter of the Religious Societies," and that the Society for the Propagation of the Gospel in Foreign Parts was an offshoot of the S. P. C. K.[11] Contemporaries observed an increase of attendance at the Lord's Supper and at the services of the Church.

That books of devotion were popular in this period is evidenced by the number of editions published and by references to them in contemporary writings. Mr. Wickham Legg thinks that *The Whole Duty of Man* is possibly the most popular book of devotion that England has ever known.[12] But between 1678 and 1764 fifty-two editions appeared of *A Week's Preparation towards a Worthy Receiving of the Lord's Supper,* while Robert Nelson's *Companion for the Festivals and Fasts of the Church of England* went through so many editions that Boswell guessed it had the greatest sale of any work ever printed in English except the Bible. Taylor's *Holy Living and Dying* and à Kempis' *Imitation of Christ* were also popular, as were William Law's books, especially his *A Serious Call to a Devout and Holy Life.*

These books fall into two classes, the ones intended as aids to devotion in connection with the rites of the Church and those aiming at personal discipline, the regulation of one's inner and outer life. It was from Jeremy Taylor that Wesley got the essence of the rules and regulations which he gave to the Holy Club at Oxford and to his helpers in the later Methodist Societies, and it was from Taylor that Wesley took the method of self-examination which appears in his Diary.[13] Regulation of devotion and of life, the "Imitation of Christ," was part of the religious life of many in the early eighteenth century, as the books of devotion and self-discipline attest.

Among those to whom such books appealed were many of the High Church party. It is true that the party in the days of Queen Anne is now remembered more for political quarrels than for private devotion; but the lapse of years should make possible a more unbiased appraisal of High Church virtues and weaknesses. High Church was sometimes an epithet for any who showed unusual devotion to the Church. According to a pamphlet published in 1705, possibly written by John Norris, anyone who appears "to have a hearty zeal for the Church, is at all strict in the observation of its rules and orders, expresses any concern for its safety, or is found to be in those measures which are necessary for its security and preservation" is likely to be called a High Churchman.[14]

But there are attempts at more precise definition. Hallam described the party as distinguished by great pretensions to sacerdotal power both spiritual and temporal, by a repugnance to toleration, and by a firm adherence to the Tory principle in the State.[15] These characteristics must be set against the background of the Commonwealth, when the Church of England was inundated by a tidal wave of Presbyterianism, Independency, and Sectarianism. The good Churchman could not look back with equanimity upon "the late unhappy times when Hell was broke loose" [16]; and a nervous zeal for the Establishment was excited by real and suspected enemies. The persecution of Dissenters was not sufficient, and ministers who had refused to conform to the liturgy, even though they were Churchmen at heart, fell under the suspicion and active persecution of the Church. After the Revolution of 1689, many good men refused to take the oath of allegiance to William and Mary because of a scruple as to the legality of the succession, and these Nonjurors became a party half in and half out of the Church of England. Others who remained loyal to the new sovereigns were suspicious of the bishops who succeeded the deposed prelates, and the reign of Anne saw an unlovely bickering and controversies which threatened more serious trouble.

In 1709, a firebrand of extreme High Church views, Dr. Sacheverell, attacked the Dissenters in scurrilous language and was impeached at the bar of the House of Lords. He was suspended for a time and made a tour of England which turned out to be a triumphal journey. Sacheverell belonged to the group of High Churchmen who were known as "high-flyers," and what he himself defined as a High Churchman must be judged accordingly. The High Churchman, in Dr. Sacheverell's mind, was one who stood for the divine right of episcopacy, for apostolic succession, for the use of liturgy instead of extemporary prayers, for the "primitive Doctrine and Discipline of the Ancient Church." He believed separation from the Church of England to be schism, and therefore held the Dissenters to be in a dangerous state. Moreover, he observed "the traditional customs as well as the written laws of the Church, and he always bowed very low before the Altar and at the name of Jesus." [17]

The more militant High Churchmen were intent upon asserting the independence of the Church from the State, claiming that Convocation stood upon the same high ground of freedom as Parliament. They were suspicious of Dissenters and insistent upon depriving them of such privileges as tolerant Whigs had granted, even plotting to deprive them of educational advantages in their own academies as they had already been excluded from the Universities. There was much talk about ancient observances; the authority of the ecumenical councils and of the early Fathers was exalted; and the practice of the primitive Church held up as the rule and guide of Christianity. On the constitution of the Church and apostolic succession, the High Churchmen seem to have been agreed. Bishop Beveridge (1637-1708), who was highly regarded by the moderate Nonjurors although he had accepted a bishopric under the new regime, was clear in his pronouncements concerning the ministry: "Thus therefore, it is, that the apostolical office hath been handed down from one to another ever since the apostles' days to our time, and so will be to the end of

29

the world, Christ himself being continually present at such imposition of hands; thereby transferring the same Spirit, which he had first breathed into his apostles, upon others successively after them. . . ." [18] Legg quotes from another sermon printed by Episcopal command, which went through four editions. This sermon declares roundly that an ordination to be good and valid requires that the ordainer or ordainers have a power transmitted to him or them "by a continued Succession from Jesus Christ." This, says the preacher, means simply "that none is a lawful Minister, who is not Episcopally ordain'd." [19]

In his poem, "The Parish Priest," [20] Samuel Wesley, Jr., portrays a clergyman who answers to Norris' description but who is also a High Churchman in a sense close to that of the definitions of Hallam and Sacheverell. This parish priest, Samuel Wesley's father-in-law in fact, was zealous to protect the doctrines of his flock.

> Amongst his Corn no Tares neglected spring;
> That free-born Subjects ought to rule their King,
> That Sense and Revelation disagree,
> That Zeal is still at war with Charity;
> That Dust-born Reptiles may their God disown,
> And place their foolish Reason in his throne.
> No Colours false deceiv'd his wary Eye,
> Nor lukewarm Peace, nor Atheist Liberty.
> Scripture and Fathers guide his Footsteps right:
> For Truth is one, but Error infinite.
>
> With Love to Souls, and deepest Learning fraught,
> His Master's Gospel undisguis'd he taught.
> He show'd the Pow'r of Kings, the Mitre's Sway,
> Which Earth can neither give nor take away.

30

. . . .

And God the faithful Sower pleas'd to bless,
And crown'd his Harvest with a vast Success.
While forty Years his heav'nly Doctrine charms,
No single Son forsakes the Church's Arms:
No Romish Wolf around his Fences prowl'd,
Nor Fox Dissenter earth'd within his Fold.

It would be unfair to assume that High Church meant only zeal against popery and dissent. Samuel Wesley's lines concerning the daily life of his father-in-law during his forty years of parish ministry should also be quoted:

He mourn'd with those who Pain or Want endure,
A Guardian Angel to the Sick and Poor;
Where the two best of Charities he join'd,
To cure the Body, and to heal the Mind.

. . . .

Oft as the Year brought back the glorious Day
When Infant Jesus in a Manger lay,
Or when from Death the God triumphant came,
Or when the Holy-Ghost descends in Flame,
Around his Board the welcome Needy sate,
And crowd his Parlour, not besiege his Gate.
T' obey their Word his Children waited near,
And learnt their Saviour's Image to revere.
This Charity perform'd, the wealthier Guest
Was call'd to share his hospitable Feast;
The Poor invited first, his Table grace,
And Riches only held the second Place.

. . . .

Such was the Man by Friends and Foes confest,
Worthy the glorious Name of Parish Priest.

Although High Church was too often a party cry during the age of Queen Anne, one must not be tempted to assess the religious lives and belief of the High Churchmen as those of belligerents only. Indeed, the whole excited period must be judged with more moderation than has often been shown by those concerned to use ancient examples in modern controversies. The historian needs to be admonished, in Professor Trevelyan's words, not "to forget that there was more in the religious sense of the nation than the feuds out of which, incidentally, our political liberties in large part arose." As he points out, the religious life of many families and parishes moved on little concerned with High and Low Church.[21]

On the whole, the tendencies in English religious life thus far described were on the side of uniformity, control, discipline, or of corporate religion. Rationalism tended to repress individual aberrations and to secure belief that was uniform for all rational beings; the religious societies attempted to subdue natural impulses and substitute the restraints of habit and rules; while a high conception of the Church made for a subordination of individual to corporate religion. Nevertheless, there was an individualistic element in rationalism; each man was to use his own reason. The societies promoted individual piety; and there was a high type of personal religion in many who were passionately devoted to the Church and its ministries.

Personal religion, understood as individual attitudes and tempers rather than the performance of outward duties, was emphasized by many in the early eighteenth century. Robert Nelson may be taken as an example of a High Churchman who understood religion to be of the heart. Nelson was a nonjuring

32

layman whose writings were widely influential. The tenor of his work may be discerned in a short paragraph concerning prayer and the means of grace. "These are happy instruments of enabling us to work out our salvation," wrote Nelson; "but except we bring forth the fruit of the Spirit, 'love, joy, peace, long-suffering, gentleness, goodness, faith, meekness, temperance'; except we 'crucify the flesh with the affections and lusts' thereof; except we live in the Spirit, and walk in the Spirit, we shall not inherit the kingdom of heaven, that infinite happiness that is promised to all devout souls." [22] Christian perfection is not merely a perfect performance of outward devotions, although they "more or less advance our Christian perfection as they tend to recover the image of God in our souls, and to work in us all Christian virtues." But "the temper of our minds must be changed, our hearts renewed, our inward affections purified and sanctified in order to make our outward things pleasing in God's sight." [23]

One of the forces making for individualism in England was undoubtedly Puritanism. During the seventeenth century, both in the Church of England and without among Presbyterians and Independents, Puritanism was an individualistic leaven. True, the more conservative Puritans desired a rigid Church discipline; but the total effect of the Calvinistic emphasis upon the independent relation of the human soul to God was in the direction of individualism. In the same way, while the Puritan remembered that the powers that be are ordained of God, he never forgot his prior allegiance to the Great White Throne; he must obey God rather than man. Social historians have seen in Puritanism one of the prime factors in the nascent capitalistic society, a principal influence in the formation of economic individualism. "In all countries alike," wrote R. H. Tawney, "the social theory of Calvinism went through the same process of development. It had begun by being the very soul of authoritarian regimentation. It ended by being the vehicle of an almost Utilitarian individualism." [24] Certainly, among those whose spiritual genealogy went back to seventeenth-century Puritanism, there were found many who insisted upon individualistic religion.

Isaac Watts, the hymn writer, may be taken as the most familiar example of this tendency toward individualistic religion. He played no small part in Wesley's own religious experience; and Watts's hymns have always been a standard part of the Methodist Hymnbook. In 1707, Watts published his hymn, "Breathing after the Holy Spirit; or, Fervency of Devotion Desired." The lines are well known:

> Come, Holy Spirit, heavenly Dove,
>   With all thy quickening powers;
> Kindle a flame of sacred love
>   In these cold hearts of ours.

His doctrine of the love of God producing man's love is not only Johannine but Wesleyan:

> Come, Holy Spirit, heavenly Dove,
>   With all thy quickening powers;
> Come, shed abroad a Saviour's love,
>   And that shall kindle ours.

Certitude, which Wesley called Assurance, appears also in Watts's hymns, along with the note of joy. Indeed, his hymn, "Why should the children of a King go mourning all their days?" is one of the great hymns which rebuke melancholy and "evangelical sadness."

> Dost thou not dwell in all thy saints,
>   And seal the heirs of heaven?
> When wilt thou banish my complaints,
>   And show my sins forgiven?
>
> Assure my conscience of her part
>   In the Redeemer's blood;
> And bear thy witness with my heart,
>   That I am born of God.
>
> Thou art the earnest of his love,
>   The pledge of joys to come;
> And thy soft wings, celestial Dove,
>   Will safe convey me home.

Hymns are not theology; but if words mean anything, Watts was giving expression in 1708 and 1709 to the essentials of a religion which emphasized the individual's experience, and the emotional rather than rational aspects of experience. Personal faith, the life of God in the soul of man and consequent assurance and joy, are all in the verses of the Nonconformist Isaac Watts. Methodists ought not to forget also that John Wesley died with the words of one of Watts's hymns on his lips:

> I'll praise my Maker while I've breath.

But the tendency toward an individualistic, emotional religion was found in less respectable circles.

That England, in the early eighteenth century, was not a land of ordered quiet, of properly suppressed feelings, a land governed easily according to the best formulations of Mr. Locke, is, of course, evident to the most superficial reader of history.

One has only to remember the uprisings of '15 and of '45 and the stirrings during the American Revolution, not to mention other wars, to understand that the century was a turbulent one. The fear of fanaticism and enthusiasm which recurs throughout the period is evidence of the *existence* of fanaticism and enthusiasm, not of their absence. The fear aroused by "papists," Quakers, French Prophets, and, later, Methodists testifies to the shock that England had received during the Civil War; but it also evidences the continuance of tendencies toward religious fanaticism. From the triumphal progress of Sacheverell to the Gordon riots, in the excesses of French Prophets, in the scenes at early Methodist meetings, there is plentiful evidence of the emotional instability of the English people. With all their faults, the English of the eighteenth century remained a vigorous, sentimental race, capable alike of storming the heights of Quebec, of weeping over the misfortunes of Pamela, or of sobbing to the rhythm of Whitefield's magic voice.

During the Commonwealth period there had been a welter of mystical and semi-mystical sects which added no little to the confusion of the time. Familists, Brownists, Seekers, Ranters, Quakers, and numerous individual mystics were united in little save a belief in the immediate communion of man with God.

The claim to immediate inspiration, what was called "enthusiasm," was no unimportant matter in the seventeenth century; and philosophers, theologians, and statesmen joined to combat the pretensions of those who asserted a revelation from God Himself. In some form or other the inner light and prophecy were live questions long after the Restoration. Mystics like Jakob Boehme, the German shoemaker (1575-1624), were influential not only in theology but also in literature.[25]

As an illustration of the crasser expression of religious emotionalism, one may recall the outbreak of fanaticism coupled with the activity of the French Prophets, or Camisards, which provoked Shaftesbury's *Characteristics*. Emissaries of these prophets went throughout the land prophesying destruction and claiming immediate inspiration as their authority. For the most part they were recruited from the humbler ranks of society; but at least two gentlemen joined them, to the scandal of the squirearchy. Even after the fiasco of a prophesied resurrection in Bunhill Fields, in 1708, the movement did not die out; and there were isolated followers of the "prophets" down at least until the middle of the century.[26]

If there were comparative quiet and freedom from fanaticism in the England of Walpole, it was not because emotion had been dissected out of English life. The masses of the people still lived in an atmosphere of "wonder." It was not until 1736 that the law punishing witchcraft by death was stricken from the statute book. The upper classes were becoming relatively free from grosser superstitions, but belowstairs and in rural districts fairies and witches were realities. Such beliefs, divorced from the grim reality of bloody assizes, were no unwholesome fare; and a recent historian quotes Wordsworth's testimony to the growth of his own imagination partly through the influence of fairy tales and ballads heard in his childhood.[26] In many parts of England, men and women lived in simpler and perhaps more normal touch with nature, giving freer scope to their fancies and to their emotions and ready to respond to an appeal to the heart.

In the early eighteenth century, therefore, one finds in England no dead uniformity of religious life. There was a rationalism which made for a minimum of belief, and that to be acceptable to all everywhere, always, and at all times. There was also a strong emphasis upon corporate religion, the mediation of grace through the Church and its ministries. But there was also in many groups a religion of the inner life, from the inner light of the Quakers to the personal devotion of the High Churchman. And affecting many in the humbler ranks of society were prophetic and mystical movements which persisted, although somewhat as echoes, after the turbulence of Cromwellian times.

CHAPTER III

WESLEY'S TRAINING AT EPWORTH AND OXFORD

"FROM a child," wrote John Wesley in his old age, "I was taught to love and reverence the Scripture, the oracles of God; and, next to these, to esteem the primitive Fathers, the writers of the first three centuries. Next after the primitive church, I esteemed our own, the Church of England, as the most scriptural national Church in the world." [1] These were Wesley's childhood loyalties, the authorities of a good High Churchman, and in the Epworth rectory he learned to reverence them.

In the Isle of Axholme, in northern Lincolnshire, cut off from the rest of England during a part of the year by the waters which overspread the lowlands, Samuel Wesley's family lived in proud isolation. The country, as the late Dean of Winchester remarked, was one "in which a man should possess his soul in patience, yet where reaction might breed volcanic energy." [2] And the Wesleys, disdaining social equality with the people of the land, were disliked by many of the parishioners and by the squirearchy who differed from the rector in politics. Under such conditions the influence of the home would be doubly great, and the children would reflect in unusual degree family ideas and characteristics.

Samuel Wesley was of good family; and although he was relegated to a living in a far-away corner of England, it was a good living, and he was not cut off from the intellectual and political life of the nation. Three times, in 1701, in 1711, and apparently once later, he was proctor for the diocese of Lincoln at Convocation in London. Since these were the times when the controversies between the Lower House and the Bishops were at their height, the whole panorama of England's political and religious conflicts must have been unrolled in the parsonage at Epworth when the rector returned from his missions.

In religion, Samuel Wesley was a High Churchman, as were most of the country clergy. Moreover, he was a convert, having been educated at a dissenting academy before he decided to enter the Established Church; and like many converts he seems to have held his adopted opinions with the greater zeal. It is true that some historians have refused to believe that Samuel Wesley held high notions of sacerdotal power, a repugnance to toleration, and a firm adherence to Tory principles; but the facts are against them. In 1775, John Wesley declared that he himself was "an High Churchman, the son of an High Churchman, bred up from my childhood in the highest notions of passive obedience and non-resistance." [3] He was speaking here of the political aspects of High Churchmanship. Some of the other tenets he had abandoned; but he knew what they were. In 1745, he thought it providential that he had not persisted in them: "And yet had we continued in the impetuosity of our High Church zeal," he wrote in *A Farther Appeal,* "neither should we have been willing to converse with Dissenters, nor they to receive any good at our hands." [4] His elder brother, Samuel, understood his father's aversion to any one tainted with the views of seventeenth-century Dissent. On Samuel Wesley's death, Samuel Wesley, Jr., wrote that his father had been shocked by those

> Who Law's and Gospel's bonds in sunder rend,
> And blush not Bradshaw's saintship to defend;
> Alike the Crown and Mitre who forswore,
> And scoff'd prophanely at the Martyr's gore.[5]

John Wesley published this in the first volume of the *Arminian Magazine,* which appeared in 1778.

If any further proof is needed, there are the elder Samuel Wesley's own words to his brother-in-law, that he was happy to have brought up his children in his own principles and practices, "to a steady opposition and confederacy against all such as are avowed and declared enemies to God and his clergy, and who deny or disbelieve any articles of natural or revealed religion, as well as to such as are open or secret friends to the Great Rebellion, or to any such principles as do but squint towards the same practices; so that he hopes they are all staunch High-Church, and for inviolable passive obedience." [6]

It would seem, indeed, that Samuel Wesley was not simply a mild High Churchman, but that he belonged to the "high-flyers." When Sacheverell was impeached, his defense was more moderate and better written than had been expected from one of such temperament, and there was considerable speculation as to the author, the most likely guesses being Smalridge or Atterbury. In his *History of England*, John Wesley solved the problem by declaring that his father wrote Sacheverell's defense.[7] There is no other evidence for this, but it seems improbable that John Wesley would have made such a statement on insufficient authority, and this authority was no doubt either his father or Sacheverell himself, whom John Wesley as a boy visited at his father's request.

As to Samuel Wesley's militant orthodoxy, it is enough to cite his membership in the Lower House of Convocation which censured Whiston's Arian views, a subject on which the elder Wesley felt so strongly that his wife had engraved upon his tombstone the words: "As he liv'd so he died in the true Catholic Faith of the Holy Trinity in Unity, and that Jesus Christ is God incarnate: and the only Savior of Mankind. Acts iv: 12."

In the enforcement of discipline, too, Wesley was of the strictest sect, punishing adulterers by public penance, compelling them to stand barefooted and wrapped in a white sheet in the various churches of the parish. It was, in fact, partly this rigid discipline of the rector which aroused his parishioners to opposition during the earlier years of his incumbency. He was strict also, according to the standards of the day, in keeping the fasts and ceremonies of the Church. He advised reading prayers on every holiday and on Wednesdays and Fridays, and he would like to have read prayers also on the eves of holidays. It was his custom to administer the Lord's Supper once a month, which was the practice of pious clergymen in that period.[8]

But Wesley was not only a High Churchman and something of a politician; he was also a poet. True he was a very minor poet, but he was important enough to have been lampooned by Garth, by Swift, and by Pope. He wrote a more or less metrical version of the Old and New Testaments and numerous occasional pieces. But he was the friend of many of the well-known literary men of the day, and Swift and Pope both held him in high regard in spite of his poetry. From his journeys to London the rector must have come back with news of other matters than the squabbles of High and Low Church; and the lonely rectory in the lowlands of Lincolnshire was at least in second-hand touch with the literary world. Quick-tempered but capable of sustained enthusiasm, a scholar although somewhat pedantic, a poet if a minor one, Samuel Wesley gave life and ambition to his household; and if he did not inspire love in his children, from his sons, at least, he called forth the deepest respect.

Less needs to be said of Susannah Wesley, for she is one of the most praised women in Christendom. Like her husband, Susannah came of good family. Her father was a distinguished Noncomformist preacher, Dr. Samuel Annesley, whose uncle was an earl. She was, according to contemporaries, a woman of great charm, some thought of greater beauty than her sister who was painted by Lely. At an early age she was reading the Fathers and making up her mind about theological problems concerning which her elders wrangled—and making up her mind that her distinguished father was wrong. Mrs. Wesley was of strong will, learned for a woman of her day, possessed of patience and of an ability for discipline which has remained a marvel to all students of Methodism.

In politics Mrs. Wesley was of the same belief as her husband; in fact going even further, since she refused to pray for King William. She showed an unfeigned belief in the supremacy of her husband, so that his poetic tribute to her, which is sometimes taken as a sign of the rector's overweening autocracy, is as truly a reflection of her sentiments as of his:

> She graced my humble roof, and blest my life,
> Blest me by a far greater name than wife;
> Yet still I bore an undisputed sway,
> Nor was't her task but pleasure, to obey;
> Scarce thought, much less could act, what I denied,
> In our low house there was no room for pride.[9]

Writing to John, in February, 1735, she made clear her belief that "the visible order of providence" and civil government could not be established "and the due subservience of one man to another preserved without ensigns of authority, and difference in houses, furniture and apparel, all which are marks of distinction, and as such, in obedience to the will of God and not for vain glory, they ought to be used, and he that breaks his rank and goes out of character so far as he does so, so far he breaks the eternal order of the universe and abuses his Christian liberty." [10] It was not from Samuel alone that the Wesley children learned to be Tories.

The same principle Susannah carried over into religion, so that she firmly convinced the young collegian, John, that faith is not assent to that which reason approves, as that budding theologian had contended. "I am, therefore," wrote John to his mother in 1725, "at length come over entirely to your opinion, that saving faith (including practice) is an assent to what God has revealed because He has revealed it and not because the truth of it may be evinced by reason." [11]

Susannah's mind, unlike that of her poetic husband, was methodical to a fault. Her theological ideas were held with tenacity but with pedestrian logic, and the little treatise on theology which she wrote for one of her daughters is a dry, rationalistic compendium. The story of her training and governance of the family has been often told, but must be remembered by all who would assess the mind of her distinguished son. At John's request she wrote out, in her old age, an account of her principal rules in educating her children; and John included the letter in his published *Journal*.

"When turned a year old (and some before), they were taught to fear the rod, and to cry softly; by which means they escaped abundance of correction they might otherwise have had, and that most odious noise of the crying of children was rarely heard in the house, but the family usually lived in as much quietness as if there had not been a child among them." [12]

With nineteen children, all told, although several died in infancy, such an arrangement had its advantages. But the methodism of Susannah had only begun.

"They were so constantly used to eat and drink what was given them, that, when any of them was ill, there was no difficulty in making them take the most unpleasant medicine; for they durst not refuse it, though some of them would presently throw it up. This I mention to show that a person may be taught to take anything, though it be never so much against his stomach. In order to form the minds of children, the first thing to be done is to conquer their will, and bring them to an obedient temper. . . . In the esteem of the world they pass for kind and indulgent whom I call cruel parents, who permit their children to get habits which they know must be afterwards broken."

That Mrs. Wesley brought up her children by these strict rules is, of course, well known. They were to do this; they were not to do that. But she extended her rules also to their religious training.

"The children of this family were taught, as soon as they could speak, the Lord's Prayer, which they were made to say at rising and bed-time constantly; to which, as they grew bigger, were added a short prayer for their parents, and some collects; a short catechism, and some portions of Scripture, as their memories could bear."

After the fire which destroyed Epworth rectory, the children were scattered out among several families; and there they learned bad habits.

"When the house was rebuilt, and the children all brought home, we entered upon a strict reform; and then was begun the custom of singing psalms at be-

ginning and leaving school, morning and evening.
Then also that of a general retirement at five o'clock
was entered upon, when the oldest took the youngest
that could speak, and the second the next, to whom
they read the Psalms for the day, and a chapter in the
New Testament; as, in the morning, they were directed to read the Psalms and a chapter in the Old;
after which they went to their private prayers, before
they got their breakfast or came into the family."

This is enough to give an idea of Mrs. Wesley's
method, although the whole letter is interesting and
should be read if Susannah's mind is to be understood.
In the letter it is hinted that there was some difficulty
in getting Samuel Wesley, Sr., to abide by the rules.
"Rules," "habits," "obedience," are the great words.
There is no way of knowing whether Mrs. Wesley
had read Locke's works on education; but the belief
that anything can be taught, regardless of natural
inclination, provided proper habits are built up is
nothing if not Lockian.

It was no mean feat to command a household of so
many children who had a poet for a father, but
Susannah Wesley's pragmatic genius was sufficient.
Nor did her reverence for authority override her
practical sense. When her husband was absent and
his curate dry, she herself read prayers in the rectory;
and the neighbors were admitted at their request.
The Rector objected, but he did not actually forbid
the gatherings; and Susannah went her way sure that
this was the sensible thing to do. A letter which she
wrote to John when he was at Charterhouse is the last
word in practicality. The boy had written her of

some students who had met a ghost near Oxford; his mother replied:

"I do not doubt the fact; but I cannot understand why these apparitions are permitted. If they were allowed to speak to us, and we had strength to bear such converse,—if they had commission to inform us of anything relating to their invisible world that would be of any use to us in this,—if they would instruct us how to avoid danger, or put us in a way of being wiser and better, there would be sense in it; but to appear for no end that we know of, unless to frighten people almost out of their wits, seems altogether unreasonable." [13]

Even Mrs. Wesley's ghosts had to be practical.

No little scorn has been poured upon John Wesley for having engraved upon his mother's tombstone a verse which says that she

> Mourned a long night of griefs and fears,
> A legal night of seventy years,

because it was not until her old age that she found the peace and love which her father had experienced for forty years, although he did not preach about it. Even Methodist historians usually preserve a discreet silence about the epitaph. Mrs. Wesley was a remarkable woman and is, in many ways, the founder of Methodism; but it is possible that John was better acquainted with his mother than are his modern critics.

Such was the home in which John Wesley spent the first eleven years of his life, and the influences upon his mind are apparent enough. From his mother he

must have received his notions of methodicity and of
the importance of habit, and from her also he possibly
learned the lesson of moral independence, the ground-
ing of action upon consideration. At six he would
not accept bread or fruit if offered out of ordinary
mealtime, but would reply, "I thank you, I will think
of it." But from his father he possibly derived his
urge to travel which later sent him to America, to
Germany, and, in fifty years, to almost every corner
of the three kingdoms. From his father, too, came his
poetic bent, which was never as pronounced as in his
brother Charles, but cropped up now and again, not
only in poetry but in a suppressed and seldom revealed
emotional strain. From both of them came his intellectual curiosity, which, while disdaining the critical
scholarship to which his father would have urged him,
manifested itself in a lively interest in all that was
being done or written in that lively age.

While there is not enough evidence concerning his
childhood to satisfy those psychologists who believe
that mortal fate is fixed at a tender age, there is some
material for those who would understand the mind of
the foremost religious leader of the century. In the
first place, it is certain that the rectory of Epworth
was hospitable to the supernatural. The famous ghost
story, that of Old Jeffrey, the Jacobite ghost who
haunted the rectory when John was sixteen and in the
Charterhouse in London, cannot be taken as determining the set of John's mind. It is rather an indication
of what that set was. The care with which the
schoolboy assembled and massed the evidence testifies
at once to his curiosity about such matters and to the

state of "expectancy" which existed in the Wesley household. Even more direct evidence is in the letters which John wrote to his mother, retailing stories of haunted houses, of boys who were snatched into the air by diabolical means, of men who saw ghosts and turned white as ashes. These are schoolboy tales, but they were obviously written to a mother who would listen to them sympathetically.

In his fifth year, the rectory was burned down, and John was at the last moment snatched from the burning building. The overjoyed rector dropped to his knees and gave God thanks for the salvation of the boy. That the incident left a deep impression on the boy's mind is evidenced by the fact that one of the earliest prints of Wesley showed, below his picture, a burning building and the words, "Is not this a brand plucked from the burning?" Forty years afterward, Wesley recalled the very day and hour on which he was rescued. There is reason to think that the incident heightened Wesley's sense of vocation.

Isolated in a distant parish, surrounded by people known, even much later, for their churlish character, who cared little for the Rector and less for his politics, the Wesleys developed no little self-esteem. Of good birth themselves, they could not avoid some accentuation of family pride in their surroundings. It is noteworthy that Wesley seems to have had much trouble about the virtue of humility. The word occurs again and again in his self-examinations. When Wesley felt that he did trust in Christ and that his sins were taken away, he immediately began to pray for those "who had in a more especial manner despitefully used me and persecuted me." [14] It was a Christian act, but one suspects that for Wesley it was a very Christian act. His own opinions were often held with obstinacy, although at other times he was the most humble of men. But there was in him an aptitude for government, and his childhood would make this more pronounced.

It may have been during his childhood at Epworth that Wesley contracted a fear of the sea. His biographers have ignored this fear, possibly thinking it of no account or at most an idiosyncrasy; but, as will appear later, Wesley's fear of the sea plagued him no little during his American experience, and his struggle with it was tied up with his whole religious problem. The sea, Wesley once said, using for him strangely emphatic language, he had both "dreaded and abhorred" from his youth. It is impossible now to determine the origin of this fear, although it may quite possibly have been caused by some mishap in a childhood excursion to the sea, or, more probably, by a misadventure in the overflowed area around Epworth, for during part of the year the rector had to visit Wroote, in his parish, by boat. In London and at Oxford John apparently forgot this fear so that it reappeared the more unexpectedly on his voyage to America.

One other result of his home experiences must be noted. Wesley was apparently by nature rationalistic, but as has been seen, he had a poetic strain in his make-up. In many things his father and mother agreed: in High Church opinions, in politics—in the main—and in their ideas of social class. But in their characters and in their ideas of training they were worlds apart. "Reason and piety," said his mother. "Child," said his father, "you think to carry everything by dint of argument; but you will find how little is ever done in this world by close reasoning." [15] It was his mother who most influenced Wesley's method of thinking. In a home where normal association with other children was impossible, the Wesleys were thrown upon themselves, and the result was unhappy for several of them. There is reason to think that John Wesley's emotional nature was buried under the methodical and reasoned life which he led even as a child. Some psychologists have thought that John's devotion to his mother was one of the reasons for his failure to make a successful marriage, but the reason may lie deeper than that. Susannah had a strain of asceticism in her, and she discouraged emotion in herself and in others. In Oxford, John recalled somewhat wistfully that his mother had more than once said that she loved him too well and would strive to love him less. The little boy who went up to Charterhouse in 1714 was trained to a pragmatic regime in which emotion had little play. He was sufficiently master of himself to be able to undergo the hardships of a public schoolboy with reasonable equanimity, and he obediently and methodically ran thrice around the schoolhouse yard every morning for exercise. But his emotional life was not dead; it only slept.

It is unnecessary to dwell upon John Wesley's experiences at the Charterhouse. There he seems to have relaxed a little the religious discipline to which he had been accustomed; and he was not happy. In later life, Wesley assumed that his childhood unhappiness was owing to a lack of religion; and he strove to supply a similar lack in the lives of the children at his school in Kingswood and elsewhere by a forbidding attack upon their sensibilities. Their lives, too, were doubtless unhappy, although they heard enough of religion. Schoolboys of Wesley's days, bullied by older students and subjected to a brutal educational system, were likely to be unhappy. But his own experiences underlie Wesley's later emphasis upon happiness through religion.

The Oxford to which John Wesley went up in 1720 as a student of Christ Church was at a low ebb educationally and religiously. Outward loyalty to the Church was a matter of pride, but any strict observance of its religious requirements was far to seek. Instruction was little better. Satirists of the century made merry with the formal disputations which were a large part of the requirements for degrees, and sober historians admit that tutors were woefully lax in the performance of their duties.[16] What Wesley actually studied cannot be determined exactly. In his diaries appear Latin and Greek classics, Hebrew and French and English literature. Following his ordination he records a formidable and diversified list of books which he read, ranging from the Bible to Juvenal and from Locke to Milton.[17] Certainly he could not escape logic, and it was in many ways a subject suited to his mind and earlier training. After his election to a fellowship of Lincoln College, smallest of the Oxford colleges but in good repute for learning, Wesley became Greek lecturer and moderator of the classes.

As moderator Wesley would preside at the disputations. An unfriendly critic writing during the very time when Wesley was an undergraduate describes these disputations as follows:

"The persons of this argumentative drama are three, viz. the Opponent, the Respondent, and the Moderator. The Opponent is the person who always begins the attack. . . . The Respondent sits over-against the opponent, and is prepared to deny whatever he affirms, and always comes off with flying colours. . . . The Moderator is the hero, or principal character of the drama, and is not much unlike the goddess Victoria, as described by the poets, hovering between two armies in an engagement, and with an arbitrary nod, deciding the fate of the field. . . . Academical disputations are two-fold, ordinary and extraordinary, ordinary disputations are those which are privately perform'd in college every day, or twice or thrice a week (according to different customs or statutes) in term-time; extraordinary disputations I call those which are perform'd in the public schools of the university, as requisite qualifications for degrees: the method of both is the same, and equally arduous is the performance." [18]

The description which the writer gives of the public disputations is ludicrous in the extreme, and the sample of Latin argumentation, with the syllogistic fencing of opponent and proponent and the decisions of moderator, were intended for satire. But there is much truth in it,[19] and Wesley himself, in later years, frequently spoke disparagingly of the whole system. Nevertheless, logic remained part of his equipment, and he later gave thanks for his experience as moderator, since it gave him advantage as a controversialist. Indeed, the experience of a moderator, who, according to the satirist, "struts about between the two wordy champions, during the time of action, to see that they do not wander from the question in debate," was no mean preparation for an eighteenth-century contender in the printed battles of the day. But it was an experience calculated to cramp the imagination if it did not kill it. At the best it was a strengthening of that reverence for exact disciplining of thought which had been inculcated into the child of the Epworth rectory.

During these years, Wesley read something of Locke, how much cannot be determined. In his old age, he read or re-read the *Essay* and objected particularly to Locke's disparagement of Aristotelian logic, concluding that the philosopher must have had "an unskilful master and read bad books upon the subject." [20] He makes his own predilection clear in another objection to Locke's remarks about logic, declaring that "the true use of it (logic) is the noblest means under heaven to prevent or cure the obscurity of language." "To divide simple terms," he continued, "according to the logical rules of division, and then to define each member of the division according to the three rules of definition, does all that human art can do, in order to our having a clear and distinct idea of every word we use." [21]

"Clear and distinct ideas" play no small part in

Wesley's theological and philosophical writings. These he concluded to be the necessity of all knowledge and the aim of learning, but he did not go further with Descartes. Whether he read Locke's *Essay* earlier or later, he accepted the dictum that man has no innate ideas, but gets all his knowledge through the senses, excepting only some religious knowledge. And Wesley also decided early that knowledge should be limited to useful knowledge, approaching therein the pragmatic strain implicit in Locke and his followers. In January, 1727, he wrote to his mother:

"I am shortly to take my Master's degree. As I shall from that time be less interrupted by business not of my own choosing, I have drawn up for myself a scheme of studies, from which I do not intend, for some years at least, to vary. I am perfectly come over to your opinion that there are many truths it is not worth while to know. Curiosity, indeed, might be a sufficient plea for our laying out some time upon them, if we had a half dozen centuries of life to come; but methinks it is great ill-husbandry to spend a considerable part of the small pittance allowed us in what makes us neither a quick nor a sure return." [22]

Thus he had come over to his mother's opinion, which was not his father's, who wished his son to follow the path of critical learning. Knowledge should be not obscure but useful. In his later life, he expressed his belief that God has purposely limited our knowledge, exactly proportioning it "to our state." "We may know whatever is needful for life or godliness, whatever is necessary either for our present or eternal happiness. But how little beside can the most

penetrating genius know with any certainty! Such
pains, so to speak, hath God taken to hide pride from
man; and to bound his thought within that channel
of knowledge wherein he already finds eternal life." [23]
In Oxford, then, Wesley came to the conclusion that
knowledge is common and useful. To possess abstruse
and esoteric learning was to lay oneself open to
"pride" in the eighteenth-century sense, lifting oneself above the common lot of man.

But Wesley could not restrain his restless mind. In
his earlier, undergraduate days, he had read many
plays and romances, including one work which he
called the "Pyrates," perhaps *Robinson Crusoe.* His
preference, throughout his life, for "the sentimental
and romantic in literature" has been noticed by more
than one student.[24] Moreover, he was a poet; and
while he forsook the formal and trivial lines of his
youthful muse, he added no little to English hymnody
both by original composition and by translation and
editing. In his youth the preponderance of influence
upon his mind was undoubtedly toward discipline,
order, conformity. But the other strain was not lost,
and there was for Wesley the possibility of a continuing conflict between the two, at least until they could
be fused into a higher unity. In 1725, his life took a
direction which it was to hold until his death sixty-
six years later; and it was in this direction that the
two tendencies in his nature and training were to find
their confluence.

CHAPTER IV

WESLEY IN OXFORD AND AMERICA

WHEN John Wesley was about twenty-two, his father urged him to enter into holy orders. This was possibly the occasion of his beginning to think more seriously about religion. The next year he came across Jeremy Taylor's *Holy Living and Holy Dying*. His account of this event in his life is found in the story of his religious progress which begins the treatise, *A Plain Account of Christian Perfection*, published in 1765. "In reading several parts of this book [*Holy Living and Dying*]," he said, "I was exceedingly affected; that part in particular which relates to purity of intention. Instantly I resolved to dedicate all my life to God, all my thoughts and words, and actions; being thoroughly convinced, there was no medium; but that every part of my life (not some only) must either be a sacrifice to God, or myself, that is, in effect, to the devil." [1] Five years later, when he laid the cornerstone of City Road Chapel in London, a great moment for him and for Methodism, Wesley again dated the beginning of the Methodist Movement in the year 1725. [2]

In recent years, the importance of Wesley's experience in 1725 has been recognized, and some have gone so far as to call this his "conversion." Others have adopted the terminology of the mystics and have referred to this as his "awakening." The latter term is perhaps the right one, if it is remembered that Wesley was not a mystic in the exact sense of the word, and that he did not go through the full course of awakening, purgation, illumination, and union often experienced by the mystic soul.

Influenced by Taylor, Wesley began to keep a diary, which he continued for sixty-five years. In 1726, according to the account in *Christian Perfection,* he began to read à Kempis, *The Imitation of Christ.* "The nature and extent of inward religion, the religion of the heart, now appeared to me in a stronger light than ever it had done before. I saw, that giving even all my life to God (supposing it possible to do this, and go on farther) would profit me nothing, unless I gave my heart, yea, all my heart to him. I saw, that 'simplicity of intention, and purity of affection,' one design in all we speak or do, and one desire ruling all our tempers, are indeed 'the wings of the soul,' without which she can never ascend to the mount of God." [3] A year or two afterward, Wesley read William Law's two great books, *Christian Perfection* (1726) and *A Serious Call to a Devout and Holy Life* (1729). "These convinced me more than ever," he wrote, "of the absolute impossibility of being half a Christian; and I determined, through his grace (the absolute necessity of which I was deeply sensible of), to be all-devoted to God, to give him all my soul, my body, and substance." [4] From this time Wesley sought nothing less than Christan Perfection.

It is necessary to stress what has been too often forgotten, in spite of Wesley's reiterated statement, that

59

Wesley in Oxford, before he ever went to America, held the doctrine of Christian Perfection essentially as he held it throughout his life. Indeed, it is impossible to understand Wesley's religion and theology without grasping the central fact, that Christian Perfection, holiness, was the controlling idea in his life and teachings and the continuous goal of his experience; and it should be remembered that he at this time was "deeply sensible" of the "absolute necessity" of grace. To make his ideas clearer one needs to look closer at William Law's teaching concerning perfection.

This little book, *Christian Perfection,* which Law wrote in 1725, is one of the most attractive religious books in the English language. Many of Law's sayings must have been doubly attractive to a young man whose family tradition was a well-turned phrase: "But how unlike are Christians to Christianity"; "if therefore there be not an Entire Change in the Way to Heaven, if the once strait Gate be now a wide and open passage to all full, fat, and stately Christians . . ."; "More senseless than the Man, who should think he had hard Usage to be saved from a Shipwreck, unless he were carried off upon a Cedar Plank." But Law's ideal of Christian Perfection, no less than his language, was also acceptable to Wesley's mind.

Sometimes perfection appears in Law as a simple imitation of Christ in outward behavior, "a right Performance of all the Duties of Life, as is according to the Laws of Christ." He insists that "every Duty or Virtue of the Christian Life is founded in Truth

and Reason, and is required because of its Fitness to
be done, and not because God has Power to command
what he pleases." But Law insisted also that perfection is a "Perfection of the Heart," a "Habit of the
Mind"; and he who has this must have been born
again. "Christianity is another Birth, that brings
into a Condition as new as when we first saw the
Light. We begin again to be, we enter upon fresh
Terms of Life, have new Relations, new Hopes, and
Fears, and entire Change of Everything that can be
called good and evil." [5] This is not simply a matter
of adding virtue to virtue. Attention will be called
later to Law's belief that human nature is diseased,
that mankind is "a Race of fallen Spirits." [6] If he
had not believed it before, Wesley would have learned
from Law a doctrine of original sin which necessi-
tates "a new principle of life." Law's language as to
the nature of perfection is explicit: "It is not therefore any Number of moral Virtues, no partial Obedience, no modes of Worship, no external Acts of
Adoration, no Articles of Faith, but a new Principle
of Life, an active Change of Temper, that makes us
true Christians." [7]

On January 1, 1733, Wesley preached at St. Mary's,
Oxford. In this sermon, to which reference will be
made again, Wesley declared that the condition of
one who is "in a state of acceptance with God" is not
attested by "baptism, or any other outward form,
but a right state of soul, a mind and spirit renewed
after the image of Him that created it." More specifically, he spoke of seeking "that habitual disposition
of soul which, in the sacred writings, is termed holi-

61

ness; and which directly implies, the being cleansed from sin . . . and by consequence, the being endued with those virtues which were also in Christ Jesus; the being so 'renewed in the spirit of our mind,' as to be 'perfect as our Father in heaven is perfect.' " Nor did Wesley think of this holiness as something that might be attained by human endeavor alone. "Our gospel, as it knows no other foundation of good works than faith, or of faith than Christ, so it clearly informs us, we are not His disciples while we either deny Him to be the Author, or His Spirit to be the Inspirer and Perfecter, both of our faith and works . . . . He alone can quicken those who are dead unto God, can breathe into them the breath of Christian life, and so prevent, accompany, and follow them with His grace, as to bring their good desires to good effect." His next paragraph goes further. "From what has been said, we may, thirdly, learn, that none is truly 'led by the Spirit,' unless that 'Spirit bear witness with his spirit, that he is a child of God'; unless he see the prize and the crown before him, and 'rejoice in hope of the glory of God.' " [8]

Thirty-two years later, Wesley wrote to a friend concerning this sermon, that it "contains all that I now teach concerning salvation from all sin, and loving God with an undivided heart. In the same year I printed (the first time I ventured to print anything) for the use of my pupils, *A Collection of Forms of Prayer,* and in this I spoke explicitly of giving 'the whole heart and the whole life to God.' This was then, as it is now, my idea of perfection, though I should have started at the word." [9]

In other points, too, Wesley was holding doctrines which continued to characterize his preaching throughout his life. To his brother he wrote in 1731: "(1) As to the end of my being, I lay it down for a rule that I cannot be too happy, or therefore too holy; and thence infer that the more steadily I keep my eye upon the prize of our high calling the better, and the more of my thoughts, and words, and actions are directly pointed at the attainment of it. (2) As to the instituted means of attaining it, I likewise lay it down for a rule that I am to use them every time I may. (3) As to prudential means, I believe this rule holds of things indifferent in themselves: whatever I know to do me hurt, that to me is not indifferent, but resolutely to be abstained from; whatever I know to do me good, that to me is not indifferent, but resolutely to be embraced." [10]

That he was seeking holiness, Christian Perfection, is sufficiently clear. Concerning his second point, the use of the "instituted means," Wesley's sermon, written in 1732 for his pupils, "On the Duty of Constant Communion," is a sufficient illustration. In this sermon he sets forth as one of the reasons for constant communion: "the benefits of doing it are so great to all that do it in obedience to him; viz., the forgiveness of our past sins, the present strengthening and refreshing of our souls. . . . Now, when we are convinced of having sinned against God, what surer way have we of procuring pardon from him, than the 'showing forth the Lord's death'; and beseeching him, for the sake of His Son's sufferings, to blot out all our sins?" "The grace of God given herein," he adds, "confirms

63

to us the pardon of our sins, and enables us to leave them." "This is the food of our souls: This gives strength to perform our duty, and leads us on to perfection." The Lord's Supper, according to Wesley, is a real "means of grace" and not a figurative or poetic gesture.[11] In 1787, Wesley reprinted this sermon in the *Arminian Magazine;* and in the note prefixed to the sermon he says that he had added very little but retrenched much, "as I then used more words than I use now." But he asserted: "I thank God, I have not yet seen cause to alter my sentiments in any point which is therein delivered." [12]

But there can be no question that, in 1732, Wesley's High Churchmanship was excessive. It is probable that John Clayton, one of the Oxford Methodists, had influenced the group in the direction of an excessive reverence for certain supposed authorities of the Early Church. Particularly did Wesley esteem the *Apostolic Constitutions,* which he later decided—and rightly—were not of such antiquity or authority as he had supposed. But the high authority of the Fathers of the Primitive Church was an article of faith which he had inherited from his father, had had confirmed in Oxford, and, as will appear later, was never entirely discarded. Wesley was also influenced in his earlier period by reading Fleury's *Manners of the Ancient Christians.* In his study of the ancient Church he found matter congenial to his ideas of Christian Perfection. In the *Apostolic Constitutions,* the episcopal blessing of catechumens is that God "may give them a new heart, and renew a right spirit in their inward parts, that they may both know and do thy will with full purpose of heart, and with a willing soul." [13] It was this for which Wesley was striving; and commandments to austerity of life and godliness fitted into the ideals of the Oxford Club. In the *Apostolic Constitutions*, wearing gold, dressing the hair, and like superfluities were forbidden; and men were admonished to be industrious, "for no one of those who are dedicated to God ought to be idle." [14]

After 1729, when "a serious man" warned him that he must seek companions, that the Bible knows nothing of solitary religion, Wesley sought holiness, not by himself, but as a member of a religious society. The Oxford Club, the beginning of which he found when he returned to Oxford after serving for a time as his father's curate, was the new religious society with which his name and Methodism are forever linked. The history of this society is too well known to need repetition here. The serious studies of the members, not only in devotional works but in the Bible, their meticulous keeping both of the rules of the University and of the observances of the Church, their charities, especially their work with prisoners, earned for them the contempt of those to whom serious striving after a high religious ideal was matter for ridicule. It is true that Wesley spoke of religion as "the cheerfullest thing in the world" [15] and identified holiness with happiness, but the asceticism of the group is beyond question. As has been suggested, their excesses were perhaps inevitable to a group of serious young men who were in deadly earnest about religion in surroundings decidedly unfavorable to such endeavor. But Wesley believed that "singularity" was necessary.

When he was being examined for priest's orders, his examiner had said to him: "Do you know what you are about? You are bidding defiance to all mankind. He that would live a Christian priest ought to know that, whether his hand be against every man or no, he must expect every man's hand should be against him." [16] And Wesley adduced the contempt in which he and his group were held as evidence of their rightness. Indeed, he was in danger of taking some little pride in it.

In a pathetic paragraph, he begged his mother to grant him that "little part of Thursday evening" which she formerly used to correct his judgment, that she might now correct his heart. Humility is the "surest and safest way" to renounce the world; "But how the question recurs, How am I to do this? To own the necessity of it is not be he humble." [17] He had early objected to Jeremy Taylor's doctrine that one must hold oneself the worst in every company. But he agreed that it is possible to have "absolute humility" before God.[18] But what did this humility before God imply? The truth is, that Wesley was wrestling with the problem of assurance. Can a man be humble and at the same time know himself a Christian?

As far back as 1725, Wesley wrote to his mother concerning Bishop Taylor's views, objecting to an interpretation which he could not accept but which he could not answer to his own satisfaction. He quoted Taylor on repentance: "Repentance contains in it all the parts of an holy life from our return to our death. A man can have but one proper repentance—viz., when the rite of baptism is verified by God's grace coming upon us and our obedience. And after this change, if we ever fall into the contrary state there is no place left for any more repentance." [19] Such a position implied the denial of any real assurance to the Christian: "A true pentitent must all the days of his life pray for pardon and never think the work completed till he died. Whether God has forgiven us or not we know not, therefore still be sorrowful for ever having sinned."

This seemed to Wesley to contradict Taylor's teaching concerning the grace given by the Holy Spirit in the Lord's Supper. "Now, surely," he wrote his mother, "these graces are not of so little force, as that we can't perceive whether we have them or no; and if we dwell in Christ, and Christ in us, which He will not do till we are regenerate, certainly we must be sensible of it." [20] And in a later letter he put his finger on the difficulty. "That we can never be so certain of the pardon of our sins as to be assured that they will never rise up against us, I firmly believe. We know that they will infallibly do so, if ever we apostatize, and I am not satisfied what evidence there can be of our final perseverance till we have finished our course. But I am persuaded we may know if we are *now* in a state of salvation, since that is expressly promised in the Holy Scriptures to our sincere endeavours, and we are surely able to judge of our own sincerity." [21] Already he was convinced of the truth which he was to hold throughout his ministry, that a man may know that he is saved.

All this lies behind the stern precisianism of his con-

duct, the meticulous observance of forms and ceremonies, the anxious spirit which he betrays particularly in his letters explaining his refusal to succeed his
aging father at Epworth.[22] In methodical fashion,
reflecting the character of his mind and of his training, he marshalled his arguments to his father. He
must have as his only consideration, the glory of God.
But that means to promote holiness in ourselves and
others. These must go together. At Oxford, this
holiness is most nearly possible because of his religious
friends, of retirement, of freedom from trifling acquaintance, of freedom from worldly cares, of opportunity for public prayer twice a day, and of weekly
communion. There is also abundant opportunity to
benefit others. This is evidenced by experience, which
"is worth a thousand reasons."

In his search for perfection Wesley had sought help
wherever he could find it, but a sound instinct forbade
his accepting anything which would depreciate the
value either of good works or of the Church. The
tenacity with which he clung to these two is illustrated in his reaction to European Protestant ideas
and to mysticism. Two or three years before he sailed
for America, he "fell among some Lutheran and Calvinist authors, whose confused and indigested accounts magnified faith to such an amazing size that
it quite hid all the rest of the commandments. . . . I
did not then see [he added] that this was the natural
effect of their overgrown fear of Popery; being so
terrified with the cry of merits and good works, that
they plunged into the other extreme. In this laby-
rinth I was utterly lost; not being able to find out

what my error was, nor yet to reconcile this uncouth hypothesis either with Scripture or common sense." [23] There is shrewd criticism here, but it is to be noted that faith is lumped with "the rest of the commandments." Wesley never finally gave over his distrust of too great emphasis upon faith *alone;* and he was later to resolve the difficulty by a psychological analysis of "salvation." [24] Also he came later to a truer appreciation of the non-intellectual elements in faith. But at the time he fell back upon the Anglican compromise as he understood it, being helped by Beveridge, Taylor, and Nelson, although their differing interpretations of Scripture confused him. At least, the Anglican position, he thought, preserved both faith *and* good works.

By the mystics, of whom he later spoke with unusual harshness, Wesley meant apparently the Quietists, who taught that man must wait quietly and passively without moral striving or institutional helps for the moving of the Spirit of God. In 1736, he wrote to his brother, Samuel, from Georgia: "I think the rock on which I had the nearest made shipwreck of the faith was the writings of the Mystics; under which term I comprehend all, and only those, who slight any of the means of grace." [25] Later he drew up a longer indictment against the mystical writers, accusing them of relying on inward tempers for salvation. Groping as he was for a more satisfactory experience, Wesley was sure of some things. He sought an inwardly realized religion, but he was certain that the Scriptures and reason and the means of grace must be preserved.

After declining to accept the succession to Epworth, Wesley seems to have reconsidered; but it was too late, and the parish was given to another. This may have made easier Wesley's acceptance of an invitation to accompany General Oglethorpe to Georgia as missionary to the Indians. Charles was to go along as secretary to Oglethorpe.

In setting forth his reasons for consenting to go to Georgia, Wesley expressed a fear that "favourable judges" would think more highly of him than they should, evidence that he feared an interpretation of his motives directly opposite to that which modern writers have given to them. His chief motive, he wrote to Dr. Burton, one of the Georgia trustees, "is the hope of saving my own soul." [26] Methodists, who are reputed to have considerable interest in their souls, have been strangely unkind in their comments on this statement. Wesley was seeking perfection, and when he spoke of saving his soul he was thinking of this goal which he held always before him, not merely of saving his soul in heaven. If seeking Christian Perfection is a legitimate goal, then there is nothing illegitimate in avowing it. The fact that Wesley was willing to go to America with this in view is, indeed, startling; but this is perhaps no compliment to the startled.

That Wesley should think his pilgrimage easier among the red Indians is understandable when one remembers how the Indians were idealized by the eighteenth century. They were supposed to have escaped the corruptions of civilization and to have retained their primitive simplicity. Wesley expected to learn the "sense of the gospel of Christ" by preaching to them, for they were as little children who would "know of every doctrine whether it be of God." With them he could mortify the flesh, for he would have no incitements to abuse his natural appetites.

Wesley's second motive in going to America was his desire to impart to the heathen "a saving knowledge of the gospel of Christ." He felt that he could not successfully preach to the heathen until perfection was reached. "It is not for me, who have been a grievous sinner from my youth up," he wrote, "and am yet heavy laden with foolish and hurtful desires, to expect God should work so great things by my hands; but I am assured, if I be once *fully* converted myself, He will then employ me both to strengthen my brethren and to preach His name to the Gentiles, that the very ends of the earth may see the salvation of our God." More than is here must not be read into this letter. At some later time he inserted the word "fully," indicating that he realized that his search had been for perfection. He does not, however, say that he was a sinner at the time he wrote, and the foolish and hurtful desires which he talks about are such imperfections as he was to learn later are associated with man's natural infirmities. But he was groaning for perfection, and he was fully persuaded that among the simple, idyllic Indians of America he might attain the goal.

Father Piette thinks that Wesley contemplated removing the Holy Club and Oxford to Georgia, there to establish in an idyllic wilderness the society of seekers after God.[27] There is some evidence for this, since

71

several of the Club expected to go, and Benjamin Ingham did accompany Charles and John Wesley. If Wesley intended such a transfer of the Holy Club, it would explain more satisfactorily his acceptance of the Georgia mission so soon after refusing the parish of Epworth. It would also illustrate again the romantic side of Wesley's character and religion. But, however that be, Wesley departed for Georgia to save his own soul as well as to preach Christ, being, as he said later, devoted to the Bible, the Primitive Church, and the Church of England.

The expedition to America, with all its disappointments and disillusionments, storms at sea, struggles with the ungrateful colonists, including a terrible experience with a dissolute woman who tried to destroy his reputation, and his unfortunate love affair with Sophia Hopkey, had importance for Wesley in three things: he learned more about himself, about people of a class with which he had little acquaintance, and about a type of religion to which he was a stranger.

In Georgia he learned not only that the red Indians were really savages and not the picturesque, noble creatures of eighteenth-century imagination, but that the whites, many of them, were also savages. Heretofore, he had dealt with the lower classes as a gentleman scholar and a clergyman. He had served them and preached to them and taught them, but it was as a gentleman receiving the gratitude of the humble poor. Now he met men face to face in situations which gave full vent to their passions and evil will. His belief in natural depravity received no setback here; it is likely that he saw more clearly than ever

that Christian Perfection is an ideal not to be obtained
but by the grace of God.

Wesley's natural sensitiveness, which was protected
even in the prison of Oxford and among the poor by
the proximity of familiar objects and people and by a
refuge in his rooms in Lincoln College, was increased
by the sight of human sufferings in surroundings
which accentuated them and the seeming callousness
of fellow human beings. His account of the impression produced upon him by the sufferings of one of
the women emigrants in childbirth is poignant evidence. "This," wrote Wesley in his *Journal*, "is the
second time I have been witness—there being only a
door between us—of one of the deepest distresses
which life affords. The groans of the sick person had
very short intermissions. And how were they filled
up by the assistants? With strong cries to God?
With counselling her that was encompassed with sorrows of death to trust in Him? With exhortation to
each other to fear Him who is able to inflict sharper
pains than these? No; but with laughing and jest-
ing, at no time convenient, but at this least of all." [28]
Wesley was an Oxford don of limited experience, and
America was a school wherein he learned much. The
importance of his experiences there is frequently overlooked or restricted to his contact with the Moravians.

It was on the voyage to America that he began to
discover that, with all his self-discipline and education of mind and will, he had not attained to mastery
over his emotional life. This discovery was the more
important because Wesley was aiming, not merely at
right conduct or at salvation by performance of

duties, but at inward peace and holiness. On January 25, 1736, in the great storm which he so graphically describes in his *Journal*, Wesley was confronted by his own fear of death and by the spectacle of simple German peasants, the Moravians on board, singing and waiting on the other passengers, unafraid.[29]

Curnock observed that this was a crucial hour in the history of Wesley, and Father Piette thinks that Wesley learned here that religion is not an affair only of the intellect and of the will.[30] In the first place, the Oxford don was humiliated by a revival of his fear of the sea in its most intense form, a fear all the more excruciating in that it was possibly a survival of some childhood experience in the fenlands. With all his disciplining of himself, his development of right habits, and with all his intellectual training he was at the mercy of an emotion. Not that his fear was marked, for the officers seem to have been as afraid as Wesley; and his conduct was exemplary. But to a sensitive man it was enough that he was afraid.

Moreover, the contrast between the gentleman and scholar and the simple peasants was in itself humiliating. Not only had they demonstrated their humility by attending other passengers in the most servile duties, but their self-possession and unfeigned trust in God stood out in painful contrast to the fear of the leader of the Oxford Methodists. Here was something which Wesley had not met before. He was not only being humbled, but he was also learning something new about Christian humility before God.

Other of Wesley's experiences in America, particularly those in which he learned that he was an impressionable young don and not the cast-iron creature of habit and reflection that he seems to have thought himself, were likewise revealing to him. That Sophia Hopkey was in love with him Wesley seems not to have found out; but that he was in love with her he suspected—to his own misery. His belief in the way of renunciation, the conviction which he then held concerning the celibacy of the clergy, both combined to make him interpret his own emotions as the wiles of Satan. "So I was once more 'snatched as a brand out of the fire,' " [31] he wrote when Mr. Causton, the girl's guardian, had interrupted a conversation with Sophia which was getting on dangerous ground. There is pathos in the young clergyman's self-abasement when one remembers his goal and the tormenting sense that he was preserved for some great end.

"She went, and I saw myself in the toils. But how to escape I saw not. If I continued to converse with her, though not alone, I found I should love her more and more. And the time to break it off was past. I felt it was now beyond my strength. My resolutions indeed remained. But how long? Yet a little longer, till another shock of temptation, and then I well knew they would break in sunder as a thread of tow that has touched the fire. I had many times prayed that if it was best our intercourse should break off, and that if I could not do it she might. But this I saw less and less reason to expect. So that all these things were against me, and I lay struggling in the net; nay, scarcely struggling, as even fearing to be delivered." [32]

As a love affair, it is amusing; as part of the epic of a soul, it is tragedy.

75

Wesley had disciplined his will and his mind, to use the old-fashioned terminology; but he had not been able to control his feelings. His emotional life was rising up in the very new world into which he had come, to reveal how large a part of life is beyond our thought and resolutions. More than once the Oxford don in the American wilderness must have recalled his father's words: "Child, you will find how little is ever done in this world by close reasoning." His mother had taught him to develop proper habits— habits of thought, habits of speech, habits of action. Man can accomplish anything by right habits. Method is the thing. But even a methodist may be afraid of the sea. Even a methodist may awake to the stirrings of love when lonely and homesick in the southern savannah-land. Even a methodist can wax angry when evil men—and worse, men of low degree—oppose one's every effort for their good. In all this Wesley was learning that one must love God not only with all one's mind and with all one's strength, but also with all one's "heart." This dawning recognition of his emotional lack lies behind the self-analysis which Wesley made on board ship returning to England:

"By the most infallible of proofs, inward feeling, I am convinced,

"1. Of unbelief; having no such faith in Christ as will prevent my heart being troubled; which it could not be, if I believed in God, and rightly believed also in Him;

"2. Of pride, throughout my life past; inasmuch as I thought I had what I find I have not:

76

"3. Of gross irrecollection; inasmuch as in a storm I cry to God every moment; in a calm, not:

"4. Of levity and luxuriancy of spirit, recurring whenever the pressure is taken off, and appearing by my speaking words not tending to edify; but most by my manner of speaking to my enemies." [33]

But in spite of these disappointments and despairs it must not be assumed that the Georgia expedition was either all sorrow or fruitless. The Charleston Hymnbook, which Wesley published in 1737, is a study in his spiritual condition. Dr. Simon remarked on the evangelical quality of many of the hymns which Wesley edited and published and wondered that he did not take them more to heart. The answer is that from the first Wesley held much closer to the so-called evangelical position than has usually been allowed. At least the main lines of his faith are evident in such verses as these from the 1737 hymnbook:

> God's Image which our Sins destroy
>   Thy Grace restores below,
> And Truth and Holiness and Joy
>   From Thee, their Fountain, flow.

> We wou'd no longer lie
>   Like Slaves beneath thy Throne:
> O let us *Abba*, Father, cry
>   And thou the Kindred own.

> Ten Thousand Thousand precious Gifts
>   My daily Thanks employ;
> Nor is the least a chearful Heart
>   That tasts those Gifts with Joy.

> Alas, O Lord, we cannot love
>   Unless thou draw our Heart!

> But there's a Voice of sovereign Grace
> Sounds from thy sacred Word,
> Here ye despairing Sinners come
> And trust upon the Lord.
>
> 'Tis not by Works of Righteousness
> Which our own Hands have done;
> But we are saved by sovereign Grace
> Abounding thro' thy Son.[34]

These verses are not untrue to Wesley's earlier convictions unless it be in the greater insistence upon faith, and it is very easy to overemphasize this. Wesley had always believed in faith, faith joined with works. And he had always believed that love is the gift of God and that men are saved by the grace of God. Moreover, in spite of all his self-torture, Wesley was not living in unrelieved misery. Curnock remarks that the fourth Savannah Diary shows him so busy and happy that he has not time to be much tempted, and it was from Georgia that Wesley wrote to Mrs. Chapman his beautiful letter on "Christian Cheerfulness." [35] In his search after Christian perfection he was practicing, in his mistaken devotion to some documents which he imagined to represent the early Church, an annoying High Churchmanship which offended reasonable men in the colony. He was still fighting for Christian humility and looking for a converted heart. But he had made some gains.

In estimating the influence of his Georgia experiences one must not overlook the books which Wesley was reading. Further study convinced him that the *Apostolic Constitutions* were of later date, and therefore of less authority, than he had thought. He was, consequently, somewhat relieved from some of his extremely High Churchmanship. But he was also reading works which he afterwards listed as the most precious of all to him, outside the Bible. These were the *Imitation of Christ* (which Wesley always called the "Christian Pattern") "and the small remains of Clemens Romanus, Polycarp, and Ignatius" and the *Life* of James Haliburton, onetime Professor of Divinity in the University of St. Andrews.[36] The importance of faith is expressly taught in three of these. "Let us cleave then to His blessings," wrote Clement, "and consider what are the means of possessing it. . . . For what reason was our father Abraham blessed? was it not because he wrought righteousness and truth through faith?" [37] And Clement adds that those worthies who were descended from Abraham "were highly honoured, and made great, not for their own sake, or for their own works, or for the righteousness which they wrought, but through the operation of His will. And we, too, being called by His will in Christ Jesus, are not justified by ourselves, nor by our own wisdom, or understanding, or godliness, or works which we have wrought in holiness of heart; but by that faith through which, from the beginning, Almighty God has justified all men." [38] It is hard to believe, in the light of Wesley's later teaching, that he overlooked that exquisite saying of Ignatius, in his epistle to the Ephesians: "For the beginning is faith, and the end is love." [39]

It was probably in Georgia that Wesley first met with the *Life of Haliburton,* a book which, Wesley thought, described the life of God in the soul of man better than any he had seen.[40] This book tells of the Scot's conversion in moving language: "It was in this extremity God stepped in. . . . Towards the beginning of February, 1698, this seasonable relief came. I was then, as I remember, at secret prayer, when he discovered himself to me, when he let me see, that there are *forgiveness with him and mercy, and plenteous redemption*. I now with wonder beheld Christ in his glory, *full of grace and truth*. I saw that he, who had before rejected all my offerings, was well pleased in the Beloved, being fully satisfied, not only that there is forgiveness of sins, through the redemption which is in Jesus, but also, that God by this means might be *just* in *justifying* even *the ungodly that believe in him*. . . . And yet more, when he let me see, that to me, even to me, was the word of this salvation sent; that even I was invited to *come*, and *take the water of life freely*." [41]

Reference will be made in another chapter to a book Wesley read at this time, that set forth a definition of faith in words almost identical with those used by Wesley. For the present, it is sufficient to recall that in 1735, 1736, and 1737, Wesley was reading A. H. Francke's *Nicodemus: or, A treatise on the Fear of Man*. Would he who thought himself "a brand plucked from the burning" for some great purpose have overlooked this sentence: "A single man, setting aside the fear of flesh and blood, and going forth in the name of the living God, hath frequently saved a whole nation"? [42]

In the light of his reading, as well as in consideration of express statements which he made concerning grace and faith before leaving Oxford, it is impossible to claim that Wesley was taught the *doctrine* of justification by faith in 1738, *after* he returned to England. But his gains in America were largely in fields other than theological. In February, 1738, he reflected on his stay in America:

"Hereby I trust He hath in some measure 'humbled me and proved me, and shown me what was in my heart.' Hereby I am come to know assuredly that, if 'in all our ways we acknowledge God,' He will, where reason fails, 'direct our path,' by lot or by other means which He knoweth. Hereby I am delivered from the fear of the sea, which I had both dreaded and abhorred from my youth." [43]

In the wilderness, he had been unable to rely upon his position as Fellow of Lincoln, or as John Wesley, Gentleman, and his reason was often helpless where there was no precedent to guide. In this condition, he had cast his cares upon the Lord; and, however superstitious the method, at bottom it was trust which saved him. His reference to conquering fear is explained by his *Journal* of January 13th. In "a thorough storm," on the homeward journey, he had lain down without fear; and the next day he had applied the word of God to every soul on board with a consequent loss of "that fearfulness and heaviness" which he had almost continually before.[44] Already he was learning, not intellectually but by experience, the psychological value of humble faith.

In his wider acquaintance with men he had learned not only the depth of human depravity but the good residing in those who were outside the ecclesiastical fold to which he belonged. His extreme High Church views were not gone, but he had come to respect the Moravians. His acquaintance with them had shown him a simple people whom he believed to live in the simplicity of the Apostolic Church, and their devotions had opened to him the riches of German hymnody. In his Diary are frequent references to German hymns he was translating. Several are in the hymn book he compiled which was published in Charleston in 1737. Not only these hymns but those which he later translated, some of them added thus to the treasuries of English devotion, must have been first read and appreciated in America. Attention has already been called to the evangelical note in the hymns of the Charleston book, but the student ought not to overlook the deepened emotional values which Wesley gained in this way. That Wesley translated for his hymn book such a hymn as C. F. Richter's, "My soul before thee prostrate lies," is evidence that he felt the power of such verses as these:

> Ye Sons of Men, here nought avails
> Your Strength, here all your Wisdom fails;
> Who bids a Sinful Heart be clean?
> Thou only, Lord, supreme of Men.

> When my warm'd Thoughts I fix on thee
> And plunge me in the Mercie's Sea,
> Then ev'n on me thy Face shall shine
> And quicken this dead Heart of Mine.

> So ev'n in Storms my Zeal shall grow,
> So shall I thy hid sweetness know,
> And feel (what endless Age shall prove)
> That thou, my Lord, my God art Love! [45]

CHAPTER V

WESLEY'S RELIGIOUS EXPERIENCE

IN 1738 Wesley returned to England under conditions which increased the nervous strain noticeable in his earlier religious quest. He left Georgia with his enemies apparently triumphing. They had indicted him for various alleged offenses (mainly, it is true, of an ecclesiastical nature), and his return boded an uneasy session with the trustees of the colony. The latter treated him with courtesy and stood by him, but they accepted his resignation with a readiness which did not salve his feelings. Several summaries of his stay in America and of his spiritual history evidence the growing strain under which he was laboring.

He had summed up the Georgia years by citing his gains. He had learned to know what was in his heart; to beware of men; to trust God to direct his path. He had been delivered from his fear of the sea. He had become acquainted with many of God's servants, particularly the Moravians, and had gained access to the writings of holy men through his acquirement of German, Spanish, and Italian. The gospel had been preached in Georgia. Moreover, the trustees now had a chance to learn the truth about their colony. He was going to tell them, and he did.[1]

On the voyage home he had summed up his spiritual history, beginning with the well-known words: "I went to America, to convert the Indians; but oh, who shall convert me?" He thought that, if the gospel be true, he was safe; but in a storm he sometimes doubted. He had been taught not to lay too much stress on outward works or on faith without works, and he believed that he had not. He had avoided both the Lutheran and the mystical extremes; and he had learned the good rule in interpreting Scripture, *Consensus veterum: quod ab omnibus, quod ubique, quod semper creditum.*[2] Thus he mused about himself. But later, he grew more self-condemnatory.

Now he had learned that, whereas he went to America to convert others, he "was himself never converted." His later corrections of this and other statements will be considered in due course. When he returned from America he had decided that his heart was "altogether corrupt and abominable," that he was "a child of wrath"; that he had only the faith of devils. The faith which he lacked was "a sure trust and confidence in God, that, through the merits of Christ, my sins are forgiven, and I reconciled to the favour of God." "I want that faith which none can have without knowing that he hath it. . . . And he is freed from doubt, 'having the love of God shed abroad in his heart, through the Holy Ghost which is given unto him'; which 'Spirit beareth witness with his spirit, that he is a child of God.' "[3]

In short, Wesley had decided that he was not a Christian, and that to be a Christian he must have a kind of faith which would drive out doubt and fear

and would be accompanied by the witness of the
Spirit that he was a child of God. In this state of
mind, Wesley met a young German, a Moravian missionary on his way to Georgia, Peter Böhler. During
the next three months, until Böhler sailed, Wesley saw
the Moravian missionary several times. They went to
Oxford together and talked much; but Wesley says
that he did not understand Böhler, and Böhler's comment was: "My brother, my brother, that philosophy
of yours must be purged away." [4]   A month later,
Böhler convinced Wesley of unbelief, although, according to his *Journal*, he had already come to that
conclusion before arriving in London. Böhler advised Wesley to preach faith until he had it, and then
to preach it because he had it. At subsequent meetings, Böhler discoursed on the holiness and happiness
which attend faith. Wesley had read Haliburton,
and he was ready to adduce the Scottish writer as an
example of instantaneous conversion.[5]   Böhler convinced him that in the early days of the Church, conversion was instantaneous; and several were brought
to Wesley to testify to their conversion in the same
manner. "Here ended my disputing," said Wesley;
"I could now only cry out, 'Lord, help Thou my unbelief.' " [6]

Father Piette has argued that Böhler was not teaching Wesley justification by faith, but the primary
place of the love of God in Christian experience; and
there is ground for the argument.[7]   When Böhler
sailed for America, he wrote to Wesley, urging him to
"taste, and then see, how exceedingly (*vehementer*)
the Son of God has loved you, and loves you still; and

that so you may continually trust confidently (*confidere*) in Him, and feel His life in you and in your flesh." He was obviously pleading here for Wesley to *realize* the love of God, and calling Wesley's failure to grasp the necessity of this, unbelief. "Beware the sin of unbelief," he wrote, "and if you have not conquered it yet, see that you conquer it to-morrow through the blood of Christ." [8] Toward the close of the letter Böhler associates himself with Wesley and his companions by changing from the second person to the first. He would have Wesley and his brother Charles and Hall admonish one another "to believe, and then to walk circumspectly in the sight of God, to fight lawfully against the devil and the world, and to crucify and to tread all sin under our feet, as far as we are permitted through the grace of the second Adam. . . ." [9] The fact that Wesley's translation of Böhler's Latin letter has certain strange omissions and changes points to a misunderstanding of the Moravian's meaning.[10] Wesley had decided he was not a Christian, and he was sure that Böhler thought the same. Later, he understood better what his German friend was driving at.

Wesley was approaching the resolution of the inner conflict which had developed slowly for many years by reason of the submergence of his emotional nature, becoming critical when, disappointed in himself and in men, he had met experience after experience which had torn away the intellectual and disciplinary covering of his natural feelings. He now sat down once more to sum up his spiritual pilgrimage. In the light of his belief that he had overlooked the power of faith in Christian living, his former life seemed less than Christian. Again we set down the record as it is, without consideration of his later and more mature judgment.

In his Oxford days, said Wesley, he had aimed at inward holiness, "the image of God." But he had not found assurance or comfort. Nor could the mystics help him, for they only substituted inward works for outer works. At Savannah he had been beating the air. "In this vile, abject state of bondage to sin, I was indeed fighting continually, but not conquering. Before I had willingly served sin: now it was unwillingly; but still I served it. I fell, and rose, and fell again. Sometimes I was overcome, and in heaviness; sometimes I overcame, and was in joy. For as in the former state I had some foretastes of the terrors of the law; so had I in this, of the comforts of the gospel. During this whole struggle between nature and grace, which had now continued above ten years, I had many remarkable returns to prayer, especially when I was in trouble; I had many sensible comforts, which are indeed no other than short anticipations of the life of faith. But I was still 'under the law,' not 'under grace' (the state most who are called Christians are content to live and die in); for I was only striving with, not freed from, sin. Neither had I the witness of the Spirit with my spirit, and indeed could not; for I 'sought it not by faith, but as it were, by the works of the law.' " [11]

Wesley's meaning is clear, although his analysis is slightly different from his earlier summaries. He was seeking inward peace and assurance, and he was looking for a permanent plane of living where he should conquer always, instead of fighting and sometimes falling. Later it will be seen how Wesley came gradually to understand that life is not made up of such permanent planes of existence where men, having achieved, go on at the same exalted level. Also he was later to understand that the assurance of salvation which he coveted is not always to be found in those who are indubitably Christians. But, for the time, his own strivings had prepared him psychologically for Peter Böhler's teaching, *as Wesley understood it.* Faith is the gift of God; it may be had instantaneously. "I was now thoroughly convinced," Wesley wrote in a summary of his religious experience, "and, by the grace of God, I resolved to seek it unto the end, (1) by absolutely renouncing all dependence, in whole or in part, upon *my own* works of righteousness; on which I had really grounded my hope of salvation, though I knew it not, from my youth up; (2) by adding to the constant use of all the other means of grace, continual prayer for this very thing, justifying, saving faith, a full reliance on the blood of Christ shed for *me;* a trust in Him, as *my* Christ, as *my* sole justification, sanctification, and redemption." [12]

Two things should be noticed here. In the first place, he had not been aware that he was trusting in his own works. Yet this problem was before his mind years before. He was not an ignorant man hearing for the first time of justification by faith, but a trained student of theology who had tried to avoid either extreme, trusting in faith without works or in

88

works without faith. But now he identified his condition with that of those who believe in salvation by works *alone*. In the second place, he determined to seek this faith by prayer, in addition to the use of "all the other means of grace." Nothing in his new attitude excluded the means of grace; he still sought his new life within the institutions of the Church.

On Wednesday, May 24, 1738, he opened his Testament (evidently practicing a sort of bibliomancy) at the words, "There are given unto us exceeding great and precious promises, even that ye should be partakers of the divine nature." Later he read, "Thou art not far from the kingdom of God." At St. Paul's in the afternoon, the anthem was "Out of the deep have I called unto Thee, O Lord; Lord, hear my voice . . . O Israel, trust in the Lord: for with the Lord there is mercy, and with Him is plenteous redemption. And He shall redeem Israel from all his sins." In the evening he went to a society in Aldersgate Street where some one was reading Luther's preface to the *Epistle to the Romans.* "About a quarter before nine, while he was describing the change which God works in the heart through faith in Christ, I felt my heart strangely warmed. I felt I did trust in Christ, Christ alone for salvation; and an assurance was given me that He had taken away *my* sins, even *mine,* and saved *me* from the law of sin and death." [13]

Any interpretation of John Wesley's personal religion is determined by the significance given to his Aldersgate Street experience. Traditionally, Methodists and non-Methodists alike have seen in this experience the evangelical conversion of Wesley. But of late years more and more scholars have classified this as a mystical rather than an evangelical conversion. Dimond points out the likeness between the mystic "Awakening, Purgation, and Illumination" and Wesley's religious crisis in 1725, "the discipline during the intervening period, and the conversion in 1738." [14] The proper approach to an evaluation of the 1738 experience is by a study of Wesley's subsequent religious life and of his own more mature conclusions concerning his "conversion" and his whole religious experience.

In the first place, Wesley persisted for some time in the belief that, prior to May 24, 1738, he had not been a Christian. On October 30, 1738, he wrote his brother Samuel, who did not look with a friendly eye on what he considered his brother's extravagances: "By a Christian I mean one who so believes in Christ as that sin hath no more dominion over him; and in this obvious sense of the word I was not a Christian till May the 24th last past." [15] But Wesley was troubled by his persistent spiritual unevenness.

At the time of his "conversion," Wesley was astonished that he did not feel those "transports of joy" usually associated with conversion. He concluded that in this experiences vary.[16] On January 4, 1739, there is a pathetic summary of his condition, in which Wesley declares explicitly: "I affirm I am not a Christian now . . . . that I am not a Christian at this day I as assuredly know as that Jesus is the Christ." His reasons are that he does not have the fruits of the Spirit, love, peace, and joy. "I do not love either the Father or the Son." He knows this because he feels it; "there is no word more proper, more clear, or more strong." Moreover, he still is "hankering after a happiness in loving and being loved by one or another." "Though I have endured hardships, though I have in all things denied myself and taken up my cross, I am not a Christian. My works are nothing, my sufferings are nothing; I have not the fruits of the Spirit of Christ. Though I have constantly used all the means of grace for twenty years, I am not a Christian." [17]

This cannot be dismissed as a mood, for Wesley was not given to moods. It is plain that he had been disappointed in not finding the inner peace and joy which he craved. Moreover, he had not found the freedom from all wrong desires and wandering thoughts which he had expected. When his doctrines are examined, it will be seen how his own experience parallels the working out of his theories concerning sin in believers and concerning the stages of the Christian life which succeed forgiveness of sins and adoption into the family of God. Wesley's high ideal of the Christian life led him to doubt his own Christianity when he did not have the assurance which he craved and the perfection which he longed for; moreover his new estimate of the place of emotion in the religious life led him to anticipate an evenness and an intensity of feeling which he did not have.

Canon Overton, a sympathetic Anglican biographer of Wesley, thought that the outburst of January, 1739, was the last evidence of spiritual uneasiness in Wesley's experience. "Henceforth," said Canon Overton, "during the whole of his long life hardly the shadow of a doubt about his spiritual state crossed his path; clouds and darkness constantly swept over his outer life, but there was perpetual and unclouded sunshine within." [18] The facts do not bear this out.

In April, 1739, Wesley wrote to James Hutton, describing the great work at Bristol, but saying: "I am still dead and cold, unless while I am speaking." [19] But far more important is a letter which Wesley wrote to his brother, Charles, in 1766, twenty-eight years after the Aldersgate experience, concealing significant parts of his thought in shorthand or Greek.

"In one of my last I was saying that I do not feel the wrath of God abiding on me; nor can I believe it does. And yet (this is the mystery) I do not love God. I never did. Therefore I never believed in the Christian sense of the word. Therefore I am only an honest heathen, a proselyte of the Temple, one of the God-fearers. And yet to be so employed of God! and so hedged in that I can neither get forward nor backward! Surely there never was such an instance before, from the beginning of the world! If I ever have had *that faith*, it would not be so strange. But I never had any other evidence of the eternal or invisible world than I have now; and that is none at all, unless such as fairly shines from reason's glimmering ray. I have no direct witness, I do not say that I am a child of God, but of anything invisible or eternal.

"And yet I dare not preach otherwise than I do, either concerning faith, or love, or justification, or perfection. And yet I find rather an increase than a decrease of zeal for the whole work of God and every

92

part of it. I am borne along, I know not how, that I can't stand still. I want all the world to come to him whom I know not. Neither am I impelled to this by fear of any kind. I have no more fear than love. Or if I have any fear, it is not that of falling into hell but of falling into nothing.

"I hope you are with Billy Evans. If there is an Israelite indeed, I think he is one. O insist everywhere on *full* redemption, receivable by *faith alone!* Consequently to be looked for *now.* You are *made*, as it were, for this very thing. Just here you are in your element. In connexion I beat you; but in strong, pointed *sentences* you beat me. Go on, in your *own way*, what God has peculiarly called you to. Press the *instantaneous* blessing: then I shall have more time for my peculiar calling, enforcing the *gradual* work." [20]

This letter must be understood in reference to its historical setting. In the early part of the 1760's, beginning at Otley, there had been an outburst of claims to perfect love. Many professed that they had passed suddenly from the status of justified souls to that of sanctified. The doctrinal implications will be reviewed in another chapter, but the meaning for Wesley was that he was faced again with claims to a greater intensity and constancy of emotional states than he had himself attained. He who had preached that men are to strive for a love which casteth out even the suggestion of evil and which gives a high and unchanging level of emotional stability, had not himself received such a salvation. Moreover, he had preached that a man could not stand still, that he must either go forward or backward. His own experience seemed to contradict his doctrine.

The truth is that Wesley had from the first been seeking nothing less than perfection. He found that a trained will and disciplined mind do not mean perfection, for the emotions are unruly. Then, in the enthusiasm of 1738 and immediately afterward, he had expected complete peace and joy and constant dominion over every taint of sin, inward and outward, as a result of the realization of the boundless love of God through faith. But he had been compelled, through the years, to readjust his doctrines, as his sermons on "Wandering Thoughts," "Sin in Believers," and the like, testify. There must be another stage in the Christian life: the justified man must be sanctified. But Wesley himself had not reached this high plateau of the Spirit, where, as he believed at first, men may be free from even the suggestion of evil.

Indeed, Wesley was by nature and training little fitted for experiences of emotional intensity. Throughout his life he had rationed his time and allotted his tasks with a methodicity impossible to more romantic natures. Sometimes, even in his old age, he looked back with a kind of nostalgia to the ordered days at Oxford. "Let me be again an Oxford Methodist!" he cried to Charles in 1772. "I am often in doubt whether it would not be best for me to resume all my Oxford rules, great and small. I did then walk closely with God and redeem the time." [21] Feelings are desirable, but Wesley could not rid himself of his reliance upon reason administering by the rules of

logic. In 1786, he wrote to Elizabeth Ritchie that he
had not heard or read of anything like his own experience. Count Zinzendorf had said that there are
three ways by which God leads his people: by apposite
texts of Scripture, by impressions, by plain and clear
reasons. Wesley had been led by reason and Scripture,
but rarely by impressions. "I see," he wrote, "abundantly more than I feel." And there is something
pathetic in the line with which he concludes: "I want
to feel more love and zeal for God." [22]

"I want to feel." This is a recurring note in Wesley's long years. Not that he was by any means devoid of feeling, but there was not that ebullience of
emotion which some seem to have. The reader who
comes to Wesley's *Journal* with the idea that he was
a preacher of feeling cannot but be surprised at the
paucity of reference to the great evangelist's own
feelings. There are occasional entries: "The longer
I spoke the more strength I had, till at twelve I was as
one refreshed with wine"; "I explained the nature of
inward religion, words flowing upon me faster than
I could speak"; "I intended to have given an exhortation to the Society; but as soon as we met, the Spirit
of supplication fell upon us, so that I could hardly
do anything but pray and give thanks." But compared to the mass of the *Journal* such entries are rare.
The high emotional experiences recorded there are
of other people. Wesley himself had earnests of the
feeling which others had, and he would have liked to
feel more. In the 1737 hymn book, he transcribed
Addison's hymn, "When all thy mercies, O my God";

but the latter lines of the first stanza he changed to read,

> Why my cold heart, art thou not lost
> In wonder, love and praise?

It is illustrative of the ease with which theories can be made that this, on first glance, seems only a proof of Wesley's preconverted state of soul. But Wesley never changed the lines. To the time of his last hymn book, he continued to reprint the hymn as he had printed it almost half a century before. Apparently, to the end it was to him a remarkable fact that he felt no more than he did.

With these facts in mind, one is prepared to understand Wesley's reinterpretation of his own experience, a reinterpretation which made possible one of his great intuitive syntheses. By readjusting his ideas concerning his own experience he was enabled to see the deeper significance of the doctrines he had been preaching concerning the progressive nature of the Christian life. So long as he thought of himself as having been a sinner before 1738, so long he was unable to appreciate some aspects of the Christian life and so long his own spiritual history puzzled him.

A few years after Wesley wrote to his brother that he did not have the love of God in his heart, he issued the first volume of his *Works*, the first collected edition, for which he had bought new paper and new type. In the first volume, which appeared in 1771, Wesley set forth reasons for the new collected edition in thirty-two duodecimo volumes. One of the reasons was that typographical errors and others which obscured the sense must be corrected. Then he added a paragraph which should long ago have given students a key to one of the most important changes in his thought. "But as necessary as these corrections were," he wrote, "there were others of a different kind, which were more necessary still. In revising what I had wrote on so many various subjects and occasions, and for so long a course of years, I found cause for not only rational or verbal corrections, but frequently for correcting the sense also. I am the more concerned to do this, because none but myself has a right to do it. Accordingly I have altered many words or sentences; many others I have omitted, and in various parts I have added more or less as I judged the subject required: So that in this edition, I present to serious and candid men, my last and maturest thoughts: agreeable, I hope, to Scripture, Reason, and Christian Antiquity." [23]

It was for this edition that Wesley corrected his first two journals, modifying or recanting some strong expressions which he had used indicating that, before his conversion in 1738, he had not been a Christian. In the summary of his condition which concludes the last Savannah Journal, Wesley made several corrections. To the statement, "that I, who went to America to convert others, was never myself converted to God," he added: "I am not sure of this." To his judgment that all his sacrifice and striving were but "dung and dross," since they were not ennobled by faith, he appended the statement: "I had even then the faith of a *servant,* though not that of a *son.*" And the collection of condemnations which were summed up in the conclusion, that he was then

97

"a child of wrath," he withdrew with the simple words, "I believe not." He had defined the faith which he lacked as "a sure trust and confidence in God, that, through the merits of Christ, my sins are forgiven, and I reconciled to the favour of God." He amended this by inserting after the words, "The faith I want [lack] is," the explanation, "the faith of a son." And in the first summary which occurs in the Journal account of May 19-24, 1738, Wesley corrects his exclamation, "Oh let no one deceive us by vain words, as if we had already attained this faith!" "That is," runs the correction, "the proper Christian faith." [24]

The importance of these corrections lies partly in the fact that they were introduced into the copy which Wesley so carefully prepared for the edition which was to carry needed corrections of his writings. He had definitely moderated his former estimates of his condition before 1738, estimates which had been written down under the influence of those troublous days when he returned from the struggles in Georgia to the difficulties at home. Now, he set forth his corrections so that there might be no mistake about it.

But Wesley had not reckoned with his printer. William Pine of Bristol has been well called the world's worst printer. He omitted whole pages and so bungled the text that Wesley added a page of errata to each volume, calling attention, sometimes sharply, to the omissions and errors of his printer.

It is part of the irony of history that Wesley was defeated first of all by his printer, and secondly by his editors and biographers. The corrections to the Savannah Journal did not become a part of the text until 1829-1831, when Thomas Jackson edited the Third Collected Edition of Wesley's *Works*. Jackson stated that for these corrections he had the authority of Wesley's own corrections of the First Collected Edition, and subsequent editors and biographers have only copied Jackson's note. Indeed, a recent writer has gone so far as to question the authenticity of the corrections, declaring that they cannot be used in any account of Wesley's thought, on the ground that they were never authorized for publication during Wesley's lifetime.[25] For this reason it is necessary to state clearly the authority for the statement made above, that Wesley included these corrections in his copy for the 1771-74 edition of his *Works*. All that was necessary to assure anyone of Wesley's inclusion of these retractions and modifications was to turn to the back of the volume containing the First and Second Journals. In volume xxvi of *The Works of the Rev. John Wesley, M.A. . . . Bristol: Printed by William Pine, in Wine Street. MDCCLXXIV*, is a list of errata containing every one of the corrections about which so much ado has been made. When the second edition was printed in 1809, the editor simply overlooked or ignored the errata, and Jackson was the first to include them; but even Dr. Curnock, to whom all students of Methodism owe so much, failed to notice that Wesley had included these corrections of earlier statements concerning his religious experience in the errata attached to the first edition. 52158

So much has been said about the authenticity of Wesley's corrections because they are vital to a correct interpretation of his experience. But this is not the only evidence that Wesley did not, in later life, regard his experience of May 24, 1738, as a conversion in the usual sense that the word carries in evangelical circles. It has been strangely assumed by many who write or speak about Wesley, that he dated everything in his religious experience from the Aldersgate episode, and that he made that the starting point of Methodism. As a matter of fact, after the first year or two, he never mentioned the occurrence in his writings. In his *Short History of the People Called Methodists,* which he appended to his *Concise History of the Church,* he makes no reference to the Aldersgate experience, the only mention of anything connected with it being the statement: "In all our steps we were greatly assisted by the advice and exhortations of Peter Böhler, an excellent young man, belonging to the society commonly called Moravians" [26]; and he is speaking here of the organization of the societies, not of his personal experience. The Methodist societies he dates back to 1729, which is, of course, the date of the Holy Club of Oxford. When Wesley delivered the address at the laying of the cornerstone of the City Road Chapel in London, April 21, 1770, he reviewed the history of Methodism. It was an epochal occasion for him, the establishment of Methodism in permanent and respectable headquarters in the capitol. But he began his story of Methodism with his acquaintance with à Kempis and Bishop Taylor; and of Aldersgate Street and of Peter Böhler there is never a word.[27]

Wesley did often refer to 1738 as an epoch in his and in Methodist history; but his references must be

100

taken for what they mean and not changed into a mythical chronology referring to his conversion. Wesley understood, of course, that his new understanding of justification by faith—whether this was a restatement of Luther's or Calvin's doctrine will be considered later—meant a change in his theological and evangelistic message. Therefore his references: "Forty years ago I knew and preached every Christian doctrine which I preach now"; "And this is the doctrine which I have constantly believed and taught for near eight and twenty years." In another sense, 1738 was an epochal year. It marked what Wesley recognized as the third stage in the rise of the Methodist Societies. In his *A Short History of the People Called Methodists,* written in 1781 and appended to his *Concise Ecclesiastical History,* he wrote:

"On Monday, May 1, our little society began in London. But it may be observed, the first rise of Methodism, so called, was in November, 1729, when four of us met together at Oxford; the second was at Savannah, in April, 1736, when twenty or thirty persons met at my house; the last was at London, on this day, when forty or fifty of us agreed to meet together every Wednesday evening, in order to a free conversation, begun and ended with singing and prayer." [28]

To attempt to place in their historical perspective the events of 1738 is not in any way to minimize the importance of Aldersgate Street for John Wesley and for Methodism. But it is necessary to emphasize that attempts to interpret that experience as an evangelical conversion which transformed Wesley from a sinner to a saint, or from a naturalistic humanist to a Christian, are in contradiction to Wesley's own judgment and misreadings of the facts. There can be no doubt that Wesley changed his mind about the Aldersgate experience: the alterations in the *Journal* included by Wesley in the 1771 edition of his *Works*, with the express statement that important changes were to be made, puts this beyond a doubt. And the other evidence is equally convincing. It must be taken, therefore, either that Wesley, in his later years, suffered a retrogression of spirit and became a man unable to understand his own spiritual history, or that his later views represent his mature judgment, that they are the Wesleyan interpretation.

According to the corrections which Wesley made in his *Journal*, he was before 1738 a servant of God, having Christian faith, but lacking the full, filial faith which characterizes "adult" children of God. In 1736, Spangenberg had been describing the fruits of faith. Wesley cried: "If this be so, I have *no* faith!" "That wise man, Mr. Spangenberg," replied: *"Habes fidem, sed exiguam:* You have faith, but it is weak." In 1771, Wesley recalled this, and wrote to Benson: "Here, in this very point, is your mistake. You was as *really* a believer when you came to Kingswood as you are now. . . . You have faith, but it is weak. This was *your* case too." [29] In 1785, Wesley retold the same story to Mary Cooke, adding: "The very same thing I say to you, my dear friend. You have faith, but it is only as a grain of mustard-seed." [30] Wesley had decided that Aldersgate Street marked a stage in his religious experience, and a very important stage; but it was neither the beginning of his Christian life nor the end of it.

And this seems a true analysis. For fifteen years, or thereabout, before 1738 he had been seeking Christian Perfection. In doing so, he had disciplined himself as few men have. His methodical and rationalistic nature made this his natural course; and he did not give over this discipline till death. But his emotional life was suppressed. His mother had taught him so; and his own ascetic beliefs had emphasized the tendency. But in Georgia he had found his reason and will insufficient. All too painfully he was reminded of his lack of emotional stability and of peace. He believed the love of God and man to be the essence of religion; but he had not realized that love. The vital, vivid sense that God loves and forgives had not been a part of his own experience.

The fusing of his personality demanded an emotional experience, and apparently the evening when his heart was "strangely warmed" saw the time when, in Dimond's words, "a powerful self-sentiment became identified, in ways too profound and secret for self-analysis, with a disinterested religious sentiment, the object of which was God revealed in Christ." [31] Or, it might be expressed by saying that Wesley had reached the stage when all his energies and interests were channeled into his devotion to God. His conversion, in short, was not an evangelical but a mystical conversion—that is, the conversion of a religious man to a higher state of religious devotion. His is nearer the type of Pascal than of Augustine. But he was too much the Briton of the eighteenth century to experience the mystical union with God which characterized the classical mystics. His strangely warmed heart signifies what Piette calls an "intense perception of the love of God." [32] And this perception of the love of God awoke in him an answering love. It was not highly emotional, and it was never to be. But it was an unwavering devotion.

Wesley never claimed to have attained perfect love or Christian Perfection; but no student of his life can fail to be impressed with the consistent quality of his long years of almost unbelievable activity. The troubled hours, noted above, seem to have broken in only when he struggled to find a satisfactory explanation of apparent inconsistencies in his experience. But these hours were few, and there is no trace of them whatsoever during the last twenty years of his life. He was cheerful, he never complained, and he maintained a level of activity which is yet a wonder to the readers of his *Journal*. There are evidences of some emotional peaks in his experience, but not many. Although quick tempered and not by nature a humble man, Wesley lived for nearly sixty-five years on an ethical plane worthy of a saint. At the same time, he tried diligently to find some solid, rational expression of his faith; and, while his theology was often inconsistent and is certainly not fully adequate for later generations, he himself was never satisfied until he had reached a mental synthesis agreeable with his own intellectual presuppositions. Beauty did not, indeed, play any large place in Wesley's life; but he made no inconsiderable contribution to hymnology, and he was quick to appreciate the place of song in

Christian societies. There is reason then for including Wesley, along with St. Francis, Wyclif, and Luther, among those in whom Christian ideas and experience have reasserted themselves "with fresh, creative energy." This Professor Lyman has done, illustrating his thesis, that religious creativity "is proportionate to the vital union effected between the four typical religious motives—the ethical, the mystical, the aesthetic, and the philosophic." [33]

To use another terminology, Wesley was a mixture of classical and romantic tendencies. Always he maintained his passion for holiness, which demanded of him the constant imitation of Christ, which led him not only to form religious societies, but to use constantly the means of grace. But orientated with this was a conscious religious experience, embracing trust and insight and the fruits of the Spirit, love, joy, and peace.

This analysis of Wesley's religion may be confirmed by a study of what is a normative element in religious life: his experience of prayer. For almost sixty-six years, as the Diaries extant indicate, Wesley gave a large place to prayer. In the earlier Diaries, he used much the short prayers known as "ejaculatory," but always he notes the hours when he spent at least a few moments in prayer. And his last days were, in this, much as his first. For Monday, February 21, 1791, the pertinent entries are: "5 prayed . . . 7.30 . . . prayer . . . 10 . . . prayer . . . 5.45 . . . prayer . . . 7 . . . prayer." The next day, he notes again: "4.30 prayed . . . 7.30 . . . prayer . . . 4 . . . prayed . . . 8 . . . prayed." On Wednesday, the 24th, he wrote: "4.45

105

prayed . . . 6.30 prayed . . . 2 . . . prayer . . . 9.30 . . . prayed." [34] This was six days before his death.

At times in the *Journal*, prayer is powerfully emotional; but these are almost always the prayers of other people. In 1764, Wesley told of a prayer by a woman in society. The prayer "was perfectly an original; odd and unconnected, made up of disjointed fragments, and yet like a flame of fire. Every sentence went through my heart, and I believe the heart of every one present. For many months I have found nothing like it. It was good for me to be there." [35] This is perhaps what Wesley meant by "passive prayer." "At some times," he wrote in 1769, "it is needful to say, 'I will pray with the Spirit and with the understanding also.' At other times the understanding has little to do, while the soul is poured forth in passive prayer." [36] Wesley thought that prayer is "but the desire of the soul expressed in words"; and for this reason he doubted that there is much value in teaching children to repeat prayers before they are awakened.[37]

Wesley was alive to the subjective value of praying. He was sure "that the end of your praying is not to inform God, as though He knew not your wants already; but rather to inform yourselves; to fix the sense of those wants more deeply in your hearts, and the sense of your continual dependence on Him who only is able to supply all your wants." [38] But on the whole, Wesley's prayers were of the simple type which Heiler calls "prophetic prayers," asking for whatever is felt as a real want. In 1770, Wesley wrote to Mrs. Barton: "For many years I had a kind of scruple with regard to praying for temporal things. But three or four years ago I was thoroughly persuaded that scruple was unnecessary. Being then straitened much, I made it matter of prayer; and I had an immediate answer. It is true we can only ask outward blessings with reserve, 'If this is best; if it be thy will.' " [39] Wesley here refers to a personal scruple which may have inhibited his own praying; but he had before held that prayer may be for temporal as well as for spiritual blessings. He had written to Bishop Warburton in 1762, that he believed "God now hears and answers prayer even beyond the ordinary course of nature; otherwise the clerk was in the right who, in order to prevent the fanaticism of his rector, told him, 'Sir, you should not pray for fair weather yet; for the moon does not change till Saturday.' " [40]

But if Wesley thought that prayer is the desire of the soul expressed in words and believed that one may sometimes pray with little exercise of the understanding, he would have nothing of prayer which depended upon impulse. "In like manner," he wrote to a correspondent in 1748, "you are as really moved by the Spirit to pray, whether it be in public or private, when you have a conviction it is the will of God you should, as when you have the strongest impulse upon your heart." [41] And he urged his people to have fixed times for prayer, that they might acquire a "taste" which they had not. "Whether you like it or no," he advised a preacher, "read and pray daily. It is for your life; there is no other way: else you will be a trifler all your days and a pretty, superficial preacher.

Do justice to your own soul; give it time and means to grow. Do not starve yourself any longer." [42]

Nor did Wesley care for the "mental prayer" of the mystics. He believed that "the Scripture by 'prayer' almost always means vocal prayer. . . . It is therefore our wisdom to force ourselves to prayer—to pray, whether we can pray or no. And many times while we are so doing the fire will fall from heaven, and we shall know our labour was not in vain." [43]

In prayer, then, as in the rest of his religious life, Wesley valued "feeling," but did not much trust it. Habit remained as real to him as in his Oxford days. Man must seek by constant, regular activity, even in prayer; and if "the fire fall," the religious man is to be thankful.

No account of Wesley's religious life would be complete without reference to his constant use of the means of grace. It has apparently been assumed by some that his defense of the Church of England was owing to an inconsistent conservatism which moved him to oppose any change of allegiance on the part of the Methodists. In fact, Wesley was devoted to the Church of his childhood. He accounted her liturgy the best of any national Church in the world, and when he prepared the liturgy for the American Methodists he made only such changes as seemed to him advisable for doctrinal or prudential reasons.[44] His *Journal* is full of references to the services which he attended, and he was moved deeply by her anthems and psalms. If he moderated his views of the Church and her orders, he maintained his belief in the value of the sacraments. It should not be forgotten that Wesley received the Lord's Supper on an average of once every five days "throughout his apostolic life." [45] The ordinances of the Church were to him a real part of the ministry of the love of God.

In prayer, in attendance upon the ordinances of the Church, in activity Wesley spent his saintly life, seeking that Christian Perfection which was to him the summation of religion.

For him, whatever may have been true of some of his followers, the search was never ended in any final status; he lived, as the *Minutes* of 1770 phrased it, moment by moment. There was stability in his life, but it was the stability of growth, of a Pilgrim's Progress; yet on the whole, the progress was that of a Happy Pilgrim. In his old age, some of his preachers said to him: "Mr. Wesley, you often ask us about our experience, we should like to be favoured with yours." Wesley's reply was to quote two stanzas of one of his brother's hymns, which were not an assertion but a prayer.

> Jesus, confirm my heart's desire
>   To work, and speak, and think for thee;
> Still let me guard the holy fire,
>   And still stir up thy gift in me;
>
> Ready for all thy perfect will,
>   My acts of faith and love repeat,
> Till death thy endless mercies seal,
>   And make my sacrifice complete.[46]

CHAPTER VI

THE BASES OF WESLEY'S THEOLOGY

FOR many years it was customary to speak of Wesley as a great evangelist and organizer whose doctrines were borrowed from German Pietists and English Dissenters. Recently this view has been challenged, but it is yet taken for granted by many that he was a reviver of half-forgotten doctrines. There is no intention to claim great theological originality for Wesley, but it is argued here that Wesley's position, theologically as well as otherwise, gives him importance for modern religion. It is necessary, therefore, to turn to a consideration of his thought.

The student who would understand Wesley's mature conclusions concerning Christianity must keep certain facts in mind. In the first place, he must remember that Wesley's background was Anglicanism of the seventeenth and eighteenth centuries. Many seeming inconsistencies in Wesley will disappear when one ceases to cramp him into the mold of German Pietism or of English Dissent. In the second place, the student must keep in mind that Wesley was typically British in his major interest: holiness. From Hobbes to the nineteenth century, British philosophers and theologians have been chiefly moralists. It is not an historical accident that both the Oxford Movements, that of Wesley in the eighteenth and that of Newman in the nineteenth century, were orientated to this idea. If one seeks for symbolic coincidences, they may be found in the sermons which heralded the two movements. In 1733, Wesley preached at Oxford on "The Circumcision of the Heart"; in 1833, Keble preached at Oxford the sermon which Newman said ushered in the Tractarian Revival, on "National Apostacy." [1]

But one must not lose sight of another fact, that Wesley's thought developed and matured through the years. It has long been recognized that he changed his views on several important matters about 1738, but too many have assumed that this was the only, or at least the last change which he made. But just as his interpretations of his own religious experience developed until he was almost seventy years old, so also his theology changed. The student of Wesley must make up his mind whether he calls the theology which Wesley held in 1733, or that which he held in 1738, or that which he held in 1770, "Wesley's theology." It is assumed in this book that the views which Wesley reached in his later period represent his mature convictions. The changes must not be exaggerated; but they must be recognized. It is therefore necessary to trace their development in order to explain his mature views.

So much preliminary statement is required, and even this is not sufficient. Professor Clement C. J. Webb referred to the difficulty of recovering the theology of the Oxford Movement in the nineteenth century because of the changes in thought since that time. The doctrine of evolution and the wide acceptation of the results of biblical criticism have naturalized certain categories until it is with effort that the student can think himself back into the earlier part of the last century. But the Oxford Movement itself has added to the difficulty. Certain conceptions of Catholic theology have been so grafted to the idea especially of High Churchmanship that it is not easy to enter into the spirit of Anglicanism as it was before either Tractarianism or Evangelicalism. John Wesley was of the eighteenth century; and he was nourished in High Church Anglicanism as that was understood in the latter seventeenth and early eighteenth centuries. One must be content to see him, therefore, in the light of his time. It may be that he is the more meaningful in that he stood close to an older and almost lost world.

To understand Wesley's thought one must begin with his assumptions, with those beliefs which underlay all his later amplifications and changes. And here one cannot ignore the mental atmosphere of his home and early training. Wesley was, for example, from an old-world family where, in spite of education and considerable sophistication, spirits and goblins yet lived. Nor is this to be dismissed as preparation only for superstition. Such an atmosphere kept minds pliable when mechanistic philosophies would have stamped out all the poetry of life. However deplorable as intellectual error, it was good that some in the eighteenth century never got completely away from old-world views; else would posterity have been the poorer for the lack of that poetry which is one of the gifts of that century to ours.[2] It is in this light that one should view the understratum of credulity in Wesley's mind. It leavened the too intellectualistic and too materialistic bent which was his both by nature and training.

In accord with his practical interests Wesley was concerned with theology principally as it bore on practical matters. Speculative doctrines Wesley usually accepted according to the prejudices of his education or to the appeal that the doctrine made to his common sense. He believed most heartily in the Trinity, but he would not contend for the term. He thought that Servetus was not really anti-trinitarian, although he dared not use the words "Trinity" or "Person." "I dare," commented Wesley, "and I think them very good words. But I should think it very hard to be burned alive for not using them; especially with a slow fire, made of moist, green wood." [3] Wesley's doctrine of the atonement seems to have been the conventional substitutionary theory, but he gave it a simple statement: "God will not inflict on that (justified) sinner what he deserved to suffer, because the Son of His love hath suffered for him." [4] Justifying faith, for him, was a confidence that "Christ died for *my* sins, that He loved *me*, and gave Himself for *me*." Wesley's religious needs and his practical interests demanded this much; they did not demand more. It is true that the work of Christ had great importance in Wesley's eyes, for this work is the ground of man's salvation. But this is not to say that Wesley attached great importance to any doctrine of the atonement. The love of God in Christ was the essence of the matter for him.

For Wesley, God is, of course, the *reality* of realities. Of the two classical modes of conceiving God, as *being* or *activity*, the latter was always uppermost in Wesley's mind. While he did not use the jargon of modern theology, he clearly had in mind that which is meant by transcendence and immanence; and his position can be stated only by saying that God is both transcendent and immanent.

God is an objective reality, to use the modern terminology. Wesley would have had nothing of the talk about God as a "projection" of human ideals; but to assume that for this reason Wesley is to be catalogued with those who relegate God to immeasurable distance from mankind is to mistake his real meaning. When he speaks of eternity, he is careful to warn his readers against assuming that God is any less mindful of his children. Man must remember that "nothing is little or great, that no duration is long or short before Him." [5] Man may be aware of the infinite distance between God in heaven and man on earth, but this distance means nothing to God. But it is not only that this distance means nothing to God, but that God is actually near to man.

If God is transcendent, He is also immanent. How God sustains the universe, man does not know. "Perhaps what the ancient philosopher speaks of the soul, in regard to its residence in the body, that it is *tota in toto, et tota in qualibet*, might, in some sense be spoken of the omnipresent Spirit, in regard to the Universe." [6] In his third discourse "Upon our Lord's Sermon on the Mount," Wesley recorded his belief, "that God is in all things, and that we are to see the

114

Creator in the glass of every creature; that we should use and look upon nothing as separate from God, which indeed is a kind of practical Atheism; but, with a true magnificence of thought, survey heaven and earth, and all that is therein, as contained by God in the hollow of His hand, who by His intimate presence holds them all in being, who pervades and actuates the whole created frame, and is, in a true sense, the soul of the universe." [7]

It would be folly to expect of Wesley a philosophical consistency untrue, not only to his nature and interests, but to his time. He did not work out the implications of his belief in the immanence of God for a philosophy of natural law. Indeed, there are times when he speaks of God in terms which show that he is, at the moment, thinking in the traditional way of a God outside his creation, as the God of the Deists was outside. But it is evident that Wesley's belief in God's closer, more intimate relation with nature, expressed in such passages as that quoted above, was his real answer to the mechanistic, deistic theories of his time. God is both transcendent *and* immanent. It will be shown later that he would have nothing of the deterministic philosophy associated with Calvinistic transcendence, and it would be equally wrong to claim his suffrage for the determinism implied in modern immanental philosophy. He held to a simpler theology. "That fine poet," Alexander Pope, was in error when he wrote:

> He sees with equal eye, as Lord of all,
> A hero perish, or a sparrow fall.

115

This would be to reduce life to a uniformity which man cannot allow. God feedeth the fowls of the air; but "are not ye much better than they?" God does deviate from his general laws. Again Wesley quoted Pope to disagree with him:

> Shall burning Etna, of a sage required,
> Forget to thunder, and recall her fires?
> On air or sea new motions be imprest,
> O blameless Bethel! to relieve thy breast!
> When the loose mountain trembles from on high,
> Shall gravitation cease, if you go by?
> Or some old temple, nodding to its fall,
> For Chartres' head reserve the hanging wall?

To this Wesley replied, simply, yes. "If it please God to continue the life of any of his servants, He will suspend that or any other law of nature." [8]

This attitude of Wesley may, in part, be attributed to the more credulous side of his nature; but it is rooted deep in his instinctive rebellion against a mechanized conception of the Universe. God is not a great machinist viewing his works with Olympian satisfaction.

Wesley's theology demanded a closer correlation of God with His world than contemporary thought allowed. He voiced this belief, in terms of traditional theology, by insisting that God has not precluded Himself "from thus exerting His sovereign power from working miracles in any kind or degree, in any age, to the end of the world." [9] It is hard for modern readers to understand that this point of miracles and when they ended was a crucial one for pre-nineteenth-century theologians. The whole relation of theology to a mechanized Universe was determined by the answer to this question: "Did God ever work miracles, and, if so, when did He stop working them?" The Catholic said: "God has never stopped; He may work miracles at any time." The Protestant said that God "worked them in apostolic times, perhaps until the close of the third century." The skeptic said: "God may never have worked them"; and he could adduce Hume's brilliant essay in support. As theology came to terms with eighteenth-century natural philosophy, it tried to push miracles more and more into the background. God's world is a beautiful machine, like Paley's watch; its ordering must not, cannot be disturbed. True, we continue to worship God because He is a Great Mechanic; but He must not tamper with the machine.

Against such a conception, the Romantic poets took up a semi-pantheism, a belief in "something interfused." According to Professor Whitehead, they revolted against the lifeless mechanism of the Newtonian world-machine toward a more organic conception of life.[10] It must not be thought that Wesley was consciously attempting a philosophic correction of Newtonian physics. But he did come down on the side of a more fluid universe as against the carpenter idea of God. And he did it by taking the Catholic position, that the relations of God and his world remain as they have always been, intimate and effective. Miracles ceased after the third century, not because God had withdrawn from his world, but because the love of men had grown cold. Man may live, if not in

117

expectation of God's intervention, at least in assurance of its possibility.

If God is not limited in His relations with his Universe by mechanical barriers, He is limited by His own nature. He cannot, for example, destroy out of the soul of man "that image of Himself wherein He made him"—a point to which the argument must return. Moreover, God is not only sovereign but governor.[11] Here Wesley adopted the argument of Grotius. God is not only powerful but just, and this precludes Him from foreordaining part of His creatures to life everlasting and part to damnation. Everywhere Wesley insists upon the goodness, the mercy, the love of God. However great, however far off according to human comparisons, God is the loving One whom men may love. To forget this is to ignore the heart of the Wesleyan message.

It is sometimes assumed that all Wesley had to say about man is contained in his doctrine of original sin. Nothing could be farther from the truth. Only in the larger setting of his doctrine of man can one understand his doctrines of sin, of evil, and of salvation.

In the first place, Wesley accepted the contemporary doctrine of a "universal chain of being" (*Scala Naturae*). In his *A Survey of the Wisdom of God in the Creation: or, a Compendium of Natural Philosophy,* Wesley made use of Bonnet's *Contemplation of Nature* to expound this doctrine. "The whole progress of nature is so gradual, that the entire chasm from a plant to man, is filled up with divers kinds of creatures, rising one above another, by so gentle an ascent, that the transitions from one species to another, are almost insensible." [12]   In other words, man is but one species in a chain of beings which stretches from the plants to man.   Wesley was sure that the chain went on to include angelic beings also.

But what is the demarcation between man and the brutes?   Wesley did not believe that the line of division is reason.   If one uses the word understanding, instead of reason, then it is plain that brutes also have understanding.   He was sure, as he set forth in a very ingenious sermon on "The General Deliverance," that the brutes had lost by the Fall of Man, and that, in consequence, some of them "have, at present, little more understanding than the earth on which they crawl, or the rock to which they adhere." [13]   But the dividing line between man and beast is not mental.

Man is made in the image of God, and what this means Wesley explains repeatedly.   "God did not make him mere matter, a piece of senseless, unintelligent clay; but a spirit like himself, although clothed with a material vehicle.   As such he was endued with understanding; with a will including various affections; and with liberty, a power of using them in a right or wrong manner, of choosing good or evil. . . ." [14]   In this there is similarity to the brutes, which have will and affections and a measure of liberty, although these have been impaired, if not lost, in the Fall.   But their affections and liberty are directed toward "loving obedience to man," while man's nature is capable of "loving obedience to God."   This is the impassable barrier between man and the brutes, that they cannot know and love God. [15]   But Wesley hoped that the consummation when the "creature itself also shall be delivered from the bondage of corruption, into the glorious liberty of the sons of God," may mean that the brutes will be moved up the Scale to the position which man now occupies, while men are made "equal to angels." [16]

Man, in his primitive purity, had, according to Wesley, both the natural and the moral image of God. The natural image was his "power of self-motion, understanding, will and liberty." The moral image of God was man's original perfection. "This was the supreme perfection of man . . . the continually seeing, and loving, and obeying the Father of the spirits of all flesh." [17] But in the Fall man lost "the moral image of God, and, in part, the natural." [18] Sin and evil are the results of man's possessing the natural image of God—that is, of his possession of liberty to choose how his affections are disposed. Having this liberty, man chose evil. He lost, therefore, the moral image of God, holiness and righteousness.

That Wesley regarded human nature as corrupt is too well known to need proof. This comes, in part, from his theological heritage. It has been mistakenly assumed that Wesley learned from William Law a mystical doctrine of the essential divinity of human nature. The assumption is the result of confusing Law's earlier writings with his later ones, written under the influence of Jakob Bœhme. Human nature, according to Law, in his *Christian Perfection* (1726), is diseased; mankind is "a Race of fallen Spirits." [19] Nor did the High Church Arminianism in which Wesley was trained teach the natural

120

religious or moral ability of man. Arminianism was a doctrine of grace, presuming original sin in man. But the main support of the doctrine of original sin was for Wesley unquestionably his own observations. Before going to America, he had pictured the savages as living an idyllic life; but, after his return, he referred over and over to their depravity. Their "natural religion" seemed to him the grand answer to all doctrines of man's natural goodness. In the beginning of his treatise on original sin, Wesley devotes pages to a survey of history and of the contemporary world in proof of man's corruption. Some of his examples are strikingly modern: "There is a still more horrid reproach to the Christian name, yea, to the name of man, to all reason and humanity. There is war in the world! war between men! war between Christians! . . . Now, who can reconcile war, I will not say to religion, but to any degree of reason or common sense?" [20]

This original sin of man is not simply the sum total of his evil acts but an inherent disposition toward evil. Sin, for Wesley, is actual transgression, but this rooted in an evil tendency which man has by the Fall of Adam. As one commentator remarks, Wesley never freed himself entirely from the belief that sin is a *substance*. The Christian may triumph over actual sin; but inbred, original sin remains in him until it has been removed by sanctification. But Wesley's common sense saved him from more than one awkward theory. In dealing with the practical needs of his people, he was a shrewd analyst and a helpful adviser, although his theoretical explanations sometimes

121

limped. It was plain to him that there is something radically wrong in the world; and so radical is this wrongness that Wesley could not see it simply as the mass of individual transgressions. The roots lie in a corrupt human nature made worse by a bad education. He freely criticized social wrongs, but he saw them always as the result of a corrupt heart.

Man lost not only the moral image of God, but, in part at least, he lost the natural image. His will became infirm, since his affections were not guided by an unerring reason. Likewise, his liberty ceased to be freedom "wholly guided by his understanding." In all this Wesley's emphasis upon understanding, or intelligence, must be noted. This emphasis is even more noticeable when it is inquired how the Fall of man affected his understanding. Before this lapse, man's spirit probably "discerned truth by intuition"; his knowledge was limited, but he was not subject to error. But with the Fall man's knowledge ceased to be by intuition; he knew not immediately but mediately.[21] What Wesley thought about the nature of man's knowledge can be learned by studying his psychology, which in many respects was thoroughly Lockian. Especially did Wesley adopt the empirical side of Locke's psychology, whether or not directly from Locke. But Wesley was unwilling to push his empiricism to its logical conclusion. There are no innate ideas, all ideas being received through the senses; but Wesley would not go on to question whether the senses may not be deceived as to the external world. Certainly, he would not agree that the external world exists only in the representation of the senses.

In fact, Wesley would not go even so far as Locke in some matters. Whereas Locke concluded that "secondary qualities," colors and the like, being somewhat confused and vague, must be attributed to the mind of the observer, Wesley contended for the objective reality of both primary and secondary qualities. "When I say," wrote Wesley, " 'That cloth is of red colour,' I mean its surface is so disposed as to reflect the red (that is, the largest) rays of light. When I say, 'The Sky is blue,' I mean it is so disposed as to reflect the blue (that is, the smallest rays of light)." His decision was: "Colour therefore is a real material thing. There is no illusion in the case, unless you confound the perception with the thing perceived." [22]

Except when the Holy Spirit has restored in man the image of God, the divine ways and purposes may be known to man, aside from revelation, only in God's works. And the intuitive knowledge possible even to the man in whom the image of God has been restored was greatly restricted by Wesley. Like Locke, Wesley distrusted mysticism. Professor Clement C. J. Webb thinks that there is some connection between an empirical psychology which finds in sensation the only avenue to reality and religious movements stressing the feelings as "the test of spiritual contact with the object of religious faith." [23] There is doubtless some truth in this observation, but Wesley did not depend much upon "feelings," whatever his psychology.

Man, corrupted by the Fall, has lost the moral image of God, and, in part, the natural image also. How is this to be restored? Since the natural man is incapable of good, and impaired in will and understanding, it would seem that one is thrown back upon the irresistible grace of Calvinistic theology. But for Wesley the "natural man" is a logical abstraction. Like the economic man or the caricatures set up today by amateur psychologists, anthropologists, and theologians, the "natural man" does not exist. The truth is that "there is no man that is in a state of mere nature; there is no man, unless he has quenched the Spirit, that is wholly void of the grace of God. No man living is entirely destitute of what is vulgarly called *natural conscience*. But this is not natural: it is more properly termed, *preventing grace*. Every man has a greater or less measure of this, which waiteth not for the call of man. Every man has, sooner or later, good desires, although the generality of men stifle them before they can strike deep root, or produce any considerable fruit. Everyone has some measure of that light, some faint glimmering ray, which sooner or later, more or less, enlightens every man that cometh into the world. And everyone, unless he be of the small number whose conscience is seared as with a hot iron, feels more or less uneasy when he acts contrary to the light of his own conscience. So that no man sins because he has not grace, but because he does not use the grace which he hath." [24]

This is Wesley's way of escape from the theological and psychological dilemma which the doctrine of original sin poses for all who adopt it. To understand how Wesley could hold to the doctrine of orig-

124

inal sin and at the same time reject Calvinism, one must grasp this essential fact, that, for Wesley, the "natural man" is only a logical fiction. In this world man exists as a natural man plus the prevenient grace of God. And this grace is not the forgiving favor of God granted in what the Reformed theologians called justification; this grace is empowering grace. "Stir up the spark of grace which is now in you," exhorted Wesley, "and he will give you more grace." On this road man may go, accepting greater and greater grace until God restores in him the lost image.

It is thus true to say that Wesley did not believe that man can by his own unaided efforts achieve any good thing. It is true that Wesley poured scorn on talk about natural morality and natural piety. There is no innate knowledge of God, no natural intuition of divine things. But there is possibility of good in man, for God has given him grace, a light which lightens every man that cometh into the world. Twentieth-century readers may remark that there is little difference between a doctrine of natural ability and a doctrine of prevenient grace; but the eighteenth century saw a deal of difference. By the doctrine of prevenient grace two important truths could be preserved. In the first place, proper emphasis could be laid upon man's proneness to evil, a proneness which modern men, aware of social imperfections and of man's instinctive tendencies, will be the last to deny. In the second place, the *divine initiative* could be safeguarded. Religion is not the evolution of man's nature; it implies the emergence of new factors in the total situation. And a great company has always testified that man's religious life begins and ends in God.

The contrast of Calvinistic theology with Wesley's is plain if one will consider the differing explanations which the two theologies offer of this dilemma of man dead in trespasses and sin. In accordance with Catholic theology, Wesley posited a prevenient grace which enables man to accept increased grace and to go on by the help of God to higher stages of the Christian life. The Anglican Articles were ambiguous, and both Catholic and Calvinistic interpretations were put upon them. The tenth Article declares that man cannot "turn and prepare himself by his own natural strength and good works, to faith, and calling upon God"; wherefore "we have no power to do good works pleasant and acceptable to God without the grace of God preventing us, that we may have a good will, and working with us, when we have that good will." Although the latter phrase is almost a direct quotation from Augustine, the Article was never quite satisfactory to the Calvinists. In 1643, the Assembly of Divines proposed a revision of the Articles, desiring to interpolate in Article X words which would make clear that preventing grace works "so effectually in us, as that it determineth our will to that which is good." [25] On the other hand, the Article was freely interpreted according to the Catholic conception of grace. It was in this sense that John Wesley's father understood it. Samuel Wesley believed that no man can do an "action properly and perfectly acceptable to God by his own natural abilities, abstracted from the assistance of God's Spirit, but by His common assistance he may pray, abstain from sin, and practice duty; and, if he continues in these good actions, he will have still more aid, and go on to perfection." [26]   In contrast with this position, the Calvinists could see salvation possible only by the irresistible power of divine grace overwhelming helpless and hopeless man.   The distinction is between man empowered to choose and man compelled to obey; and in that distinction, however hidden under theological subtleties, is the essential difference between two philosophies.

It has been pointed out above that present-day critics of Newtonian science stress the metaphysical implications of that science by which man becomes "the puny and local spectator," the "irrelevant product of an infinite, self-moving engine."   Professor Whitehead has drawn the parallel between the irresistible grace of Calvinism and Jansenism and "the irresistible mechanism of nature" with neither of which man can co-operate.   It was precisely along this line that Wesley made one of his most fundamental attacks upon Calvinism.   In two short papers, "Thoughts on Necessity" and "A Thought on Necessity," published in 1774 and in 1780 respectively, Wesley connects a mechanical philosophy of the world, a necessitarian psychology, and Calvinism. [27]   The mechanical philosophy he sets forth in a paraphrase of the words of Henry Home, Lord Kames (1696-1782): "The universe is one immense machine, one amazing piece of clock-work, consisting of innumerable wheels fitly framed, and indubitably linked together.   Man is one of these wheels, fixed in the middle of this vast automaton. And he moves just as necessarily as the rest, as the sun or moon, or earth. Only with this difference (which was necessary for completing the design of the Great Artificer) that he seems to himself perfectly free. . . ." This is of a piece with the materialistic explanation of mind, which Wesley exhibits in another quotation: "The soul is now connected with a material vehicle, and placed in the material world. Various objects here continually strike upon one or other of the bodily organs. These communicate the impression to the brain; consequent on which such and such sensations follow. These are the materials on which the understanding works, in forming all its simple and complex ideas; according to which our judgments are formed. And according to our judgments are our passions; our love and hate, joy and sorrow, desire and fear, with their innumerable combinations. Now, all these passions together are the will, variously modified; and all actions flowing from the will are voluntary actions; consequently, they are good or evil, which otherwise they could not be. And yet it is not in man to direct his own way, while he is in the body, and in the world."

The associationist psychologist, David Hartley (1705-1757), began with Locke's sensationalism, as did Wesley also, and his scheme seemed "plausible" to Wesley. "Who can deny," he asked, "that not only the memory, but all the operations of the soul, are now dependent on the bodily organs, the brain in particular? insomuch that a blow on the back part of the head (as frequent experience shows) may take away the understanding, and destroy at once both sensation and reflection; and an irregular flow of spirits may quickly turn the deepest philosopher into a madman?" But this psychology implies determinism. "In all cases the choice must be determined by that motive which appears the best upon the whole. But motives are not under our power. Man is passive in receiving impressions of things, according to which the last judgment is necessarily framed. This the will necessarily obeys, and the outward action necessarily follows the will."

Wesley followed the quotations just given by examining Jonathan Edwards' psychology and by an insistence on the dependence of Calvinistic theology upon deterministic philosophy. To Wesley, the picture of man helpless to co-operate with God was essentially the picture of man helpless before the Newtonian world-machine or helpless in the grasp of mechanical causes and effects working in himself. It is true that Wesley himself had no satisfactory answer to the questions raised by the determinists; he could only affirm his faith in the intention of "the God of Nature" to make man free and reasonable. Man is not a machine, however intricate and wonderful. Nor—logician and logic-chopper that Wesley sometimes was—could he be satisfied with the finely-spun distinctions with which Edwards explained voluntary action. "The actions of men are quite voluntary," said Edwards; "the fruit of their own will. . . . Now, if men voluntarily commit theft, adultery, or murder, certainly the actions are evil, and therefore punishable. And if they voluntarily serve God, and help their neighbours, the actions are good, and therefore rewardable." But according to Calvinism their wills are *not* free, reiterated Wesley; they cannot help willing thus or thus. Here is the ancient antinomy: deterministic theories seem to demonstrate man's unfree will; but mankind knows itself to be free. It is significant that Wesley's answer is finally to quote from Milton:

> For so
> I form'd them free: and free they must remain,
> Till they enthral themselves.

Even this brief discussion will be sufficient to show that in Wesley's fundamental doctrines of God and of man he rejected determinism. Although he worked with the traditional dogmatic materials which Anglican theology handed to him, he came down on the side of human freedom. Man is evil, but he has the prevenient grace of God, empowering grace which, if used, will enable a man to go on to repentance and faith, to the Christian life. Man is not a machine; of this Wesley was sure, even if he had to express his assurance in quotations from the poets.

Before going on to a more detailed examination of Wesley's evangelical doctrines, it is necessary to ask one more question about his assumptions: What did he regard as religious authority? The tendency with many in the eighteenth century was to adopt a simplified answer. If natural phenomena could be reduced to simple terms, so also could religious authority. The final authority of Christians is the Bible; or reason, reduced to certain innate ideas, or the dogma of the Church as formulated by the ecumenical councils. It is customary to speak of Wesley as holding to some such simple religious authority: he was a Bible Christian, acknowledging no authority but the written word; he rested in the evidence of Christian experience; or, he combined the two.

Wesley called himself a Bible-Christian. He insisted that Christians should not require what is not found in the Scriptures, and that they should stand by all that is found there. "To the law and to the Testimony," was his cry. "This," he wrote, "is the general method of knowing what is 'the holy and acceptable will of God.' " [28] To find the particular rule, one has only to apply the general. But he recognized that men may err in interpretation, and he enjoined caution because of this. One should be especially careful "with respect to those parts thereof which less immediately relate to practice." That men differ in interpretation is not proof that they are not children of God; "but it is a proof that we are no more to expect any living man to be infallible, than to be omniscient." [29] But there are no mistakes in Scripture. Nevertheless, in his translations Wesley frequently anticipated the readings of later critics, and when he prepared the *Sunday Services* for America, he left out many psalms and parts of others "as being highly improper for the mouths of a Christian congregation." Here, as often elsewhere, his practical sense overrode his theory.

But Wesley had another guide whose authority for him has not been so generally recognized. In the preface to the First Collected Edition of his works (1771-1774), Wesley hoped he had written what was

"agreeable to Scripture, reason, and Christian antiquity." No one can follow Wesley with understanding
without taking into consideration his high regard for
the primitive Fathers. To Dr. Conyers Middleton,
Wesley explained this high esteem. By the primitive
Fathers he meant particularly Clement of Rome,
Ignatius, Polycarp, Justin Martyr, Irenæus, Origen,
Cyprian, Macarius, and Ephraim Syrus. "I allow,"
he said, "that some of these had not strong natural
sense, that few of them had much learning, and none
the assistances which our age enjoys in some respects
above all that went before." He did not doubt, therefore, that one could find in their writings "many mistakes, many weak suppositions, and many ill-drawn
conclusions." But he added: "Yet I exceedingly
reverence them as well as their writings, and esteem
them very highly in love. I reverence them, because
they were Christians, such Christians as are above
described. And I reverence their writings, because
they describe true, genuine Christianity, and direct
us to the strongest evidence of Christian doctrine. . . .
They never relinquish this: 'What the Scripture
promises, I enjoy. Come and see what Christianity
has done here, and acknowledge it is of God.' " [30]
The Fathers—"chiefly those who wrote before the
Council of Nice"—are "the most authentic commentators on Scripture, as being nearest the fountain,
and eminently endued with that Spirit by whom all
Scripture was given." [31] This was written, not before
1738, but in 1756. And twenty-six years later, Wesley declared that he regarded no authorities but "the
Ante-Nicene Fathers," although he would not accept

them in opposition to Scripture.[32] In 1784, he acted upon a conviction concerning the validity of presbyterial ordination which was rooted in his understanding of the practice of the Primitive Church.

Here again Wesley was in line with High Church Anglicanism. In the seventeenth century the Church of England had been remarkable for wealth of patristic learning. The appeal to antiquity was made by the Laudian divines in their controversies both with Rome and with the Puritans. And this appeal was made especially to the first six centuries, to the period of the undivided Church. But there was a tendency among English High Churchmen to narrow this still more. Bishop Andrewes, perhaps the most learned of the English divines, in the seventeenth-century sense of the word, preferred for authority the Fathers before 500 A.D.[33] Herbert Thorndike (1598-1672), whose books occupy considerable space in The Anglo-Catholic Library, thought the Fathers before the fourth century should have preëminence, giving for this reasons very similar to those quoted above from Wesley.[34] The Nonjurors made their appeal to Scriptures, reason, and the Primitive Church; and with them patristic learning almost disappeared from the English Church until the Oxford Movement. One of the first acts of the authors of "Tracts for the Times" was the publication of some of the writings of the Ante-Nicene Fathers.

In listing his authorities, Wesley always coupled reason with Scripture. Here again Wesley was a child of the Enlightenment. "It is a fundamental principle with us," he wrote to Dr. Rutherforth, in 1768, "that to renounce reason is to renounce religion, that religion and reason go hand in hand, and that all irrational religion is false religion." [35] He did not, therefore, deny the value of so-called natural theology, and when taxed with having caricatured "natural religion" in his picture of the American Indian, Wesley replied that he was there speaking of "men's natural manners." [36] He did not believe that natural religion is enough, for he insisted upon the necessity of revelation; but all religion is reasonable.

This is true, Wesley held, whether one means by reason, "the eternal reason, or the nature of things," or "the faculty of reasoning, of inferring one thing from another." The foundation of religion "stands on the nature of God and the nature of man, together with their mutual relations." And Wesley had no sympathy with mystic depreciations of reason. He contended that the Lord and his apostles were continually reasoning with their opponents, and that the Epistle to the Hebrews is "such a chain of reasoning or argumentation" as he did not know in ancient or modern times.[37]

Wesley insisted that reasoning about religion is not fruitful unless "ideas" received by intuition are considered as well as those which come through the senses. As will be seen later, he developed, in accordance with his Lockian psychology, a doctrine of faith which was, in reality, a theory of knowledge. Man may perceive certain truths directly instead of indirectly through the senses. These truths were, in fact, limited to Biblical doctrines personally applied; but Wesley believed that there was direct apprehension of these by

134

the mind. The materials of intuition, therefore, must be included by those whose reasoning on religion is to be sound.[38] In the main, however, Wesley agreed with his contemporaries that the reason must deal primarily with the natural world and derive therefrom its materials for a reasonable faith. "The little which we know of God, (except what we receive by the inspiration of the Holy One)," he wrote, "we do not gather from any inward impressions, but gradually acquire from without. 'The invisible things of God,' if they are known at all, 'are known from the things that are made;' not from what God hath written in our hearts, but from what he hath written in all his works." [39]

Whatever one thinks of Wesley's conception of reason, however inadequate his theory may now seem, it is certain that he believed in the reasonableness of religion. The Scriptures are indeed the sole rule of faith and practice; but Wesley assumed that the Scriptures are themselves reasonable and must be so interpreted. Whatever is irrational is not religion. While holding to this principle, Wesley shared the early eighteenth-century view that only practical matters are worth reasoning about. "I believe that most of the controversies which have disturbed the Church," wrote Wesley to Joseph Benson in 1788, "have arisen from people's wanting to be wise above what is written, not contented with what God has plainly revealed there." "Metaphysical disquisition" is worse than useless; it is dangerous.[40] And Wesley was also too good a psychologist to encourage his converts to "reason" about their condition. His exhortation was to simple trust and obedience. But there is no reason to doubt Wesley's sincerity when he repeatedly expressed his belief that religion is reasonable.

It has long been recognized that Wesley made a distinct contribution to modern religion by his emphasis upon Christian experience. What Wesley did, according to the usual interpretation, was to revolt against the eighteenth-century conception of religion as doctrine and conduct, and to substitute the individual's faith and feeling. Such an interpretation is only partially true.

In the first place, Wesley's interest in Christian experience is rooted in the same soil as the eighteenth-century English interest in conduct. Just as he preferred reason devoid as far as possible of metaphysical subtleties, so he was interested in experience as a practical matter: the proper study of mankind is man. In 1734, he argued with his father that Epworth was not the proper place for the true development of John Wesley's religious life. "But for the proof of every one of these weighty truths," he added, "experience is worth a thousand reasons." [41] With Wesley, religious experience, in the primary sense of the term, is the experience of God, or of the Holy Spirit. But this experience is man's experience, and most of Wesley's concern was with the manward side. He believed and insisted upon the work of the Holy Spirit, but any serious study of his writings must convince the student that Wesley was rather modest in his dealings with the Godward side of Christian experience. This is, in part, the explanation for his

136

conservatism in theology. He would go no further than he thought reasonable interpretation of Scripture would allow when he spoke of God, but man's side of experience may be analyzed and expounded.

Wesley recognized the apologetic importance of introducing into theology the evidence of Christian experience. In his letter to Dr. Middleton, Wesley says that he conceives this "to be the strongest evidence of the truth of Christianity." Attacks upon the traditional "evidences" of Christianity had not destroyed those evidences, but some of the objections were weighty and did not admit of self-evident answers. He doubted that the cause could long be maintained by appeal to these traditional evidences, and questioned "whether, if they do not obey the loud call of God, and lay far more stress than they have hitherto done on this internal evidence of Christianity, they will not one after another give up the external, and (in heart at least) go over to those whom they are now contending with; so that in a century or two the people of England will be fairly divided into real Deists and real Christians." [42] To give up the outward evidences would mean for many very little. They have neither faith nor love; they have no divine evidence of things unseen; they are neither happy nor holy; they have not learned, in whatsoever state they are, to be content; they do not walk as Christ walked.

But what does Wesley mean by experience? It is better to let him speak for himself. "I now am assured that these things are so: I experience them in my own breast. What Christianity (considered as a doctrine) promised is accomplished in my own soul.

137

And Christianity, considered as an inward principle, is the completion of those promises. It is holiness and happiness, the image of God impressed on a created spirit, a fountain of peace and love springing up into everlasting life." [43] At another time, he wrote to one of his correspondents: "We know there is nothing deeper, there is nothing better in heaven or earth than the God of love! So that we see distinctly what we have to aim at. We see the prize and the way to it! Here is the height, here is the depth, of Christian experience! 'God is love; and he that dwelleth in love dwelleth in God, and God in him.' " [44]

Experience in these quotations refers to "inward" experience: the acme of it is love; for he that dwells in love dwells in God and God dwells in him. But experience has a wider meaning for Wesley. In 1774, Wesley explained to "Miss March" his method of estimating the experience of others. "I 'sum up the experience' of persons," he wrote, "in order to form their general character. But in doing this we take a different way of making our estimate. It may be you chiefly regard (as my brother does) the length of their experience. Now this I make little account of; I measure the depth and breadth of it. Does it sink deep in humble, gentle love? Does it extend wide in all inward and outward holiness? If so, I do not care whether they are of five or five-and-twenty years' standing." [45] Here Christian experience includes not only inward but outward holiness. It is the experience of the whole man.

Wesley was alive to the possibilities of evidential value in the religious consciousness. He was especially curious about claims to experience of the Trinity. Some of his friends thought they had an experience similar to that of de Renty, the Catholic worthy whom Wesley so much admired, a direct experience of the three Persons of the Godhead. Among these was Lady Maxwell, to whom Wesley wrote in 1787: "I think there are three or four in Dublin who likewise [he has named some others in London] speak clearly and scripturally of having had such a manifestation of the several Persons in the ever-blessed Trinity. Formerly I thought this was the experience of all those that were perfected in love; but I am now clearly convinced that it is not. Only a few of these are favoured with it." [46] But Wesley was suspicious of peculiar experiences. Willing to allow for individual variations, he yet insisted upon "common salvation." [47] Whitefield had not done well to go against the judgment of the whole society, and Wesley's careful organization of his followers was designed not only to deepen but to regulate individual experience. Besides, external authorities, the Scriptures, especially as interpreted by the Ante-Nicene Fathers, and reason (as he understood it) served as a check upon the vagaries of individual inner experiences. "The conjunction of belief in the authority of an organic church with insistence upon the value and reality of individual experience as the final test," writes Dr. H. B. Workman, "gives to Methodism its special position in the Catholic Church." [48]

So much may be said of experience as an authority to which appeal may be made for the truth of Christianity. But there is another sense in which the

Christian needs authority; that is, in the sense of guidance. What is the authority for one's actions at any given time? Wesley had to meet in his day the old claim to immediate inspiration, to guidance by direct impulses upon the mind and heart. Very early in his dealings with the Moravians he found them inclined to value highly this direction "by the Spirit." In November, 1738, he gave his opinion on some matter to James Hutton. "This may seem of very little weight to some of our brethren," he wrote, "especially when urged by one so weak as me; and they may think it deserves no other answer than 'He hath not the Spirit.'" [49] Soon he learned to distrust this submission of matters to the tailors, mechanics, and other untrained men who were in the society; and he fell back upon the advice of men of like training with himself. Wesley's aristocratic system in his societies was not only because of his own predispositions, but because of his unsatisfactory experience with the impulses of his brethren.

Up until at least the middle of the 1740's, Wesley still resorted to lot or to some form of bibliomancy in determining his actions when he was at a loss how to proceed. But this disappeared, and Wesley fell back more and more upon common sense and the Bible, interpreted by the early Fathers. "How does the Spirit of God lead his children to this or that particular action? Do you imagine it is by blind impulse only? by moving you to do it, you know not why? Not so. He leads us by our eye, at least as much as by the hand; by light as well as by heat." [50]

Wesley's belief concerning immediate inspiration

140

has been dealt with more fully in a monograph by the writer, but it is necessary to say that Wesley restricted the tendency to act upon impulses supposed to be of the Holy Spirit by safeguards which were intended to prevent any great reliance upon them. In practice they were not sufficient, and the documents which he himself collected from his friends, detailing their experiences, are replete with marvels. Believing as he did in the communion of the divine and the human, Wesley could hardly exclude them *a priori;* but the dilemma was recognized, and he attempted to deal with it in his organization.

It must be remembered, however, that Wesley estimated the experience of others not only by their inner state of humble love but also by their inward and outward holiness. Experience, then, if one is to be true to the whole range of Wesley's thought, is not to be restricted to moments of experience, as in conversion, but includes the whole range of man's inner and outer life. It is in connection with this that one must observe a second meaning of experience. Not only one's own but the experience of other people has evidential value in religion. Men may learn something not only from their own seeing, but also from those who have been restored to sight.

"Now, transfer this to the case before us: and those who were blind, but now see—those who were sick many years, but now are healed—those who were miserable, but now are happy—will afford you also a very strong evidence of the truth of Christianity; as strong as can be in the nature of things, till you experience it in your own soul; and this, though it be allowed they are but plain men, and in general of weak understanding—nay, though some of them should be mistaken in other points, and hold opinions which cannot be defended." [51] This was Wesley's great evidence for the essential Christianity of Methodism. To the Bishop of London, Wesley appealed "to plain facts." "By the fruits shall ye know those of whom I speak; even the cloud of witnesses, who at this hour experience the gospel which I preach to be the power of God unto salvation. The habitual drunkard that was is now temperate in all things; the whoremonger now flees fornication; he that stole, steals no more, but works with his hands; he that cursed or swore, perhaps at every sentence, has now learned to serve the Lord with fear and rejoice in Him with reverence; those formerly enslaved to various habits of sin are now brought to uniform habits of holiness. . . . My Lord, can you deny these facts?" [52] Wesley felt that in his writings he was representing mature Christian experience. "In the *Thoughts on Christian Perfection* and in the *Farther Thoughts*," he wrote to one of his correspondents in 1766, "you have the genuine experience of the adult children of God. Oppose that authority to the authority of any that contradict (if reason and Scripture are disregarded). . . ." [53]

The collections which Wesley made of religious autobiographies have furnished materials for more than one study in the psychology of religion. But Wesley was not merely a romantic, emphasizing the worth of the inner life. He was interested in man and his conduct. He would not admit the reduction of empirical psychology to the subjectivism which resulted in Hume's skepticism, but he did accept a practical consequence of empiricism, that one must turn to an analysis of man's experience for further light on the vexed questions of the relation between mind and reality.

In the light of this study of Wesley's fundamental assumptions, one may go on to examine his reconstruction of Christian doctrine. But the assumptions must be kept in mind. And not least among these assumptions is that of the nature of religious authority. It has been too easily assumed that Wesley simply reinstated orthodox theology and the letter of the Bible as Christian infallibilities, or that he set up Christian experience as the final authority. The truth is that he felt the richness of Christian truth to be too great to allow so simple a solution. Inconsistent as his own treatment was, inadequate as was his attempt to give logical statement to his conviction, he did realize how impossible it is to fit the manifold facts of human experience into any one of the theological molds which were ready to his hand. In common with the historic Church, he recognized the Bible as the one rule of faith and practice; but he supplemented this by an acknowledgment of the priority of the primitive Fathers as interpreters, and by a recognition of the place of reason; and to this he added the authority of experience, the religious experience of man in its broadest sense, but particularly the testimony of the "adult children of God." No more consistent, no simpler authority would suffice: single and more logical molds were too rigid; the systems were too systematic.

CHAPTER VII

THE DOCTRINE OF SALVATION

ALTHOUGH Wesley expressed himself on such subjects as the nature of God, the nature of man and their relations, he was, as has been said, primarily interested in practical matters. He was sure that religion does not consist in orthodoxy or right opinions; they are but "a slight part of religion at best, and sometimes no part at all." If a man is a child of God, holy in heart and life, opinions are but the smallest part of his religion. If a man is a child of the devil, his opinions, however correct, are not religion at all. Only the ingrained convictions of a lifetime can explain this tolerance, for in other matters Wesley was, during most of his life, contentious enough. In his old age he wrote of those who lie in bed eight or nine hours or more: "I do not say now (as I should have been very apt to do fifty years ago) that all who indulge themselves in this manner are on the way to hell." [1]

One of the most beautiful letters which John Wesley ever wrote was written to his nephew, Samuel, who had joined the Roman Catholic Church. Samuel's defection troubled his uncle, but not because of his "embracing such and such opinions (were they right or wrong)." Wesley was troubled because his nephew had cut himself off from instructions which he sorely needed. His nephew lacked religion: "Christ in you the hope of glory, Christ reigning in your heart and subduing all things to Himself." "I care not a rush," he wrote, "for your being called Papist or Protestant. But I am grieved at your being an heathen. Certain it is that the general religion both of Protestants and Catholics is no better than refined heathenism." And, with delicate courtesy, Wesley recommended to his Catholic nephew true religion, "the religion which Kempis, Pascal, Fenelon enjoyed." [2]

The matter with which Wesley was most concerned was salvation. This is the doctrine which has been most expounded by his commentators and has been most extolled and condemned. It has been explained as a religion of feeling, as a revival of Luthero-Calvinian justification by faith, and as a doctrine formulated in reaction against Protestantism. A restudy of the doctrine of the Moravians, of the Reformers' faith, of the teachings of Arminius, are undoubtedly helpful; but the necessary thing is to examine carefully the teachings of that eighteenth-century son of the English Church, John Wesley.

In the first place, what did Wesley mean by salvation? He tells us in very understandable English. "We mean," he wrote, "that the moment a man receives faith . . . . he is saved from doubt and fear, and sorrow of heart, by a peace that passes all understanding; from the heaviness of a wounded spirit, by joy unspeakable; and from his sins, of whatsoever kind they were, from his vicious desires, as well as words and actions. . . . By salvation I mean, not barely,

145

according to the vulgar notion, deliverance from hell, or going to heaven; but a present deliverance from sin, a restoration of the soul to its primitive health, its original purity; a recovery of the divine nature; the renewal of our souls after the image of God, in righteousness and true holiness, in justice, mercy and truth." [3]

Salvation is here defined by a psychological analysis of the "saved" man. It is the state of the man who is the recipient of the saving grace of God. Wesley is using the framework of his theology of the Fall. Man had lost the image of God; now it is restored. He has been "born again."

This new birth is "a vast inward change, a change wrought in the soul, by the operation of the Holy Ghost; a change in the whole manner of our existence; for from the moment we are born of God, we live in quite another manner than we did before; we are, as it were, in another world." [4] In his sermon on "The Great Privilege of Those that are Born of God," Wesley draws a long and interesting analogy between this new spiritual birth and natural birth. [5] Before natural birth, the child exists, but without "senses." "All these avenues of the soul are hitherto quite shut up. Of consequence, it has scarcely any intercourse with this visible world; nor any knowledge, conception, or idea, of the things that occur therein." With birth, all is changed. "Every sense is employed upon such objects as are peculiarly suitable to it; and by these inlets the soul . . . . acquires more and more knowledge of sensible things, of all the things which are under the sun."

"So it is with him that is born of God." Man, hitherto existing without seeing or knowing the spiritual world, enters into new relationships. He is a man of a new heart and of a new life. "His soul is renewed after the image of God, in righteousness and in all true holiness. And having the mind that was in Christ, he so walks as Christ also walked." The life of God in the soul of a believer implies "the continual inspiration of God's Holy Spirit . . . . an unceasing presence of God; and an unceasing return of love, praise and prayer, offering up all the thoughts of our hearts, all the words of our tongues, all the works of our hands, all our body, soul, and spirit, to be a holy sacrifice, acceptable unto God in Christ Jesus." This implies "the reaction" of the soul; "God does not continue to act upon the soul, unless the soul reacts upon God." [6]

To Wesley, working as he did with adults to whom his preaching was new, new in emphasis and for most of them new in content, conversion was instantaneous. His converts were twice-born men. His own experience was not of this type, but he regarded instantaneous conversion as normal. But Wesley did not contend for this. From the time when a man is justified, "salvation gradually increases in his soul." And he said of the new birth: "Of the first sowing of this seed I cannot conceive to be other than instantaneous; whether I consider experience, or the word of God, or the very nature of the thing;—however, I contend not for a circumstance, but the substance: If you can attain it another way, do. Only see that you do attain it." [7]

Perhaps his best expression of the fact that there are marked differences in religious experience is in a letter which he wrote in 1785. He recalled his own dismay when he had listened to Spangenberg describe the "glorious privileges of a believer." He had immediately cried out: "If this be so, I have no faith." Spangenberg replied: *"Habes fidem, sed exiguam;* You have faith, but it is weak." Remembering this, Wesley applied it to his correspondent. "The very same thing I say to you, my dear friend. You have faith, but it is only as a grain of mustard seed. . . . There is an irreconcilable variability in the operations of the Holy Spirit on the souls of men, more especially as to the manner of justification. Many find Him rushing upon them like a torrent, while they experience 'the o'erwhelming power of saving grace.' This has been the experience of many; perhaps of more in this late visitation than in any other age since the time of the Apostles. But in others He works in a very different way:

> He designs His influence to infuse,
> Sweet, refreshing, as the silent dews.

It has pleased Him to work the latter way in you from the beginning; and it is not impossible He will continue (as He has begun) to work in a gentle and almost insensible manner." [8]

The new birth, whether instantaneous or gradual, is connected with a realization of God's love for man as shown in the redeeming work of Christ. It is in this sense that the doctrine of the Atonement can be said to have had great importance for Wesley. But

148

it was not any theory of Christ's work, but the conviction that that work made possible the application of God's love to man, which was central in Wesley's thinking. Man is forgiven for Christ's sake. And we love him because he first loved us. "How came you then to love him at first?" asks Wesley. "Was it not because you knew that he loved you? Did you, could you, love God at all, till you tasted and saw that he was gracious; that he was merciful to you a sinner? . . . And whatever expressions any sinner who loves God uses, to denote God's love to him, you will always upon examination find, that they directly or indirectly imply forgiveness. Pardoning love is still at the root of all." [9] This confidence in a pardoning God is one of the essentials of faith, and this brings the student to consider Wesley's doctrine of faith.

It is necessary at this point to make a digression, but a digression important for establishing Wesley's theological provenance. It has been too commonly assumed that Wesley grafted on to the body of Anglican doctrine, which he had inherited from his High Church father and mother, the Lutheran or Calvinistic dogma of justification by faith. Wesley's variations came "in part from Peter Böhler, by further study of the Greek Testament, and listening to some one reading Luther's Preface to the Romans": so a Methodist scholar, Dr. J. Agar Beet, writing in 1920, explained Wesley's doctrine of faith.[10] In 1935, another Methodist writer asserts that "Martin Luther is known to be, along with his [Wesley's] own independent inquiries into the Word of God, the only authority other than Scripture, that Wesley ever acknowledged for his understanding of Justification by Faith. . . ." [11]

Wesley did sometimes declare his agreement with the sixteenth-century Reformers, saying, for instance, that he believed in justification by faith as Calvin did—although, as will be shown later, Wesley added what Calvin would never have admitted. But it must be kept in mind that Wesley thought that he had found his doctrines, and they *are* apparently taught, in the writings of the early Fathers which he prized so highly. The *Life* of Thomas Haliburton, also, which Wesley read and extolled in Georgia, teaches unequivocally the free forgiveness of God obtainable by faith. It cannot be maintained that Wesley, a well-trained scholar, heard of justification by faith for the first time from the Moravians, Peter Böhler, or anyone else. That he quoted the Homily of his Church "On Salvation" when he finally agreed with what he thought Peter Böhler was teaching about this doctrine is evidence that he had in mind that familiar authority. But Wesley definitely stated where he had learned the doctrine. In 1751, he wrote to the Bishop of Exeter, that "I learned it from the Eleventh and Twelfth Articles and from the Homilies of our Church." [12] In 1762, he wrote Dr. George Horne, afterwards Bishop of Norwich, that he had taught his doctrine of justification "ever since I was convinced of it myself by carefully reading the New Testament and the Homilies." [13]

Taken generally, faith, according to Wesley, is "the demonstrative evidence of things not seen." By faith the spiritual man discerns the things of God. It is with regard to the spiritual world what the senses are to the physical world. Here Wesley falls back upon his psychology. There are no innate ideas; all come from the senses. In order, then, to have "fixed, distinct, and determinate" ideas, "a clear apprehension of the things of God," one must have "a new class of senses opened" in the soul. These are man's avenues to the invisible world; these are the senses whereby one is furnished with "ideas of what the outward 'eye hath not seen, neither the ear heard.' " [14]

In this Wesley can see no difficulty, not as much as in the explanation of the natural senses. "For there is the utmost difficulty in conceiving how matter should influence matter at all; how that which is totally passive should act. Neither can we rationally account either for gravitation, attraction, or any natural motion whatsoever, but by supposing in all the finger of God, who alone conquers the *vis inertiæ* which is essential to every particle of matter, and worketh all in all." [15] Once again Wesley is laboring with his eighteenth-century psychology (and physics) to make clear a deep conviction, this time a conviction concerning man's intuition of divine things.

The source of this definition is clear. It stems remotely, of course, from the definition of the *Epistle to the Hebrews;* but it comes almost word for word from Scougal's *Life of God in the Soul of Man,* a book which Wesley was reading as early as 1736 to one of his parishioners in America. Scougal believed that the root of religion is faith; and the chief branches, love to God, charity to man, purity, and humility. As will be seen later, Wesley changed this;

for to him the root of religion is not faith, but love. But the definition of faith which Scougal gave was retained: "Faith hath the same place in the divine life, which sense hath in the natural; being indeed a kind of sense, or feeling persuasion of divine things." [16]

What, then, is justifying faith? For Wesley, justification is "present forgiveness, pardon of sins, and, consequently, acceptance with God." This comes by faith. "Justifying faith implies, not only a divine ἔλεγχος that God 'was in Christ, reconciling the world unto himself,' but a sure trust and confidence that Christ died for my sins, that he loved me, and gave himself for me." "And," adds Wesley, "the moment a penitent sinner believes this, God pardons and absolves him." [17] Justifying faith, then, is not simply an intuitive knowledge of a general truth but a persuasion of individual application. It is the general truth appropriated in individual experience.

But salvation by faith means more than forgiveness granted to those who trust in God, for present salvation is the state of one who is not only forgiven but saved from sin: it is, in short, holiness: "Without faith we cannot be thus saved; for we cannot rightly serve God unless we love him. And we cannot love him unless we know him; neither can we know God unless by faith. Therefore, salvation by faith is only, in other words, the love of God by the knowledge of God; or, the recovery of the image of God, by a true, spiritual acquaintance with him." [18]

How faith as knowledge works out in the normal Christian life, Wesley explains more than once: "Let but the eye of the soul be constantly fixed, not on the things which are temporal, but on those which are eternal, and our affections are more and more loosened from earth, and fixed on things above. So that faith, in general, is the most direct and effectual means of promoting all righteousness and true holiness." [19]

It is easy to see all this as so many words; but if Wesley is accorded the attention which is given to other men of another century and another universe of thought, his words have substance. Faith to him was something like the intuition of the poet, by which meanings are discovered which are hidden to others. The man of faith lives in a new world, or, more exactly, he is a new man. True, Wesley was sure that by faith he discovered the truth of the Christian system as he understood it; but so are all man's intuitions bound up with his past as well as his present. Beneath all his psychological explanations and all his theological carpentry is a profound conviction, that man may live in relation to the world perceived by faith instead of to a world apprehended only by the physical senses.

That Wesley meant precisely this is set forth in unmistakable language in a sermon which he wrote in his old age, "Walking by Sight and by Faith." [20] "Do you walk by faith?" he asked. "Observe the question. I do not ask, whether you curse, or swear, or profane the Sabbath, or live in any outward sin. I do not ask, whether you do good, more or less; or attend all the ordinances of God. But, suppose you are blameless in all these respects, I ask, in the name of

153

God, by what standard you judge of the value of things? By the visible or invisible world?" And he illustrates his meaning by asking whether his hearers would rather a son should "be a pious cobbler or a profane lord"; whether they would prefer a daughter "should be a child of God, and walk on foot, or a child of the devil, and ride in a coach-and-six." "Religion," he declared, "is no less than living in eternity, and walking in eternity; and hereby walking in the love of God and man, in lowliness, meekness, and resignation." This is the sense of Charles Wesley's verses:

> The things unknown to feeble sense,
>   Unseen by reason's glimmering ray,
> With strong commanding evidence
>   Their heavenly origin display.
>
> Faith lends its realizing light,
>   The clouds disperse, the shadows fly,
> The Invisible appears in sight,
>   And God is seen by mortal eye.

Man trusts in God to forgive his sins, and they are forgiven; but faith is not only trust, it is also the opening of man's inward eyes by the grace of God, so that he no longer walks by sight but by apprehension of a new world of values. He knows, not by logic, nor by authority, but by intuition, that God has indeed loved him and given His son for him. Man is restored, in part, to his primitive state where he knows by intuition as well as by his senses. But, knowing that God has so loved him, man himself loves: the love of God and of all mankind is shed abroad in the human heart.

It is apparent that, in his discussion of faith, Wesley has had some difficulty with his intellectualistic tendencies. He would have clear and distinct ideas; and, while allowing that faith is a sure trust and confidence, he insists that faith is also intuitive knowledge. But there were certain other problems concerning the knowledge of the saved man which had to be raised. Does a man who has been forgiven know this to have been done? In other words, has he "Assurance"?

This is a very old theological question. Augustine thought that man cannot know; the Westminster Confession says that such knowledge is possible, although one may struggle long before attaining it.[21] Wesley had believed from the first that religion means happiness; and no man can be happy who doubts of his salvation. Therefore, very early in his career, Wesley declared his belief in Assurance. At least as early as 1733, he wrote that "the Holy Spirit within us is the security of our salvation; he is likewise an earnest of it, and assures our spirits that we have a title to eternal happiness."[22]

Böhler did not teach Wesley the doctrine of justification by faith; it is doubtful if Wesley understood Böhler's advice in some important respects. But there were some new things in Böhler's teaching. These were, that the fruits of justifying faith are "dominion over sin and constant peace from a sense of forgiveness."[23] Concerning the latter, Böhler taught, more specifically, that when a man is justified, which always happens in a moment, "in that moment he has peace with God: which he cannot have without knowledge that he has it." [24]   It has been somewhat generally assumed that Wesley held tenaciously to the doctrine that a Christian, to be a Christian, must know that his sins are forgiven, must have "peace with God." How far is this sustained by the facts?

In the *Minutes* of 1744, it was denied that one can be justified without knowing it, or that one who hears the gospel can go to heaven without an assurance of God's love.   In 1745, however, the Conference would not declare "a sense of God's pardoning love absolutely essential to our being in his favour." [25] There may be exempt cases.   Neither would they say that such assurance is absolutely necessary for final salvation.   In the same year, Wesley wrote to "John Smith" that he did not deny God's working imperceptibly in some a gradually increasing assurance of his love. [26]   But a man perceives the states of mind and heart, that is righteousness, peace, love, which the Spirit works in his heart.   In later life, Wesley concluded that an assurance of salvation is the privilege of all Christians, but he ceased claiming that this is essential to "justifying faith."   In his old age, he wrote to Melville Horne at Madeley: "When fifty years ago my brother and I, in the simplicity of our hearts, told the good people of England that unless they *know* their sins forgiven, they were under the wrath and curse of God, I marvel, Melville, they did not stone us.   The Methodists, I hope, know better now; we preach assurance as we always did, as a common privilege of the children of God; but we do not enforce it, under the

pain of damnation, denounced on all who do not enjoy
it." [27]

Wesley had some difficulties in stating his doctrine.
He did not teach, as he was often accused of teaching,
that a man is justified because he believes he is justified. Vinet's statement would have pleased Wesley:
"Faith does not consist in the belief that we are saved;
it consists in the belief that we are loved." [28] At
times Wesley recognized that, as a modern scholar has
put it, "confidence is nothing but faith aware of
itself." [29] Writing to Richard Tompson in 1755,
Wesley spoke of assurance as "no other than the full
assurance of faith; therefore it cannot be a distinct
thing from faith, but only so high a degree of faith
as excludes all doubt and fear. This *plerophory,* or
full assurance, is doubtless wrought in us by the Holy
Ghost; yet the mind of man is the subject of both.
I believe feebly; I believe without all doubt." [30] But
he could not get away from his predilection for clear
and distinct ideas.

The testimony of the Spirit of God, the well-known
"Witness of the Spirit," he defined as "an inward impression on the soul, whereby the Spirit of God directly witnesses to my spirit, that I am a child of God;
that Jesus Christ hath loved me, and given Himself
for me; and that all my sins are blotted out, and I,
even I, am reconciled to God." [31] The manner in
which this direct communication, immediate revelation, in short, is given to man, Wesley does not under-
take to say. "But the fact we know; namely, that
the Spirit of God does give a believer such a testimony
of this adoption, that while it is present to the soul, he

can no more doubt the reality of his sonship, than he can doubt of the shining of the sun, while he stands in the full blaze of his beams." [32]

But when one has considered Wesley's doctrines of the new birth, of justification, faith, and assurance, he may yet overlook the essential nature of religion as Wesley understood it. A religion worthy of God who gave it is no other "than love; the love of God and of all mankind; the loving God with all our heart, and soul, and strength, as having first loved us, as the fountain of all we have received, and of all we ever hope to enjoy; and the loving every soul which God hath made, every man on earth, as our own soul." "This love," he continued, "we believe to be the medicine of life, the never-failing remedy for all the evils of a disordered world, for all the miseries and vices of mankind. Wherever this is, there are virtue and happiness going hand in hand." [33]

In Christianity there has always persisted the view that love is the essence of religion, love which is, in fact, the life of God in the soul of man. Sometimes Wesley speaks of Christians living by the inspiration of the Holy Spirit, sometimes of the love of God in the heart; but his meaning is plain. To him the abiding characteristic of Christian living at its best is the love which is shed abroad in the heart by the Holy Spirit.

Professor Webb has seen as one of the characteristics of the Oxford Movement "its return to a primitive consciousness of organic participation in the risen life of Christ, with which the concentration of Western medieval piety on the Passion has less in common than it has with evangelical devotion to the Precious Blood." In speaking of this emphasis upon love as Catholic, one must remember that it is Catholic more truly in the sense that it is primitive and that it is especially characteristic of the mysticism of the Greek Fathers. Professor Webb agrees with Dr. Brilioth, that "the thought of sharing in the glory of the risen Lord preponderates over confidence in the atoning work of the Cross"; that "Easter overshadows Good Friday and makes its message only a part of its own." [34] It seems to the writer beyond a doubt that, however strongly Wesley emphasized the Atonement, he did not give it the place which it had in the thinking of Calvinistic evangelicals. With Wesley the central idea is the love of God in the heart, which is the indwelling of the Spirit. He would not have phrased it as did the Tractarians or their Greek forerunners, but he did center on the thing itself. The beginning is faith, as Ignatius put it; but the end is love.

But love is not merely a state of the soul at any given moment. In one sense, love is holiness. Religion is not simply an inward sense, nor is salvation merely a psychological state. The root of religion is in the soul; but "if this root be really in the heart, it cannot but put forth branches, and these are the several instances of outward obedience, which partakes of the same nature as the root; and, consequently, are not only marks or signs, but substantial parts of religion." [35] This statement must be carefully weighed by those who think that Wesley's doctrine was concerned only with the emotional states of the

159

believer. And, if one will recall that Wesley had clung from his earliest college years to the conviction that "without holiness no man can see the Lord," it will seem reasonable that he should not be able to forget this in his new-found zeal for a life of faith. In his very definition of religion as love, Wesley lays it down for true that outward obedience is not a *sign* of salvation or of faith but a substantial part of religion. How was this reconciled with his doctrine of salvation by faith?

In the first place, let it be stated again, Wesley's is a religion of grace. He had the religious man's conviction of the *divine initiative*. In 1730, he had written to his father that the main point to be gained is "to have an habitual lively sense of our being only instruments in His hands, who can do things either with or without instruments." At that time he felt that "how to affix this sense in us is the great question." [36] In his mystical conversion, if not before, he had achieved that sense of the divine action. If he had heard the words of Bajezid Bistani, Wesley would have understood and approved them: "For thirty years I searched for God, and when at the end of this time my eyes were opened, I discovered that it was he who had searched for me." [37]

Man is saved by the grace of God and by the merits of Christ. He was at one with all orthodox Reformation theologians in this. But how is he saved? What on man's part is the response which appropriates this grace? He had answered, that man is forgiven the moment that he has faith, confidence in the love of God. This Wesley saw was very close to Calvinism, "only a hair's breadth" away. But it was also very close to antinomianism, the doctrine that man's efforts are useless, that the law has no authority for the Christian. Therefore, Wesley could not be satisfied to rest with a doctrine of forgiveness and of the peace of the saved man.

As usual Wesley was brought to clearer formulation of his theology by practical problems. Suppose a good man does not believe in justification by faith, suppose that he will not depend upon faith to save him: will that man be lost? On December 1, 1767, when Wesley had already had to face the problem as to his own state before 1738, he wrote in his *Journal* that this much "appeared clear as day": that "a Mystic, who denies Justification by Faith (Mr. Law, for instance,) may be saved. But, if so, what becomes of *articulus stantis vel cadentis ecclesiæ?* If so, is it not high time for us to 'reject bombast and words half a yard long,' and to return to the plain word, 'He that feareth God, and worketh righteousness, is accepted of Him?' " [38]

The importance of this statement for Wesley's mature theology must not be slurred over. From his earliest manhood, Wesley had believed that "he that feareth God and worketh righteousness is accepted of Him." But when he came to know the power of a consciousness of God's love through faith, he accepted it as true that all who do not so realize the loving forgiveness of God are not Christians. God accepts only those who come by faith alone. But his Church of England training and his English common sense would not let him rest there. Neither would his ab-

sorption in morality. So significant is his development here that it must be considered in some detail.

In 1742, Wesley declared all works done before
justification to partake of the nature of sin.[39] Before
a man is forgiven he can do no good thing. In the
Conference of 1744,[40] the questions of repentance
and of works meet for repentance were up for discussion. It was decided that these must go before forgiveness. In 1745, it was added: "if there be time for
them" (this was to leave room for deathbed salvation).
But the difficulty was gotten around by calling repentance "a low species of faith." In 1745, the Conference considered the case of Cornelius (Acts x). According to the theory, Cornelius' good works, which
were said to have come up as a memorial before God,
were only splendid sins. But the Conference could
not agree to this. His works, the Conference decided,
were sinful, but they were not "abomination to the
Lord."

At first Wesley had scrupled even to use the word,
"condition," in speaking of any requirement made
of man previous to his forgiveness by faith.[41] But
this, in which he went even beyond the Reformers,
he soon gave over. In 1745, he wrote to "John
Smith": "I believe (1) that a rational assent to the
truth of the Bible is one ingredient of Christian faith;
(2) that Christian faith is a moral virtue in that
sense wherein hope and charity are; (3) that men
ought to yield the utmost attention and industry for
the attainment of it, and yet (4) that this, as every
Christian grace, is properly supernatural, an immediate gift of God, which he commonly bestows in the

use of such means as He hath ordained. I believe it is generally given in an instant; but not arbitrarily, in your sense of the word; not without regard to the fitness (I should say the previous qualifications) of the recipient." [42]

In 1779, Wesley made a clear-cut distinction. All the talk about "salvation by faith" and "salvation by works" tended to obscure what seemed to him the real point of division. Either salvation is the arbitrary breaking through of God upon man's passivity, or it is the reciprocal work of God and man. When he and his brother began to preach, "By grace are ye saved through faith," they had been astonished at the charge of preaching salvation by works which was leveled against them. At first Wesley had simply suspected the sincerity of those who so accused him; but later he hit upon the key to an understanding of their position. "This is the key," he wrote: "those that hold, Every one is absolutely predestinated either to Salvation or Damnation, see no medium between Salvation by Works and Salvation by Decrees." They are right, concludes Wesley. "As averse as I once was to the thought, upon further consideration, I allow there is, there can be no medium. Either Salvation is by Absolute Decree, or it is (in a scriptural sense) by Works." He goes on to explain that salvation by the decree of God, in the strict Calvinistic sense, is salvation without human conditions. If conditions are insisted upon, then the absolute decree breaking through upon man's passivity must be set over against salvation on conditions, as salvation by faith against salvation by works. Faith itself is a condition; and Wesley

163

could not deny man's part even in present salvation: "only he that believeth shall be saved." [43]

If there are conditions attached to man's forgiveness, there are certainly conditions attached to man's final salvation. In the point of conditions before justification, Wesley thought Calvin defective; in regard to the conditions of salvation at the end, he considered Luther woefully lacking. The only book of Luther which Wesley commented on at any length was the *Commentary on Galatians*. This Charles Wesley had read in May, 1738, seeming to get no small comfort from it. John apparently did not read it until June, 1741, when he set down his opinion thereof in no uncertain language. "I was utterly ashamed," he wrote. "How have I esteemed this book, only because I heard it so commended by others; or at best, because I had heard some excellent sentences occasionally quoted from it! But what shall I say, now I judge for myself, now I see with my own eyes? Why, not only that the author makes nothing out, clears up not one considerable difficulty; that he is quite shallow in his remarks on many passages, and muddy and confused almost, on all; but that he is deeply tinctured with mysticism throughout, and hence often dangerously [in the first edition, it was "fundamentally"] wrong. To instance only in one or two points: How does he (almost in the words of Tauler) decry reason, right or wrong, as an irreconcilable enemy of Christ. ... Again, how blasphemously does he speak of good works and of the law of God—coupling the law with sin, death, hell, or the devil; and teaching that Christ delivers us from them all alike. ... Here (I apprehend) is the real spring of the grand error of the Moravians. They follow Luther, for better for worse." [44]

Luther had touched Wesley at two of the Englishman's most tender points. Nothing could make Wesley give up his belief in the use of reason in religion nor in the primary place of holiness in the Christian life. It should be noted that Wesley's opinion of Luther did not result from the disagreements of the Methodists and the Moravians. Already in April, 1739, the day before he began to expound the Epistle to the Romans to one of the Bristol societies, Wesley spoke of "Luther in the fury of his Solifidianism." [45] Luther simply did not emphasize works enough for the man who had inherited the mediating theology of Anglicanism and whose passion was first and last a passion for holiness. It is significant that Wesley never included any writings of either Luther or Calvin in his numerous reprints for Methodists, although he had profound respect for the character and labors of both Reformers. As far as Wesley could go was to include two short biographies of the Reformers in his *Christian Library*.

With an intense conviction that "without holiness no man can see the Lord," Wesley could not exclude inward and outward holiness from the conditions of salvation, in the ordinary sense of the word. But he was equally convinced that present salvation, salvation from doubt and fear and from guilt and sin, is by faith, although a faith with conditions. Reconciliation of the two Wesley found in a distinction between salvation as a present experience and salvation as the final acceptance of man by God. In 1741 he read Bishop Bull's *Harmonica Apostolica*,[46] in which this distinction is made. At first, Wesley was repelled by the idea, but he was soon using it himself. In 1745, he was writing that justification at the last day is on the condition of "both inward and outward holiness." He thought that this ought to meet the desires of all "who have hitherto opposed justification by faith alone merely upon a principle of conscience, because you was zealous for holiness and good works." [47]

He did not himself believe that any can be finally saved who is not holy. So far as he knew, all Christians believe this. The papists introduce a doctrine of purgatory to establish this, and others believe that holiness is attained only "in the article of death." But all agree that we must be "fully cleansed from all sin, before we can enter into glory." He admitted that usually this happens at death, as will be seen when his doctrine of Christian Perfection is considered. But there is the hope that one may have holiness in this life. Any way one approaches it, this doctrine requires good works as a condition of final salvation.

With Wesley's position in mind, one can understand the meaning of the famous *Minutes* of 1770. Until the death of Whitefield, Wesley had done everything possible to avoid conflict with the Calvinists. But he had already come to a conclusion about his own experience. He had adopted that theory of the infinite grades of faith and of assurance which he set forth to more than one correspondent, and he had decided on the division of Christian experience into two stages, the condition of a servant and the condition of a son, which is a part of his mature doctrine of Christian Perfection. Accordingly, in 1770, the Conference considered the question of faith and works. These *Minutes* have often been quoted, but no excerpts will take the place of the *Minutes* themselves. It is necessary to quote the relevant parts *in extenso,* together with the section published in the *Long Minutes* which gives the setting of the discussion.[48]

"Q. 74. What is the direct antidote to Methodism, the doctrine of heart-holiness?

"A. Calvinism: All the devices of Satan, for these fifty years, have done far less toward stopping the work of God, than that single doctrine. It strikes at the root of salvation from sin, previous to glory, putting the matter on quite another issue.

"Q. 75. But wherein lie the charms of this doctrine? What makes men swallow it so greedily?

"A. (1) It seems to magnify Christ; although in reality it supposes him to have died in vain. For the absolutely elect must have been saved without him; and the non-elect cannot be saved by him.

"(2) It is highly pleasing to flesh and blood, final perseverance in particular.

"Q. 77. We said in 1744, 'We have leaned too much toward Calvinism.' Wherein?

"A. (1) With regard to man's faithfulness. . . .

"(2) With regard to 'working for life,' which our Lord expressly commands us to do. 'Labour,' literally *work,* 'for the meat that endureth to everlasting life.' And in fact, every believer, till he comes to glory, works *for* as well as *from* life.

"(3) We have received it as a maxim, that 'a man is to do nothing in order to justification.' Nothing can be more false. Whoever desires to find favour with God, should 'cease from evil, and learn to do well.' So God himself teaches by the Prophet Isaiah. Whoever repents, should 'do works meet for repentance.' And if this is not in order to find favour, what does he do them for?

"Once more review the whole affair:

"(1) Who of us is now accepted of God?

"He that now believes in Christ with a loving, obedient heart.

"(2) But who among those that never heard of Christ?

"He that, according to the light he has, 'feareth God and worketh righteousness.'

"(3) Is this the same with 'he that is sincere'?

"Nearly, if not quite.

"(4) Is not this salvation by works?

"Not by the merit of works, but by works as a condition.

"(5) What have we then been disputing about for these thirty years?

"I am afraid about words, namely, in some of the foregoing instances.

"(6) As to merit itself, of which we have been so dreadfully afraid: We are rewarded according to our works, yea, because of our works. How does this differ from, 'for the sake of our works'? And how differs this from *secundum meritis operum?* Which is no more than, 'as our works deserve.' Can you split this hair? I doubt I cannot."

The importance of these *Minutes* for an understanding of Wesley's theology cannot be minimized. The Moravians had long since perceived that Wesley had interests that could not be reconciled to Lutheran theology. "Wesley," writes a Moravian historian, "desired to give a prominent place in his system of the Christian religion to the doctrine of *an active love*, proceeding from the new birth and faith; and manifesting itself in *striving after holiness* and *Christian perfection*, and to the doctrine of the furtherance of this *active* love by the *means of grace in the church*. Zinzendorf on the other hand allowed of none other than a *grateful love*, proceeding from the experience of the heart of a *pardoned* sinner; he condemned all self-made holiness, and every merely legal duty, and act of self-denial." [49] Zinzendorf was true to Lutheran doctrine: man's good works are only those which proceed from thankfulness for justification; all others are self-acts.

The *Minutes* were understood as important by contemporaries, enemies and friends. The onslaught made against Wesley is well known, and Wesley did not regard his subsequent statement, that nothing in the *Minutes* contradicts justification by faith, as in any way a retraction of the *Minutes* themselves. He did believe in justification by faith, and in salvation by faith; but he could believe in present salvation only on conditions which man must meet and in final salvation only on the condition of inward and outward works. Fletcher of Madeley, who, Wesley hoped, would be his successor as ruler of the Methodists, saw in the *Minutes* something to be admired, that is, "the

169

candour of an aged servant of God, who, instead of stiffly holding, and obstinately maintaining an old mistake, comes down as a little child, and freely acknowledges it before a respectable body of preachers, whose esteem it is his interest to secure." [50]

In writing to Lady Huntingdon, Wesley insisted that he had had regard for the honor of God for "above these forty years" (he was writing in 1771); and he thought Mr. Fletcher's letter (in the *First Check to Antinomianism*) showed definitely that the *Minutes* "lay no other foundation than that which is laid in Scripture, and which I have been laying, and teaching others to lay, for between thirty and forty years." [51] In the light of this, Fletcher's understanding of Wesley's meaning is important. This Fletcher stated succinctly: "For my part I entirely agree with the Authour of the Minutes, and thank him for daring to break the ice of prejudice and bigotry among us, by restoring *works of righteousness* to their deserved glory, without detracting from the glory of *the Lord our Righteousness*. I am as much persuaded that the Grace of Christ *merits* in the works of his members, tho' it is mixed with dust and dross, which are good for nothing . . . . there is but one man whose works are truly meritorious; but when He works in us by his spirit, our works cannot (so far as he is concerned in them,) but be in a sense meritorious; because they are,—his works." [52] In his *Fourth Check,* Fletcher said that he had produced nearly twenty scriptures, "which declare, with one consent, that we shall be judged, not according to our faith, but according to our works. . . ." [53]

170

In the year when Wesley ordained preachers for America, he recapitulated his views. "Undoubtedly faith is the work of God; and yet it is the duty of man to believe. And every man may believe if he will, though not when he will. If he seeks faith in the appointed ways, sooner or later the power of the Lord will be present, whereby (1) God works, and by His power (2) man believes. In order of thinking God's working goes first; but not in order of time. Believing is the act of the human mind, strengthened by the power of God." [54] Wesley could no longer speak as he once did concerning good works which do not proceed from faith. When he prepared the "Articles of Religion" for the American Methodists, he omitted Article XIII, "Of Works before Justification." He could not endorse the statement of the Article, that "Works done before the grace of Christ, and the inspiration of the Spirit, are not pleasant to God, forasmuch as they spring not of faith in Jesus Christ, neither do they make men meet to receive grace .... for that they are not done as God hath willed and commanded them to be done, we doubt not but they have the nature of sin." Nor could he believe that good works after justification come without the effort of man. Therefore, from Article XII, "Of Good Works," he omitted one word. From the statement that good works "do spring out necessarily of a true and living Faith," Wesley took out the word "necessarily."

In this way Wesley conceived that he united doctrines which had been separated in Catholicism and in the Reformation. "It has been very frequently observed," he wrote in a sermon dated in 1787 and printed in the *Arminian Magazine* in 1789, "that very few were clear in their judgment both with regard to justification and sanctification. Many who have spoken and written admirably well concerning justification, had no clear conception, nay were totally ignorant, of the doctrine of sanctification. Who has wrote more ably than Martin Luther on justification by faith alone? And who was more ignorant of the doctrine of sanctification, or more confused in his conceptions of it? .... On the other hand, how many writers of the Romish Church (as Francis Sales and Juan de Castaniza, in particular) have wrote strongly and scripturally on sanctification, who, nevertheless, were entirely unacquainted with the nature of justification! insomuch that the whole body of their Divines at the Council of Trent, in their *Catechismus ad Parochos,* (Catechism which every parish Priest is to teach his people,) totally confound sanctification and justification together. But it has pleased God to give the Methodists a full and clear knowledge of each, and the wide difference between them." In a later paragraph, Wesley added: "It is, then, a great blessing given to this people, that as they do not think or speak of justification so as to supersede sanctification, so neither do they think or speak of sanctification so as to supersede justification. They take care to keep each in its own place, laying equal stress on one and the other. They know God has joined these together, and it is not for man to put them asunder; Therefore they maintain, with equal zeal and diligence, the doctrine of free, full, present justification, on the one hand, and of entire sanctification, both of heart and life, on the other; being as tenacious of inward holiness as any mystic, and of outward, as any Pharisee." [55]

In 1773, Wesley quoted the words of his High Church friend, John Byrom:

> Nor steel nor flint alone produces fire,
> Nor spark 'arises till they both conspire;
> Nor faith alone, nor works without, is right;
> Salvation rises when they both unite.

CHAPTER VIII

CHRISTIAN PERFECTION

WESLEY'S most distinctive doctrine is unquestionably that of Christian Perfection.[1] This he believed and taught during not only his great ministry, but throughout his ministerial life. From 1725 on, he sought nothing less than perfection; and to understand what he meant by this is to come nearest to an appreciation of Wesley's religious thought.

To the eighteenth century the doctrine of the perfectibility of man rapidly became an axiom. The optimism of both the Enlightenment and the Romantic Movement was partly rooted in a belief that man, once he has the right environment and training, may go on to perfection. This belief was rooted, it is true, in certain conceptions of man's nature which were far removed from the traditional religious conception and, therefore, from Wesley's primary assumptions. The fact that Methodism held to a doctrine of Christian Perfection may, at first sight, suggest analogies and affinities which may be deceiving. To understand Wesley and his relation to the thought movements of his time, one must consider carefully what he believed and taught concerning perfection, sanctification, the "Great Salvation." This is the more important since his doctrine, involving as it does the goal of the Christian life, brings once more

174

into the purview of the student Wesley's entire theology.

In considering Wesley's doctrine of Christian Perfection, one must trace out again the roots of his religious life and thought. Out of what did his conceptions of the Christian way stem? From his young manhood, not to say from his childhood, he had walked in the classical way, putting high value upon the imitation of Christ and upon the Church and its ministries. But upon his return from America Wesley had experienced vividly the love of God and had learned the value of a trust in that love as manifested in the life and work of Christ. This immediate experience, immediate both in the sense of direct and instantaneous, set for him a definite and difficult problem. Just as in his thinking of the relation of man to God Wesley had to consider the old, old problem of faith and works, so in his doctrine of Christian Perfection Wesley had to work over again in his mind the relation of immediate experience to the traditional Christian discipline and means of grace. What is Christian Perfection? How does one receive it? Is it a status or a goal? Is it gradually or instantaneously reached? Is one a Christian who is not perfect? These and other questions had to be answered; and, as in other matters, Wesley did not at once reach his final conclusions. One must follow his development of mind and of experience. In the doctrine of Christian Perfection, as in his other doctrines, his mature convictions are those which should be called "Wesleyan."

As to the origins and development of his doctrine

of Christian Perfection, Wesley had much to say. If it were possible, it would be better to reprint *A Plain Account of Christian Perfection*, which he wrote in 1765 and printed the next year. In this work he reviews, step by step, the progress of his beliefs about the "Great Salvation." The work is not entirely consistent; for Wesley was, in many ways, a journalist rather than a theologian or a historian. But the account is Wesley's own deliberate summing up of his doctrine. Aside from this publication, the most succinct account of Wesley's thoughts on Perfection is in a letter which he wrote to John Newton, Cowper's friend. The relevant parts of this letter, written in 1765, should be quoted.

"But how came this opinion into my mind? I will tell you with all simplicity. In 1725 I met with Bishop Taylor's *Rules of Holy Living and Dying*. I was struck particularly with the chapter upon Intention, and felt a fixed intention to *give myself up to God*. In this I was much confirmed soon after by the *Christian Pattern* [à Kempis, *The Imitation of Christ*], and longed to *give God all my heart*. This is just what I mean by Perfection now: I sought after it from that hour.

"In 1727 I read Mr. Law's *Christian Perfection* and *Serious Call*, and more explicitly resolved to be *all devoted to God* in body, soul, and spirit. In 1730 I began to be *homo unius libri*, to study (comparatively) no book but the Bible. I then saw in a stronger light than ever before that only *one thing is needful*, even *faith which worketh by the love* of God and man, all inward and outward holiness; and I groaned to love God with *all my heart* and to serve Him with *all my strength.*

"January 1, 1733, I preached the sermon on the Circumcision of the Heart, which contains all that I now teach concerning salvation from *all sin* and loving God with an *undivided heart.* In the same year I printed (the first time I ventured to print anything) for the use of my pupils *A collection of Forms of Prayer;* and in this I spoke explicitly of giving '*the whole heart* and *the whole life to God.*' This was then, as it is now, my idea of Perfection, though I should have started at the *word.*

"In 1735, I preached my farewell sermon at Epworth, in Lincolnshire. In this likewise I spoke with the utmost clearness of having *one design, one desire, one love,* and of pursuing the *one end* of our life in all our words and actions.

"In January, 1738, I expressed my desire in these words:

"O grant that nothing in my soul
May dwell but Thy *pure love alone!*
O may Thy love *possess me whole,*
My joy, my treasure, and my crown!
Strange flames far from my heart remove!
My *every* act, word, thought, be love!

"And I am still persuaded this is what the Lord Jesus hath bought for me with His own blood." [2]

The sources which Wesley mentioned deserve at least passing notice. They are Bishop Jeremy Taylor, the *Imitation of Christ,* William Law and the Bible. Certainly, one cannot refer this aspect of Wesley's belief either to German Pietism or to Wesley's "nonconformist ancestors." Taylor was a royalist bishop, a protege of Archbishop Laud; the *Imitation* is a production of medieval monasticism;[3] and Law was, of course, a Nonjuror. As will be seen later, the ideal of Christian Perfection comes theologically and historically from the Catholic stream of Christian thought. The Church of England, in spite of such schisms as that in which the nonjuring High Churchmen were lost, managed to preserve much that distinguished the Catholic view of Christianity. And it was along this *via media* of pre-Tractarian Anglicanism that Wesley came to his final views.

What was the conception of Christian Perfection which Wesley learned from Taylor, from à Kempis, from Law, and from the Bible? In 1733, Wesley preached at Oxford, as he notes in the letter to Newton, on "The Circumcision of the Heart." [4] It is necessary to look again at this sermon, which—it will be remembered—was preached two years before Wesley went to America and five and a half years before the experience of Aldersgate Street.

Wesley began by assuming that one of the most essential facts of Christianity is, that "If Christ be risen, ye ought then to die unto the world, and to live wholly unto God." This, Wesley observed, was a hard doctrine if taken in the "plain and obvious meaning" of the words. Moreover, those whose circumcision is of the heart and spirit, not of the flesh, have as the "distinguishing mark" of a true follower of Christ "not either outward circumcision, or baptism, or any other outward form, but a right state of soul, a mind and spirit renewed after the image of Him that created it." To live wholly to God involves, then, "a right state of the soul." But Wesley goes on to define his meaning more carefully. "Circumcision of the heart" is, in general, "that habitual disposition of soul which, in the sacred writings, is termed holiness; and which directly implies, the being cleansed from sin, 'from all filthiness both of flesh and spirit'; and, by consequence, the being endued with those virtues which were also in Christ Jesus; the being so 'renewed in the spirit of our mind,' as to be 'perfect as our Father in heaven is perfect.'" This renewal implies the possession of the virtues of humility, faith, hope, and charity. Not that these are achieved by man; for it is He alone who works in us, "it being as impossible for us even to think a good thought, without the supernatural assistance of His Spirit, as to create ourselves, or to renew our whole souls in righteousness and true holiness." But the Holy Spirit does work in man humility, faith, hope, and love. As to faith: there is no other foundation of good works than faith, or of faith than Christ; and the Spirit of God is the "Inspirer and Perfecter, both of our faith and works." Moreover, "none is truly 'led by the Spirit,' unless that 'Spirit bear witness with his spirit, that he is a child of God.'"

Love, he added, is "the essence, the spirit, the life of all virtue. It is not only the first and great command, but it is all the commandments in one. " 'Whatsoever things are just, whatsoever things are pure, whatsoever things are amiable,' or honourable, 'if there be any virtue, if there be any praise,' they are all comprised in this one word,—love. In this is perfection, and glory, and happiness." But this love implies the love of man, as well as of God. Only, man's ultimate end is God.

Although holiness is of the heart, that is, of the inner life, it is also the outward obedience of man. A gift of God, holiness requires man's struggle. "Vain hope!" he exclaims of any expectation to fulfil the commandments of God without effort, "that a child of Adam should expect to see the kingdom of God without striving, without *agonizing,* first, 'to enter in at the strait gate'; that one who was 'conceived and born in sin,' and whose 'inward parts are very wickedness,' should once entertain a thought of being 'purified as his Lord is pure,' unless he tread in His steps, and 'take up his cross daily,' unless he 'cut off his right hand,' and 'pluck out the right eye, and cast it from him'; that he should ever dream of shaking off his old opinions, passions, tempers, of being 'sanctified throughout in spirit, soul, and body,' without a constant and continued course of general self-denial!" [5]

This would seem to be a complete statement of Christian Perfection, and even the most cursory acquaintance with Wesley will cause the reader to recognize much that is characteristic of his later teaching. But is this truly a statement of the doctrine as Wesley held it after 1738? Dr. Sugden, in his comments on the sermon, thought that the section concerning agonizing to enter in by the strait way and the necessity of self-denial to achieve sanctification, was a clear statement of holiness by works.[6] But Wesley said to Newton that this sermon contained all that he later taught "concerning salvation from all

sin, and loving God with an undivided heart." And
in the light of the discussion of Wesley's doctrine of
faith and works in the previous chapter, the section
does not seem alien to Wesley's thought.

In one thing there was certainly need of correction
in order that the statement of the sermon might be
brought into line with Wesley's later belief. And in
this instance, Wesley made the correction. In the
original sermon, faith appeared as one of the virtues
wrought in the soul by the Holy Spirit, essentially an
understanding of man's calling "to glorify God, who
hath bought him at so great a price, in his body and in
his spirit, which now are God's by redemption, as well
as by creation"; and as an unshaken assent "to all that
God hath revealed in Scripture and in particular to
those important truths, 'Jesus Christ came into the
world to save sinners,' 'He bare our sins in His own
body on the tree,' 'He is the propitiation for our sins,
and not for ours only, but also for the sins of the
whole world.'" Now, by 1738, Wesley had come to
think of faith as something more than this understanding and "unshaken assent": faith is "the revelation of Christ in our hearts," by which Wesley meant
a vivid conviction of God's love, "His free unmerited
love to me a sinner," a "sure confidence in His pardoning mercy, wrought in us by the Holy Ghost." [7]
In other words, Wesley's early sermon did not need
any emendation as to the goal of the Christian Life;
but there was need to add to his former definition of
faith that it is not merely a virtue of the soul but a
vivid confidence and conviction which is in itself

powerful toward the creation of happiness and conquering love.

Such was the conception of Christian Perfection which Wesley held and which he had held from his Oxford days: a total devotion to God, which includes inner and outward holiness. This is the gift of God, but man's moral effort is assumed. It is assumed also that man's perfection means his happiness, and this implies perfect peace of mind. When Wesley went to Germany in 1738, after his experience of a strangely warmed heart, he met one, Arvid Gradin, who gave a definition of "the full assurance of faith." This was: "Repose in the blood of Christ; a firm confidence (*firma fiducia*) in God, and persuasion of his favour; the highest tranquility, serenity, and peace of mind, with a deliverance from every fleshly desire, and a cessation of all, even inward sins." This, said Wesley, "was the first account I ever heard from any living man, of what I had before learned myself from the oracles of God, and had been praying for, (with the little company of my friends,) and expecting, for several years." [8] The Holy Club, that is, had been praying for and expecting a full peace and assurance which would lift them above, not only anxiety or fear, but evil desire also. This was doubtless what Wesley meant, in 1735, when he said that, after he "was fully converted," he would be able to turn others to Him.

When he realized the love of God in experience, he evidently expected too much. Apparently he thought that he was entering immediately into the long-expected state of perfection. So his early sermons, "The Almost Christian," "Circumcision of the

Heart," and "The Witness of our own Spirit" seem to teach that the believer is "entirely freed from sin at his conversion." Wesley's spiritual struggles were owing, in part, to the fact that he did not realize how long may be the pilgrim's journey. His talk about "being fully converted," and his statement that the little company had prayed for and expected such full assurance as Arvid Gradin described, would indicate that Wesley thought at first that perfection comes with the attainment of a sure trust and confidence that one is a child of God. To be converted is to be perfect.

It is frequently said that those who separate justification and sanctification hold to a mechanical theory which minimizes the ethical character of justification. This assumes that justification is a mechanical, forensic process with no moral meaning. It is not true of Wesley. He insisted upon separating the two terms because he himself had learned that the Christian life is a development, not an event. So important did a realization of the love of God in Christ seem to Wesley, after his experience of it, that he at first supposed this the status of full peace and victory which he had long associated with perfection. But when he understood that this was not the end, he adjusted his theory to the facts. In the preface to the *Hymns* published in 1740,[9] he spoke of the justified man in terms so high that he later substituted the word "sanctified." In the first edition of his *Works* (1771-74), he corrected his sermon on "The Witness of our own Spirit," so it would be clear that he was talking about "adult" Christians; and he added this note at the end: "It may easily be observed, that the preceding discourse describes the experience of those that are strong in faith." For those who might be discouraged by reading this sermon he advised the sermon on "Sin in Believers." [10] Further evidence of the way in which Wesley had to modify his high expectations of the newly converted is in the other changes which he made in the preface to the 1740 hymnal.[11] According to the original preface, the justified Christian is freed from all darkness, having no fear, no doubt, either as to their state in general or as to any particular action. This, he decided later, is frequently the case, but only for a time. The Holy Spirit teaches them every hour what they shall do and what they shall speak. His later comment was: "For a time it may be so; but not always." Christians have no further need of reason concerning these matters. Sometimes they have no need, was his later decision, but at other times they have. The converted Christian is not troubled by temptations. Later he added that they are sometimes troubled "and that grievously." The sum of the matter is, that Wesley was forced by experience to the conclusion that a realization of the love of God and a sure trust and confidence that God has for Christ's sake pardoned his sins and that he is reconciled to God, does not mean that the convert has arrived at Christian perfection.

Further adjustments of Wesley's theory were made necessary by the facts of experience. In the sermon on Christian Perfection which he published in 1741, Wesley stated that there is no such thing as "absolute perfection on earth." [12] Man cannot control entirely his wandering thoughts; and there are defects of understanding and opinions which prevent infallibility and frequently affect one's actions. Man may have defects of temper, although there can be no sin in those who are perfect in love.

To explain this gave Wesley no little trouble, for his inherited theology was hard to reconcile with the facts as he saw them. Man is corrupt. God forgives him and gives him a new heart. Theoretically, he ought not to sin thereafter; but he does. Evidently there is sin remaining in him. Wesley believed that this remaining sin is inbred sin, the fallen nature inherited from Adam. There is, of course, more logic than anything else here. Wesley never got over thinking of sin as something substantial. He would have been nearer the solution of his problem if he had remembered the words of William Law, in *Christian Perfection*: "When by an inward Principle of Holiness we stand so disposed to all Degrees of Virtue, as the ambitious Man stands disposed to all Steps of Greatness, when we hate and avoid all Kinds of Sins, as the covetous Man hates and avoids all Sorts of Loss and Expense, then are we such Sons of God, as cannot commit Sin." [13] The expulsive power of a new affection is a better psychological explanation of sinless perfection than Wesley's theological propositions concerning inbred and actual sin. There is no denying the truth of the statement which Dr. Flew quotes from Dr. Maltby: "Our [*i.e.*, the Methodist] theological coat was cut for the figure of Total Depravity, but when it was tried on, it was found not to fit any kind of human nature." [14]

The curious may trace out the whole matter in Wesley's writings, especially in his sermons on "Sin in Believers" and "Repentance in Believers," where Wesley corrects a possible inference from some of his earlier sermons, that when a believer sins he must re-trace the whole process of becoming a Christian. In all this, Wesley was perfecting his doctrine of growth in the Christian life.

But, if inbred sin is left in the believer, this, too, must be rooted out before one can be finally saved, for without holiness no man can see the Lord. The root of sin must be taken out of the heart; man must be wholly conformed to the image of God, or, more exactly, the lost image of God in man must be restored by the grace of God. Wesley was too good a logician not to see that, when the root is gone, the fruit cannot again be produced. But he held to his point, attested by experience: wrong opinions, tempers, and actions may remain. His psychology helped him here. Man is a soul "in a shattered body." He lost his bodily per-fection at the Fall, and "for want of better bodily organs, they must at times, think, speak, and act wrong; not indeed through a defect of love, but through a defect of knowledge." [15]

If God removes the root of sin, it will be instan-taneously, as justification is usually instantaneous. This Wesley learned from those who claimed to have experienced it. Moreover, the man whose Diary shows that he was reading a work on logic when he was almost tottering to the grave, had ground for his belief: "It is often difficult to perceive the instant when a man dies; yet there is an instant in which life ceases. And if ever sin ceases, there must be a last moment of its existence, and a first moment of our deliverance from it." [16] On the assumption that sin is a material *something* the logic is impeccable.

But Wesley was sure that sanctification is gradual as well as instantaneous. In his sermon on Christian Perfection, where he denied "absolute perfection" to be possible in this life, Wesley said that there is no perfection "which does not admit of a continual increase. So that how much soever any man has attained, or in how high a degree soever he is perfect, he hath still need to 'grow in grace' and daily to advance in the knowledge and love of God his Saviour." [17] In the moment one is justified, the seed of every virtue is then sown in the soul. From that time the believer "gradually dies to sin, and grows in grace." [18] This idea Wesley repeats over and over again. There is a gradual work of grace preceding and succeeding sanctification, just as a gradual work of grace precedes justification.

In this Charles differed somewhat from John, for Charles was much taken with the mystical doctrine of the "dark night of the soul." [19] Only gradually does man go on to perfection, and that by way of manifold temptations, afflictions, and tribulations.

> 'Tis not a sudden stroke of grace
> Destroys at once the cursed race,
> When first to Christ we come
>   But by degrees insensible
>   The Lord shall all our sins expel,
> And utterly consume.

On the phrase, "by degrees insensible," John commented: "Both suddenly and gradually."

In 1767, John Wesley summed up his thoughts on Christian Perfection, saying of the matter of time: "I believe this perfection is always wrought in the soul by a simple act of faith; consequently in an instant. But I believe a gradual work, both preceding and following that instant. As to the time. I believe this instant generally is the instant of death, the moment before the soul leaves the body. But I believe it may be ten, twenty, or forty years before. I believe it is usually many years after justification; but that it may be within five years or five months after it, I know no conclusive argument to the contrary." [20]

Some supposed that, when he began to declare, "By grace ye are saved through faith," he had retracted his former belief, that without holiness no man can see the Lord. "But it is an entire mistake: These scriptures well consist with each other; the meaning of the former being plainly this,—By faith we are saved from sin, and made holy. The imagination that faith *supersedes* holiness, is the marrow of Antinomianism." [21] In even clearer language he set forth his idea in *A Farther Appeal*: "With regard to the *condition* of salvation, it may be remembered that I allow, not only faith, but likewise holiness or universal obedience, to be the ordinary condition of final salvation; and that when I say, Faith alone is the condition of present salvation, what I would assert is this: (1) That without faith no man can be saved from his sins; can be either inwardly or outwardly holy. And, (2) That at what time soever faith is given, holiness commences in the soul. For that instant 'the love of God' (which is the source of holiness) 'is shed abroad in the heart.' " [22] Faith is both "the condition and the instrument" of sanctification. "When we begin to believe, then sanctification begins. And as faith increases, holiness increases, till we are created anew." [23]

What Wesley is talking about is, in brief, this. Man lives by faith, for faith is necessary if one is to have that love in the heart which is the cause of holiness. And holiness is necessary to final salvation, so necessary that, if man cannot have it otherwise, God will give it to him who has faith in the article of death. And in order to hold to this last, that man must be sanctified before he is finally saved even if on his deathbed, Wesley must hold that faith alone, without works, may be the condition of sanctification. So he goes on torturously proving that, while works are in a sense necessary to sanctification, they are not necessary in the same degree as faith, not immediately and proximately.

Here we have the devious ways by which Wesley maintains his fundamental convictions. Holiness is essential—he will have no compromise with this. But since he admits that most do not reach the ideal in this life, then there must be provision for them to be sanctified by faith alone. Moreover—Wesley reasons by analogy, and he is sure that he is supported by Scripture and by the experience of those whose testimony he trusts—since justification is usually in a moment, by faith only, so also is sanctification.

Professor Cell has said that the "Wesleyan reconstruction of the Christian ethic of life is an original and unique synthesis of the Protestant ethic of grace with the Catholic ethic of holiness." [24]   This is a wise and a just observation. Holiness comes to man by the indwelling of the Holy Spirit, and man receives the Spirit by faith. Always Wesley thinks of man's growing spiritual nature as in dependence upon Christ. "The holiest of men still need Christ, as their Prophet, as 'the light of the world.' For he does not give them light but from moment to moment. . . . They still need Christ as their Priest, to make atonement for their holy things. Even perfect holiness is acceptable only through Jesus Christ." Moreover, men need Christ as their "Priest, their Atonement, their Advocate with the Father, not only as the continuance of their every blessing depends on his death and intercession, but on account of their coming short of the law of love. Every man living does so." [25] This is to say, in short, that man needs continuously the ever-present and ever-active love of God through Christ. It is this which energizes the Christian. He loves Christ because Christ first loved him; and from this love flows all inward and outward holiness. This simple truth lies at the heart of all Wesley's appeals to traditional theology, and more than once he reminded his readers and hearers that simple people who never heard of the theological explanations could understand the fact.

When one comes to see what Wesley means by the faith whereby we are sanctified, it is evident how Wesley combines his general and his special definitions of faith. Faith as the evidence of things not seen, the spiritual sense by which one discerns spiritual reality, is, in essence, intuitive knowledge of what one cannot prove by reason. A sure trust, on the other hand, is confidence, the belief that clings. The faith whereby we are sanctified is both, but mainly the first. It is first, according to the sermon, "The Scripture Way of Salvation," a divine "evidence and conviction . . . . that God hath promised it in the holy Scripture"; secondly, "a divine evidence and conviction . . . . that what God hath promised He is able to perform"; thirdly, "a divine evidence and conviction, that He is able and willing to do it now." To this there must be added something more, "a divine evidence and conviction that He doeth it." [26] This last Wesley himself never had.

In short, Wesley would have his people live in expectation of reaching their goal, and in certainty that they might come nearer and nearer to that love which expels sin and governs the heart and life. And they were to live by the grace of God, not as "given all at once, as if they had a stock laid up for many years; but from moment to moment." [27] Here Wesley comes close to the heart of the matter. As he said in the conclusion of the *Large Minutes*, they talked too much about justified states and sanctified states; but they lived moment by moment. They were to live in the constant consciousness of the continual favor of God.

It might seem that his stress upon the necessity of the repentance of believers and upon their acknowledgment of their imperfect attainments would make for morbidness. In healthy minds it did not. As

191

Professor Goodloe puts it: "No one of us is ever so good but that we may not become better. Repentance is not alone an acknowledgment of one's sins, it is as truly a recognition that one has not yet achieved all that is possible for him to attain. So that in this very resolve to 'press forward' is ground sufficient for genuine joy. . . . Further, repentance is necessary as a permanent attitude of mind because of the fact that no individual, with or without sin, is able at any moment in his experience to realize goodness in its fulness, but is able to increase his ability to do so. Hence as long as life exists there is opportunity for a deepening experience of grace and of the consciousness of God." [28]

But what of the "full assurance of faith," that "repose in the blood of Christ," that "firm confidence," that "highest tranquility, serenity, and peace of mind" which he had sought long before he met Arvid Gradin in far-away Germany? Wesley had considerable experience with enthusiasts who thought they had attained perfection, and he was obviously careful in guarding against excesses. Those who think themselves to have reached the goal should be reticent about it, and others should be tender with the claimants. There was, indeed, a rule by which one may judge himself to have attained perfection. This is: "a man is perfect when after having been fully convinced of inbred sin, by a far deeper and clearer conviction than that he experienced before justification, and after having experienced a gradual mortification of it, he experiences a total death to sin, and an entire renewal in the love and image of God, so as to rejoice evermore, to pray without ceasing, and in everything to give thanks." [29] But one is not so to judge because he feels "all love and no sin." However, when one known to be veracious testifies that he is perfect, he ought not to be doubted without sufficient reason.

Not only the fruit but the witness of the Spirit is the attestation of a man's sanctification. But here Wesley was again cautious. "The witness of sanctification is not always clear at first.... neither is it afterward always the same, but, like that of justification, sometimes stronger and sometimes fainter. Yea, and sometimes it is withdrawn." [30]

It should be made clear, that "holiness" for Wesley is a strongly ethical term, but ethical because it is religious. There is no "natural" ethics so far as Wesley is concerned; and there is no understanding of his moral teaching unless the essential religiousness of his ethical thought is firmly grasped: but Wesley's ethical interest was real. Of the Standard Sermons a much larger proportion deal with morality than is generally recognized; perhaps Wesley's best treatise on Christian ethics is in his thirteen sermons on our Lord's Sermon on the Mount.

In these thirteen sermons, Wesley places the hunger of the soul "after the image of God" at the center. This is the case of the soul "that truly hungers and thirsts after righteousness. He can find no comfort in anything but this: he can be satisfied with nothing else. Whatever you offer besides, it is lightly esteemed: whether it be riches, or honour, or pleasure, he still says, 'This is not the thing which I want.' Give me love, or else I die!" [31] And this love is, as he phrases it again, "the image of God, the mind which was in Christ Jesus. It is every holy and heavenly temper in one; springing from, as well as terminating in, the love of God, as our Father and Redeemer, and the love of all men for His sake." [32] Such a one cannot be satisfied with formal religion, with what "the world accounts religion." In an intense passage, Wesley presses the claim for inward religion: "The religion of the world implies three things: (1) The doing no harm, the abstaining from outward sin; at least from such as is scandalous, as robbery, theft, common swearing, drunkenness: (2) The doing good, the relieving the poor; the being charitable, as it is called: (3) The using the means of grace: at least the going to church and to the Lord's supper. He in whom these three marks are found is termed by the world 'a religious man.' But will this satisfy him who hungers after God? No: it is not food for his soul. He wants a religion of a nobler kind, a religion higher and deeper than this. He can no more feed on this poor, shallow, formal thing, than he can 'fill his belly with the east wind.' True, he is careful to abstain from the very appearance of evil; he is zealous of good works; he attends all the ordinances of God: but all this is not what he longs for. This is only the outside of that religion which he insatiably hungers after. The knowledge of God in Christ Jesus; 'the life which is hid with Christ in God'; the being 'joined unto the Lord in one spirit'; the having 'fellowship with the Father and the Son'; the 'walking in the light as God is in the light'; the being 'purified even as He is pure,'

194

—this is the religion, the righteousness he thirsts after; nor can he rest, till he thus rests in God." [33]

The great hindrances to this inward religion are pride, levity, and thoughtlessness, anger, impatience, discontent. These are healed by poverty of spirit; "holy mourning," which Wesley interprets as sorrow for our own and others' sin; and meekness. But Wesley anticipates modern psychology in his recognition that instinctive attitudes may be sublimated. They who are truly meek "do not desire to extinguish any of the passions which God has for wise ends implanted in their nature; but they have the mastery of all: they hold them in subjection, and employ them in subservience to those ends. And thus even the harsher and more unpleasing passions are applicable to the noblest purposes; even hatred, anger, and fear, when engaged against sin, and regulated by faith and love, are as walls and bulwarks to the soul, so that the wicked one cannot approach to hurt it." [34]

But insistent as Wesley is that true holiness is rooted in the inner life, this must in no way be taken as minimizing outward holiness. One must recall again his answer to those who object "that religion does not lie in outward things, but in the heart, the inmost soul; that it is the union of the soul with God, the life of God in the soul of man; that outside religion is nothing worth." His answer was: "It is most true, that the root of religion lies in the heart, in the inmost soul; that this is the union of the soul with God, the life of God in the soul of man. But if this root be really in the heart, it cannot but put forth branches. And these are the several instances of outward obedience, which partake of the same nature with the root; and, consequently, are not only marks or signs, but substantial parts of religion." [35]

He would not surrender his belief that ethical conduct is part of religion, not merely an outward sign of an inward work. As a true Englishman, he was interested in morality far more than in metaphysics; but he was sure that morality is truly rooted in the inner life and, therefore, would have nothing to do with morality completely divorced from religion. Neither would he have anything to do with religion divorced from morality. He would not put asunder what he believed God Himself to have joined.

The ethical life, or rather the life of outward Christian conduct, is to be sought not only by enriching the inner life but also by ethical striving. "Strive to enter in at the strait gate," he wrote, "not only by this agony of soul, of conviction, of sorrow, of shame, of desire, of fear, of unceasing prayer; but likewise by ordering thy conversation aright, by walking with all thy strength in all the ways of God, the way of innocence, of piety, and of mercy. Abstain from all appearance of evil; do all possible good to all men; deny thyself, thy own will, in all things, and take up thy cross daily. Be ready to cut off thy right hand, to pluck out thy right eye, and cast it from thee; to suffer the loss of goods, friends, health, all things on earth, so thou mayest enter into the kingdom of heaven." [36] Thus again he defines "serving God" as believing in him, loving him, imitating him, and obeying him.

But how does a man seek perfection in this world?

196

Perfection, in the medieval Church, was sought in retreat from the world; and, while Luther and Calvin made much of man's "calling," his "vocation" to live in the world, they never entirely freed themselves from a feeling that the worldly affairs are unimportant. A man's great business is to save his soul, and he lives in the ordinary calling of life because he has to: he seeks God *in vocatione,* not *per vocationem.*[37] How was the quest of perfection related, in Wesley's mind, with the world of common affairs?

Professor Mecklin, in his *Story of American Dissent,* has seen the "quintessence of Methodism" in a quotation from Wesley: "Here is a short, a plain and infallible rule before you enter into particulars. In whatever profession you engage you must be singular or be damned! The way to hell has nothing singular in it; but the way to heaven is singularity all over. If you move but one step towards God, you are not as other men are." This, says Professor Mecklin, expresses "the dissenting, 'come-outer' spirit of Methodism. . . . This obviously harmonizes with the dissenting tradition, developed in opposition to the churchly tradition, of spiritual separation from the world and a secularized church."[38] Professor Mecklin is here dealing with American Methodism and not with Wesley; but the spirit of which he speaks is in Wesley also, but not as an inheritance from "the dissenting tradition." In him it was from that deep spiritual tradition which has existed in the Church at almost all times. From William Law, a High Churchman, Wesley had learned that "if the doctrines of Christianity were practiced, they would make a man as different from other people as to all worldly tempers, sensual pleasures, and the pride of life, as a wise man is different from a natural [a fool]." [39]   And it will be recalled that Dr. Hayward, who examined Wesley before he was ordained to priest's orders in 1728, said: "Do you know what you are about?   You are bidding defiance to all mankind.   He that would live a Christian priest ought to know that, whether his hand be against every man or no, he must expect every man's hand should be against him." [40]   Whatever may have determined the Methodists in England or America, Wesley's "singularity" stemmed from that principle of renunciation which has been in Christianity from the beginning.

Christianity is a peculiar way of life.   Just as truly as the medieval Church thought that the highest type of Christian must live a life separated from the world, so truly did Wesley, following the *Imitation of Christ* and Christian asceticism, believe that one must be singular "or be damned."

It will be well to examine the asceticism in Wesley's teaching.   In Sermon XLII, on "Self-Denial," there is much material.   This sermon was written before the Aldersgate experience, but it was revised afterwards—Dr. Sugden thinks about 1744-45. [41]

In the second paragraph, Wesley speaks of the duty of denying oneself: "The *denying* ourselves, and the *taking up our cross*, in the full extent of the expression, is not a thing of small concern: it is not expedient only, as are some of the circumstantials of religion; but it is absolutely, indispensably necessary, either to our becoming or continuing His disciples."

This necessity arises from the fact that "the will of God is the supreme, unalterable rule for every intelligent creature; equally binding every angel in heaven, and every man upon earth." A second reason for the necessity of self-denial is that it is the will of God, that we resist and counteract the corruption of our nature. Indeed, in order to "the healing of that corruption, that evil disease, which every man brings with him into the world, it is often needful to pluck out, as it were, a right eye, to cut off a right hand,—so painful is either the thing itself which must be done, or the only means of doing it."

Such statements as the above represent Wesley's views after 1738 as well as before. "Without holiness no man can see the Lord" was Wesley's uncompromising slogan; and he made clear in his sermon on "Self-Denial" just what he meant. The second division of his sermon was to show "that it is always owing to the want either of self-denial, or taking up his cross, that any man does not thoroughly follow Him, is not fully a disciple of Christ." He illustrates this as follows: "A man hears the word which is able to save his soul .... yet he remains 'dead in trespasses and sins,' senseless and unawakened. Why is this? Because he will not part with his bosom sin, though he now knows it is an abomination to the Lord." No deep impression is made upon him because of this. "Suppose he begins to awake out of sleep, and his eyes are a little opened, why are they so quickly closed again? Why does he again sink into the sleep of death? Because he again yields to his bosom sin." In other instances, the impressions once received do not wear away.

"And yet, many of these have not found what they seek: they mourn, and yet are not comforted. Now, why is this? It is because they do not 'bring forth fruits meet for repentance.'" Another receives the "heavenly gift"; "the peace which passeth all understanding" ruled in his heart, and "the love of God was shed abroad" therein. "Yet he is now weak as another man . . . his love is waxed cold, and the peace of God no longer rules in his heart. And no marvel; for he has again given place to the devil. . . . Or he did not stir up the gift of God which was in him; he gave way to spiritual sloth, and would not be at the pains of 'praying always, and watching thereunto with all perseverance': that is, he made shipwreck of the faith, for want of self-denial, and taking up his cross daily." Another does not make shipwreck of the faith, but he does not go on to perfection. "And why is he thus, but because he hath forgotten the word of God, 'By works is faith made perfect'? He does not use all diligence in working the works of God. He does not 'continue instant in prayer,' private as well as public; in communicating, hearing, meditation, fasting, and religious conference."

Toward the end of 1739, eight or ten persons "who appeared to be deeply convinced of sin, and earnestly groaning for redemption," came to Wesley in London. They desired his help and advice; and from this meeting developed the "United Societies"—that is, the Methodist Societies of the Methodist Revival. For admittance to these societies nothing was required save "a desire 'to flee from the wrath to come, to be saved from their sins'"; but this desire was expected to produce fruits. Consequently, certain rules were drawn up for these seekers, the famous "General Rules." [42] The first division of the rules sets forth the self-denial required of the Methodists.

Aside from the common evils which Methodists were to avoid, such as drunkenness, quarreling, using many words in buying or selling, the list includes "unprofitable conversation," "doing what we know is not for the glory of God, as the 'putting on of gold or costly apparel'; the taking such diversions as cannot be used in the name of the Lord Jesus; the singing those songs, or reading those books, which do not tend to the knowledge or love of God; softness, and needless self-indulgence; laying up treasures upon earth." Fasting is enjoined under the head of "the ordinances of God." In *Advice to the People Called Methodists* (1745), Wesley was more particular. He refers to the rule of the Methodists "to abstain from fashionable diversions, from reading plays, romances, or books of humour, from singing innocent songs, or talking in a merry, gay, diverting manner; your plainness of dress; your manner of dealing in trade; your exactness in observing the Lord's day; your scrupulosity as to things that have not paid custom; your total abstinence from spirituous liquors (unless in case of necessity); your rule, 'not to mention the fault of an absent person, in particular of Ministers or of those in authority.'" [43]

It may be noted, in passing, that Wesley was emphasizing what he deemed new in the Methodists; he did not think of his people as simply reviving Puritanism or Moravianism. He believed that he was restoring primitive Christianity, and that in the combination of different qualities the Methodists were new in the world of the eighteenth century.

In many things Wesley was scrupulous and required his followers to be so. He stressed plainness of dress, insisting that Methodists should wear clothes in accord with the times, but not fine clothes. To the answer that people must dress expensively if their stations required it, he replied sarcastically that he advised all Lords of the Bedchamber and Maids of Honor at Court to do this, but not others.[44] But in many ways he required more of his Methodists than he thought absolutely necessary for all. He did not allow any belonging to his Societies to dance or play cards, but he would have his preachers say no more than: "Possibly you may be saved though you dance and play at cards. But I could not." He made allowance thus for those who were not Methodists; "else," he added, "I might send my own father and mother to hell, though they not only lived many years, but died in the full assurance of faith."[45] His mother would not allow her children to go to a dancing-school, but she had a dancing-master come to the house to instruct the children in her presence so far as she thought necessary. "To this," said Wesley, "I have no objection. If I had convenience, I would be glad to have all our preachers taught, even by a dancing-master, to make a bow and to go in and out of a room."[46] Wesley also gave instructions to his Methodists which he did not think necessary for a Fellow of Lincoln. He revised at least one novel for circulation, and his own reading was omnivorous. But he knew his people and their lack of discrimination. It was one of his own preachers who, after Wesley's death, burned the Shakespeare which the Methodist leader had read and annotated with his own hand.

There remained in Wesley also some traces of his former preference for celibacy. Although he agreed that clergymen might marry and although he himself finally married, yet Wesley congratulated those who became eunuchs for the Kingdom of Heaven's sake, taking pains to explain that marriage is an honorable estate but that he who is unmarried may give all his time and money to the Lord without let or hindrance.[47] As late as 1745, the Conference seemed undecided whether one who had reached perfection would be "capable of marriage." The answer to the questions was: "We cannot well judge. But supposing he were not, the number of those in that state is so small it would produce no inconvenience." In John Bennet's copy of the *Minutes*, Wesley added a note: "Me is H in all"; a reference to Hebrews xiii. 4, "Marriage is honourable in all." [48]

The preachers and assistants were examined more closely than were members as to their renunciations. Among the questions asked them concerning their "prudential" means of grace were the following: "Do you deny yourself every useless pleasure of sense, imagination, honour? Are you temperate in all things? instance in food: Do you use only that kind and that degree which is best both for your body and soul? Do you see the necessity of this? Do you eat no flesh suppers? No late suppers? Do you eat no more at each meal than is necessary? Are you not heavy or drowsy after dinner? Do you use only that kind and that degree of drink which is best both for your body and soul? Do you drink water? Why not? Did you ever? Why did you leave it off? If not for health, when will you begin again? today? How often do you drink wine or ale? every day? Do you want [need] it? Wherein do you 'take up your cross daily?' " [49]

All this is in the line of Christian asceticism, although it is an asceticism lived in the world, not out of it. But how is this related to man's business, to man's vocation as a workman, as a master, a member of the professions? Professor Tawney has summed up the Puritan ideal as follows: "In their emphasis on the moral duty of untiring activity, on work as an end in itself, on the evils of luxury and extravagance, on foresight and thrift, on moderation and self-discipline and rational calculation, they had created an ideal of Christian conduct which canonized as an ethical principle the efficiency which economic theorists were preaching as a specific for social disorders." [50] Wheras the axioms of Christian social ethics had been summed up for generations in the words to Timothy, "Having food and raiment, let us be therewith content. For the love of money is the root of all evil," the Puritans, according to Professor Tawney, raised a new standard. They exalted "not an easy-going and open-handed charity, but a systematic and methodical accumulation."

At first blush this seems to be precisely what Wesley did. His followers were to seek earnestly after inward and outward holiness by faith and works, practicing self-discipline and self-denial. "It is the bounden duty of all who are engaged in worldly business," he wrote in his sermon on "The Use of Money," "to observe that first and great rule of Christian wisdom, with respect to money, 'Gain all you can.' Gain all you can by honest industry. Use all possible diligence in your calling. Lose no time. If you understand yourself, and your relation to God and man, you will have none to spare. If you understand your particular calling, as you ought, you will have no time that hangs upon your hands. . . . And 'whatsoever thy hand findeth to do, do it with thy might.' Do it as soon as possible: No delay! . . . And do it as well as possible. . . . Gain all you can, by common sense, by using in your business all the understanding which God has given you. . . . You should be continually learning, from the experience of others, or from your own experience, reading, and reflection, to do everything you have to do better today than you did yesterday. . . . Having gained all you can, by honest wisdom, and unwearied diligence, the Second rule of Christian prudence is, 'Save all you can.' . . . Expend no part of it merely to gratify the desire of the flesh, the desire of the eye, or the pride of life." [51]

Numerous quotations could be added, but the heart of the matter is here. Work, diligent, intelligent work, and careful, self-denying saving are the rules of the Christian man. If this were all, then there would be no alternative to listing Wesley with those who reinterpreted the Christian doctrine of money and work in line with the individualistic economic development of the eighteenth century. But Professor

Tawney himself recognized as exceptions to the general trend Wesley's sermon on "The Use of Money" and Law's reassertion of Christianity as a distinctive way of life.[52]

In Wesley's sermon, he rules out employments that are hurtful to the worker in mind or body. He insists that a Christian must not engage in a business which hurts his neighbor. "We cannot devour the increase of his lands, and perhaps the lands and houses themselves, by gaming, by over-grown bills, (whether on account of physic, or law, or anything else,) or by requiring or taking such interest as even the laws of our country forbid. . . ."[53] We cannot, consistent with brotherly love, sell our goods below the market-price; we cannot study to ruin our neighbour's trade, in order to advance our own; much less can we entice away, or receive, any of his servants, or workmen whom he has need of. None can gain by swallowing up his neighbour's substance, without gaining the damnation of hell!" For the same reason none can engage in selling liquor or anything which would injure his neighbor's health. And concern for his neighbor's soul will prevent any from keeping "taverns, victualling-houses, opera-houses, play-houses, or any other places of public, fashionable diversion."

Such are the cautions which must be used by those who work. But there is a third rule to be added. "Gain all you can; save all you can"; but also "give all you can." The rule which Wesley lays down is short but explicit: "First, provide things needful for yourself; food to eat, raiment to put on, whatever nature moderately requires for preserving the body in health and strength. Secondly, provide these for your wife, your children, your servants, or any others who pertain to your household. If, when this is done, there be an overplus left, then, 'do good to them that are of the household of faith.' If there be an overplus still, 'as you have opportunity, do good unto all men.' " This is not to be taken as an exhortation to "tithing" or to any other method of keeping books with the Almighty. "Render unto God, not a tenth, not a third, not half, but all that is God's, be it more or less; by employing all on yourself, your household, the household of faith, and all mankind, in such a manner that you may give a good account of your stewardship, when ye can be no longer stewards." At the Judgment, the Lord will inquire of man: "In what manner didst thou employ that comprehensive talent, money? . . . first supplying thy reasonable wants, together with those of thy family, then restoring the remainder to Me, through the poor, whom I had appointed to receive it; looking upon thyself as only one of that number of poor, whose wants were to be supplied out of that part of My substance which I had placed in thy hands for this purpose; leaving thee the right of being supplied first, and the blessedness of giving rather than receiving." [54] It is estimated that Wesley himself, during his life-time, gave away £30,-000.

The point here is not Wesley's economic or social theory but his conception of the way in which the Christian man, who is going on to perfection, may follow his "vocation" in this world. Professor Cell has given an interesting analysis of Wesley's views concerning riches and has speculated as to the influence of such religious ideals as thrift, diligence, self-denial in economic history.[55] The present concern is to show that Wesley was proposing, not a religious ideal which coincided with the dominant economic individualism of the times, but a conception of the Christian man's vocation as distinctive. Decidedly, if he were taken seriously, there could be no such thing as modern business. If surplus were turned back into social channels, instead of being applied to capital holdings, then the modern capitalistic economy would be destroyed.

It is well known that Wesley was very much afraid of riches. Time and again, he pointed out with sorrow that his Methodists were becoming rich; and he was sure that, when they were rich, they would no longer be religious. In no sense was Wesley a social philosopher. In politics he was conservative; he had no social or economic outlook peculiar to him—save in his interpretation of the path of the Christian seeking perfection. Here he stands neither in the way of St. Francis nor of the Puritan—if the ordinary interpretation of the Puritan's economic morality is correct. Wesley did not believe in poverty as poverty; he would relieve all men from its thraldom. Work is good, and business is to be encouraged. But the importance of Wesley's teaching is that, for the modern, industrial world, he preserved the traditional Christian attitude. The man of God lives a distinctive life, not in monasteries, but in the world of business. He has the virtues of the modern world; but his aims are different. Each man owes all that he has to the God of all men, and he pays it to society. The first unit of society is the household of faith; next comes all mankind. For this society of God's poor brethren man must work all his days; to work for himself alone is to fatten his soul for hell.

The holiness of the inner life and the holiness of conduct, religion and ethics, Wesley joined together, not as two separate things but as different parts of the same. "In a word," he wrote in a passage which sums up his total belief, "let thy religion be the religion of the heart. Let it lie deep in thy inmost soul. Be thou little, and base, and mean, and vile (beyond what words can express) in thy own eyes; amazed and humbled to the dust by the love of God which is in Christ Jesus. Be serious. Let the whole stream of thy thoughts, words, and actions flow from the deepest conviction that thou standest on the edge of the great gulf, thou and all the children of men, just ready to drop in, either into everlasting glory or everlasting burning! Let thy soul be filled with mildness, gentleness, patience, long suffering towards all men; at the same time all which is in thee is athirst for God, the living God, longing to awake up after His likeness and to be satisfied with it! Be thou a lover of God and of all mankind! In this spirit do and suffer all things! Thus show thy faith by thy works; thus 'do the will of thy Father which is in heaven'! And, as sure as thou now walkest with God on earth, thou shalt also reign with Him in glory!" [56]

This was the ideal. Men should be filled with a great passion for God, and, living in constant awareness of the criticalness of life, should be possessed of

the Christian virtues and of the outward goodness
and obedience which are substantial parts of religion.
But as Wesley grew older he grew in comprehension:
all men are not the same, nor do all men attain unto
the same. Sometimes he had been too exacting, too
rigid. In April, 1788, Wesley the aged looked back
with regret upon his earlier narrower views. "Nearly
fifty years ago, when the Preachers, commonly called
Methodists, began to preach that grand scriptural
doctrine, salvation by faith, they were not sufficiently
apprized of the difference between a servant and a
child of God. They did not clearly understand, that
even one 'who feareth God, and worketh righteousness, is accepted of him.' In consequence of this, they
were apt to make sad the hearts of those whom God
had not made sad. For they frequently asked those
who feared God, 'Do you know that your sins are
forgiven?' And upon their answering, 'No,' immediately replied, 'Then you are a child of the devil.'
No; that does not follow. It might have been said,
(and it is all that can be said with propriety,) 'Hitherto you are only a *servant*, you are not a *child* of God.
You have already great reason to praise God that he
has called you to his honourable service.' " [57] The
path toward perfection stretches not only a long way
forward, but a long way back, and along the way any
who walks forward is of the good company.

Even among those who had felt justifying faith,
there are two kinds of Christians; there have been two
kinds from the beginning. "The one lived an innocent life, conforming in all things, not sinful, to the
customs and fashions of the world; doing many good

works, abstaining from gross evils, and attending the ordinances of God. They endeavoured, in general, to have a conscience void of offence in their behaviour, but did not aim at any particular strictness, being in most things like their neighbours." [58] From long experience, Wesley had decided that justified Christians had the choice of walking in this way or in "the more excellent way." But those who chose the lower path, while he would not say that they were in the way to hell, "will not have so high a place in heaven as they would have had if they had chosen the better part." [59]

The ideal is an ideal, but one must look to the height. "Settle it then in your heart, that from the moment God has saved you from all sin, you are to aim at nothing more, but more of that love described in the thirteenth of the Corinthians. You can go no higher than this, till you are carried into Abraham's bosom." [60] He believed in man's natural depravity, but also in man's opportunity, by the grace of God, for infinite growth. His doctrine of perfectibility was not that of the optimists of the Enlightenment, nor was it at one with the naturalistic optimism of the Romantic Movement; but Wesley saw that man's reach exceeds his grasp, and that he may go on hopefully in his pilgrimage toward the City of God. The sum of the whole matter he might have stated in a quotation from his father's friend, high-priest of eighteenth-century Classicism, "that excellent poet," Mr. Pope:

> And knows where faith, law, morals, all began,
> All end, in love of God, and love of man.

211

CHAPTER IX

THE DISCIPLINE OF LIFE

It has already been made plain that Wesley did not, either in practice or teaching, rely upon "feelings." He would have subscribed to Augustine's aphorism, "Love God and do as you please," but only on the presupposition of a disciplined character. Fully to understand Wesley's religion, one must consider at greater length the place which discipline and control played in his scheme for himself and others.

According to Wesley, the name of Methodist was given to the little group at Oxford because of "the exact regularity of their lives as well as their studies." He further said, that "the one charge then advanced against them was, that they were 'righteous overmuch'; that they were abundantly too scrupulous, and too strict, carrying things to great extremes: In particular, that they laid too much stress upon the Rubrics and Canons of the Church; that they insisted too much upon the Statutes of the University; and that they took the Scriptures in too strict and literal a sense; so that if they were right, few indeed could be saved." [1] It will be well to examine in more detail the practices of Wesley and the Oxford Methodists during the early stages and then to follow the older Wesley in the matter of "exact regularity."

212

The Discipline of Life

Certainly Wesley was by nature and training fitted for a regular way of life. No man with any natural predisposition in this direction could have escaped a bent toward some form of methodism as a result of Susannah Wesley's training and teaching. Exactly how much in Wesley's character was owing to his natural tendencies and how much to training cannot, of course, be determined; but that he was from his youth up precise in his habits, as well as rationalistic of mind, is plain to all who know his story. In his childhood he seems to have taken kindly to the barrack-like discipline of his mother; at Charterhouse he ran thrice around the yard every morning, read the Scriptures and said his prayers twice a day; in 1721, as a young collegian he budgeted his time, allowing portions for study, for correspondence and the like; in his old age his "habit of body" was expressive "of strict temperance and continual exercise. . . . In dress he was a pattern of neatness." [2]

The influence of Jeremy Taylor, of Thomas à Kempis, and of William Law was to set Wesley upon the way toward Christian Perfection. Nothing less than inward and outward holiness was to be his goal from 1725 until his death more than sixty-five years later. But these guides also set Wesley upon the path of discipline, of the imitation of Christ. The first Journal opens with the well-known words: "It was in pursuance of an advice given by Bp. Taylor, in his *Rules for Holy Living and Dying*, that about fifteen years ago [about 1725], I began to take a more exact account than I had done before of the manner wherein I spent my time, writing down how I had

213

employed every hour." [3]   À Kempis' *Imitation of Christ,* let it be said once more, is not a mystical book, but the product of monasticism.   It is a book for ordered lives, setting out rules and methods for a self-denying, sometimes ascetic, way of living.   And, in like manner, one should recall that the William Law who influenced Wesley was not William Law, follower of the mystic, Jakob Bœhme, but Law in his earlier period, the author of *A Serious Call to a Devout and Holy Life* and of *Christian Perfection.*   Part of the teaching of Law was: "either Reason and Religion prescribe rules and ends to all the ordinary actions of our life, or they do not: If they do, then it is as necessary to govern all our actions by these rules, as it is necessary to worship God." [4]

Wesley's practices at Oxford and in America are too well known to need detailed repetition, but their general character should be recalled.   A writer, sometimes said to have been William Law, summed up the habits of the Oxford Methodists in an approving paragraph: "That this society think themselves obliged in all particulars to live up to the law of the gospel.   That the *Rule* they have set themselves is not that of their own inventions but the Holy Scriptures, and the orders and injunctions of the Church, and that not as they perversely construe and misinterpret them, but as they find them in the holy canon.   That, pursuant to these, they have resolved to observe with strictness not only all the duties of the Christian religion according to their baptismal engagements, but the fasts, the prayers, and sacraments of the Church; to receive the blessed Communion as often as there is

214

opportunity; and to do all the good they can, in visiting the sick, the poor, the prisoners, &c., knowing these to be the great articles on which they are to be tried at the last day; and in all things to keep themselves unspotted from the world. It would be found that, if they rise earlier than ordinary, if they are sparing in eating and drinking or any expensive diversions, 'tis to save time and money for improving those glorious ends; and not, as is unfairly insinuated, that they make such things to be essentials in religion, much less out of a gloomy and Pharisaical spirit, to shun the company or upbraid the practices of others. These are the *Rules*, this the *Method*, they have chosen to live by." [5]

Unquestionably the Oxford Methodists carried their enthusiasm to excess. Rising early, carefully abstaining from other than godly company, treating every act as affecting eternal destiny, Wesley sometimes showed traces of that morbidity which Tyerman noticed. But meeting together to review the day and plan work for the next, visiting the sick and prisoners, catechizing children, relieving the poor and suffering, strict observance of the statutes of the University and of the Church and weekly communion were their chief characteristics. Wesley insisted that he could best pursue holiness at Oxford because he had there religious friends, retirement, and opportunity for public and private prayers and for frequent communion. Samuel Wesley, Jr., was no friend to fanaticism; but he wrote lines on the death of one of the Oxford Methodists, William Morgan, which are fair to the whole group.

Whose Zeal for other Men's Salvation shown,
Beyond the reach of Hell secur'd his own.
Glad'ning the Poor where e'er his Steps he turn'd,
Where pin'd the Orphan, or the Widow mourn'd:
Where Pris'ners sigh'd beneath Guilt's Horrid Stain,
The worst Confinement, and the heaviest Chain:
Where Death's sad Shade the Uninstructed Sight
Veil'd with thick Darkness in the Land of Light.
Our Saviour thus fulfill'd his great Design,
(For Human may be liken'd to Divine,)
Heal'd each Disease that Bodies frail endure,
And preach'd th' unhop'd-for Gospel to the Poor.

Nor yet the Priestly Function he invades,
'Tis not his Sermon, but his Life, persuades.
Humble and teachable to Church he flies,
Prepar'd to practice, not to criticize.
Then only angry, when a Wretch conveys
The Deists Poison in the Gospel Phrase.
To Means of Grace the last Respect he show'd,
Nor sought new Paths, as wiser than his God.
Their sacred Strength preserv'd him from Extremes
Of empty Outside, or Enthusiast Dreams;
Whims of Molinos, lost in Rapture's Mist,
Or Quaker, late-reforming Quietist.
He knew that Works must here our Faith employ,
And that 'tis Heav'n's great Business to enjoy.[6]

During his later years at Oxford, after 1732, Wesley was influenced by John Clayton of Manchester, who sympathized with the High Church views of the Nonjurors, Dr. Deacon and John Byrom. Concerning Clayton's influence, Wesley wrote: "The two points whereunto, by the blessing of God, we had attained, we endeavoured to hold fast: I mean, the doing what good we can; and in order thereto, communicating as often as we have opportunity. To

Mr. Samuel Lucas

A Tribute on His Eighty-Fifth Birthday, March 14, 1937

In years it has been seventy-two,
  Since he came to our town by chance.
Urged by a childs curiousity,
  He followed an army's advance.

His possessions, physically speaking,
  Were naught but those on his back,
Yet today, in the hearts of this people,
  He has riches that never shall lack.

The charm of his sweet personality,
  The winsomness of his broad smile;
Has carried him through many battles,
  And over many a weary mile.

Today, on his eighty-fifth birthday,
  As he stands looking back o'er the years.
The happiness that we, his friends, wish him
  Brings to our eyes a few tears.

G. M. BURNWORTH

these, by the advice of Mr. Clayton, we added a third, —the observing the fasts of the Church, the general neglect of which we can by no means apprehend to be a lawful excuse for neglecting them." [7] It is possibly to Clayton's influence that one must attribute Wesley's interests in the so-called *Constitutions of the Holy Apostles* and *Ecclesiastical Canons.* These, he thought, were of such early date as to make them authoritative. Wesley was also influenced by Dr. Deacon's service book and by the teaching of this very High Church group of Nonjurors, and part of his Georgia troubles came from his strictness in these matters.

It must not be inferred that Wesley was of a sour, forbidding spirit at Oxford and in America. In the first place, he was a man who rejoiced in strictness and in methodical living. In the second place, his austerity was not excessive. Mr. Edwyn Bevan favorably contrasts Wesley, in this respect, with Augustine, to whom "more and more the many colours of life seemed to him only an undesirable stain upon the white radiance of eternity." [8] Mr. Bevan is thinking of Wesley's moderation of view in his later years; but the contrast holds good for his earlier period also. "You seem to apprehend," he wrote to Mrs. Chapman from Georgia in 1737, "that I believe religion to be inconsistent with cheerfulness, and with a sociable, friendly temper. So far from it, that I am convinced, as true religion or holiness cannot be without cheerfulness, so steady cheerfulness, on the other hand, cannot be without holiness or true religion. And I am equally convinced that true religion has nothing sour, austere, unsociable, unfriendly in it; but, on the contrary, implies the most winning sweetness, the most amiable softness and gentleness." Wesley may have been thinking of Augustine, who was stricken with shame because he could not eat after fasting without some "gust of sensual pleasure," when he added: "Do you refuse no pleasure but what is an hindrance to some greater good or has a tendency to some evil? It is my very rule; and I know no other by which a sincere, reasonable Christian can be guided. In particular, I pursue this rule in eating, which I seldom do without much pleasure." [9]

Not only was Wesley not a morbid, unhappy man; he was not seeking to commute his sins by good deeds. When, in the disturbed days immediately preceding and just after his Aldersgate experience, he said hard things about his previous experience, he stopped to note that he had not been consciously trying to acquire merit by his own works. "I take religion," he wrote to Richard Morgan from Oxford in 1734, "to be not the bare saying over so many prayers, morning and evening, in public or in private; not anything superadded now and then to a careless or worldly life; but a constant ruling habit of soul, a renewal of our minds in the image of God, a recovery of the divine likeness, a still-increasing conformity of heart and life to the pattern of our most holy Redeemer." [10] The year before, Wesley had written to his mother, that "when I am entrusted with a person who is first to understand and practice, and then to teach, the law of Christ, I endeavour, by an intermixture of reading and conversation, to show him what that law is—that is, to renounce all insubordinate love of the world, and to love and obey God with all his strength." [11]

It was to attain to a "ruling habit of soul," to "a recovery of the divine likeness," that Wesley followed rules and methods. He was, it must be remembered, seeking holiness, nothing less than Christian Perfection; and he believed that there were means which God had commanded "in order to that end." These means were what Wesley called "instituted," that is, those, such as prayer, reading, meditation on the Scriptures, and frequent communion, which he believed to be commanded in the Scriptures as interpreted by the early Church. Other means were "prudential," that is, "recommended by wise and good men." Among these latter were meeting together for counsel, keeping strict account of one's time, rising early, working by method, and the like. In 1734, Wesley summed up his beliefs in a letter to Richard Morgan. "God everywhere declared (1) that without doing good as well as avoiding evil shall no flesh living be justified; (2) that as good prayers without good works attending them are no better than a solemn mockery of God, so are good works themselves without those tempers of heart from their subserviency to which they derive their whole value." [12]

In another chapter it has been shown that Wesley maintained to the end of his long life habits of regular prayer and of frequent communion. Moreover, he continued, almost to the end, the practice of meditation and of self-examination which characterized his earlier period. Sometimes, as was remarked above, he considered taking up again even the minutiae of his Oxford discipline. "Let me be again an Oxford Methodist!" he exclaimed in 1772; "I am often in doubt whether it would not be best for me to resume all my Oxford rules, great and small." [13] But it is necessary to examine in more detail his teachings concerning regularity, "methodism," in the years *after* 1738.

In 1773, Wesley wrote that "the Methodists, so called, observe more of the Articles, Rubrics, and Canons of the Church than any other people in the three kingdoms. They vary from none of them willingly, although the English canons were never established by law." [14] Although he could not acknowledge the authority of many of the canons,[15] he recorded, in 1744, that he had as curate always observed the rubrics with "a scrupulous exactness, not for wrath, but for conscience sake." And he added: "this, so far as belongs to an unbeneficed Minister, or to a private member of the Church, I do now." [16] In detailing what he meant, Wesley began by listing the "days of fasting or abstinence to be observed." These were the forty days of Lent, the Ember Days at the four seasons; the three Rogation Days; all Fridays in the year except Christmas day. There is plenty of evidence that these fast days were neglected in the eighteenth century; indeed, it is Wesley's argument, in the passage in *An Earnest Appeal* which is here cited, that he observed the canons and rubrics better than those who accused him of laxity. And Wesley continued to observe the fasts and festivals of the Church. In December, 1773, almost thirty years

220

after that quoted above was written, Wesley recorded in his *Journal*, that he celebrated "the solemn feast-days, according to the design of their institution." [17] These days included Christmas day, St. Stephen's day, St. John's day, and Holy Innocents' day. The next year, 1774, Wesley wrote: "During the twelve festival days, we had the Lord's Supper daily; a little emblem of the Primitive Church." [18] In this, of course, he was going beyond the practice of the Church of England in his devotion to what he believed to be the practice of the Primitive Church; and this, let it be remembered, was not in Wesley's so-called High Church period, but when he was seventy-one years old.

Ten years later, 1784, when Wesley abridged the Book of Common Prayer for the American Methodists, he omitted most of the holy days "as at present answering no valuable end." [19] Does this mean that Wesley had come to the opinion that the observance of fixed times for fasting or celebration has no value? Again a glance at his practice is instructive. In 1782 the Diary, which is not available for the previous forty years, once more comes to the student's aid. It has been seen that in 1773 and 1774 Wesley was observing the festivals of the Twelve Days from Christmas to Epiphany, in the latter year communicating every day. What of the years from 1782 to 1791, the years when he was deleting most of the holy days as answering no valuable end for the American Methodists? In 1782, Wesley received the Lord's Supper eight times during the Twelve Days; in 1783, eight times; in 1784, eight times; in 1785, seven times; in 1786, nine times; in 1787, seven times; in 1788, when

Wesley was eighty-five years old, twelve times; in 1789, nine times; and in 1790, the aged man communicated four times.

Of the value of fasting Wesley was never in doubt from his Oxford days until the end. He and his companions in the University fasted on Wednesdays and Fridays as well as on the regular fast days of the Church, although Wesley had had some doubts as to the obligation to observe Wednesday. Recommendations to fast are scattered through the *Journal* and the *Letters*. Sermon XXII, Discourse vii "Upon Our Lord's Sermon on the Mount," is upon the duty of fasting and sets forth at length the reasons for the practice. This was possibly written before 1738; but in 1785 Wesley advised Adam Clarke to recommend the sermon in every society.[20] Fasting, according to this sermon, has no merit in itself, but "is only a way which God hath ordained, wherein we wait for His unmerited mercy; and wherein, without any desert of ours, He hath promised freely to give us His blessing."[21] That is, fasting is one of the "means"; and to attempt to attain the end without the means is "enthusiasm."

In 1789, Wesley viewed with regret the neglect of fasting by his people. "While we were at Oxford," he wrote, "the rule of every Methodist was, (unless in case of sickness,) to fast every Wednesday and Friday in the year, in imitation of the practice of the Primitive Church; for which they had the highest reverence. Now this practice of the Primitive Church is universally allowed. 'Who does not know,' says Epiphanius, an ancient writer, 'that the fasts of

the fourth and sixth days of the week' (Wednesday
and Friday) 'are observed by the Christians throughout the world?' So they were by the Methodists for
several years; by them all, without any exception;
but afterwards, some in London carried this to excess,
and fasted so as to impair their health. It was not
long before others made this a pretence for not fasting
at all. And I fear there are now thousands of Methodists, so called, both in England and Ireland, who,
following the same bad example, have entirely left
off fasting; who are so far from fasting twice in the
week, (as all the stricter Pharisees did), that they do
not fast twice in the month. Yea, are there not some
of you who do not fast one day from the beginning
of the year to the end? But what excuse can there be
for this? I do not say for those that call themselves
members of the Church of England; but for any who
profess to believe the Scripture to be the word of God.
Since, according to this, the man that never fasts is
no more in the way to heaven, than the man that
never prays." [22]

From the beginning Wesley stressed the necessity
for regular public and private devotion. In Georgia
he began daily service, dividing the public prayers
according to what he believed to be the appointment
of the early Church. He was apparently following
Hickes' *Reformed Devotions,* itself an abridgment
and "reformation" of a Roman Catholic work. The
service was divided into the early morning service at
five; the Communion and sermon at eleven; the evening service at three. For daily devotion, there were
public prayers at five and, apparently, in the evening.

But these did not last, on week-days, more than seven or eight minutes. Dr. Curnock very shrewdly suggests that "probably long prayers, long hymns, and long, prosy sermons, more than anything else, destroyed the early morning services of the Methodists in the last years of the eighteenth century." [23]

Private devotion, prayer, meditation, reading the Bible and other books, Wesley recommended constantly by precept and example. His own habit of early rising and regular prayer and meditation is well known. But he insisted upon the same plan for others. This was not a matter of feeling or impulse. "It is therefore our wisdom to force ourselves to prayer—to pray whether we can or no," [24] is his advice to a correspondent who had been infected by Madame Guyon's quietistic doctrines. To another inquirer he wrote: "Certainly your friend will suffer loss if he does not allow himself time every day for private prayer. Nothing will supply the place of this. Praying with others is quite another thing." [25] Prayer was to be a part of the devotional exercise of the individual; to this was to be added meditation and reading. One of his preachers was rebuked for his little reading. "Fix some part of every day for private exercises," wrote Wesley. "You may acquire the taste which you have not; what is tedious at first will afterwards be pleasant. Whether you like it or no, read and pray daily. It is for your life; there is no other way, else you will be a trifler all your days, and a pretty, superficial preacher. Do justice to your own soul; give it time and means to grow. Do not starve yourself any longer." [26] Members, as well as preachers, were expected to follow the same regimen. In his letter to the Bristol Societies, in 1764, Wesley advised: "To the public, constantly add the private means of grace, particularly prayer and reading. Most of you have been greatly wanting in this; and without it you can never grow in grace. You may as well expect a child to grow without food as a soul without private prayer; and reading is an excellent help to this." [27] And for the reading, Wesley had specific directions. "The most profitable way of reading," he wrote Martha Chapman, in 1772, "is to read in an exact method: Suppose a chapter or two (as time may serve) in the Old Testament with the *Notes* [his own] in the morning; and a chapter more or less of the New Testament and *Notes* in the afternoon or evening. Next to this it might be useful to read the *Works* [again his own] in order, only not too fast. For all reading should be joined with meditation and prayer. Read a little, pray and meditate much." [28]

This introduces a somewhat neglected aspect of Wesley's work. In Wickham Legg's *English Church Life from the Restoration to the Tractarian Movement*, there is an excellent chapter on devotional works popular in the eighteenth century, including Roman Catholic works translated and adapted for Protestant use; but the author seems to be unaware of the extent to which Wesley participated in the publication and circulation of such books.

That Wesley had a high opinion of Bishop Taylor's *Holy Living* and *Holy Dying*, William Law's *Serious Call* and *Christian Perfection*, and Thomas à Kempis'

Imitation of Christ goes without saying. The latter Wesley thought should be in every house—along with his own "Instruction for Children" and his *Primitive Physic*. The *Imitation* was undoubtedly what Henry Moore called it, Wesley's "favourite guide." The third book that he published (1735), it was reprinted in full in 1750; and extracts from it were published in 1741 and reissued in 1746, 1759, 1777, 1780, and 1788. Taylor and Law were both included, in abridged form, in the *Christian Library,* the collection of fifty volumes of Christian literature which Wesley hoped to circulate as a sort of "five-foot shelf" of the world's best religious books.

Perhaps a glance at the works, in addition to those mentioned, which Wesley published for the benefit of the Methodists, preachers and members, will best clarify Wesley's intentions and interests in regard to private devotion. Most of the works which he printed were abridged—and frequently mutilated; but the concern here is not with his literary taste but with his devotional interest.

The books which may be classed as devotional include religious treatises helpful for meditation and those providing definite religious exercises. Among the former are Bishop Hall, *Meditations and Vows, Divine and Moral; An Extract from the Whole Duty of Man;* Pascal's *Thoughts on Religion, and other subjects; The Spiritual Bee: or a Miscellany of Divine Meditations, Extracts from the Letters of Mr. Samuel Rutherford; Contemplations Moral and Divine,* extracted from the works of Lord Chief Justice Hale; *A Relation of the Holy War* (Wesley's abridgment of

Bunyan) ; Baxter's *Saints Everlasting Rest; Spiritual Letters Written in Spanish,* from the writings of Don Juan D'Avila. Of works designed as guides to spiritual exercises may be mentioned: *A Collection of Prayers for Families;* Dr. Horneck's *The Happy Ascetic: or the best Exercise* (containing prayers suitable for each exercise) ; *An Extract of the Christian Sacrifice: a Treatise showing the Necessity, End and Manner of receiving the Holy Communion, together with suitable prayers and Meditations,* by Simon Patrick, late Bishop of Ely; *Devotions for Every Day of the Week, and the Great Festivals.*

Some of these works call for comment. The *Collection of Prayers for Families* had been printed separately, and Green's description of this work will be helpful. "It contains a morning and evening prayer for each day of a week. This devotional manual is admirably suited to its high purpose. The prayers are comprehensive, but brief, each covering about a page and a half." [29] *The Devotions for Every Day of the Week, and the Great Festivals* was a work, originally by John Austin, a Catholic, but adapted for Church of England use by a Mrs. Susannah Hopson. George Hickes (1642-1715), the Nonjuror, further reformed the work; and it was Hickes' version which Wesley adapted, abridged, and printed. This work had influenced Wesley in Georgia. He had used it in his public and private devotions, as it was said to have been used in nonjuring oratories. The work, too, was useful to Wesley when he compiled his Charlestown Hymnbook, although he could not include some of Austin's hymns. Hickes pro-

vided daily devotions, divided into Matins, Lauds,
Vespers, and Compline. In his edition, Wesley
changed these to Morning, Noon, Afternoon, and
Evening. The character of the work as issued by Wesley is described thus by Green: "Wesley has inserted
'The Office' for each day of the week, and under the
head of *Devotions for the Great Festivals,* the Office
of our blessed Saviour, the Office of the Holy Ghost,
the Office of the Saints, and the Preparatory Office for
Death. Under the head of *Occasional Devotions* are
the Office for a Family, two Litanies, and a number of
Prayers. . . . Generally the Psalms written by Austin are given in full in the earlier part, in the latter
several are omitted, but there is little or no verbal revision; a few only of the hymns and of the shorter
prayers are given, and the passages of Scripture are
not as a rule inserted." [30]

This much detail has been given in order that the
reader may understand the nature of the devotional
works which Wesley hoped to circulate among his
people. That the *Christian Library* was not exten-
sively sold was a matter of deep regret to him, for he
felt that he had provided abridgments and corrections of a rich treasury of Christian literature. And
he had. If his emendations were not always wise, his
intentions are evident enough. Aside from doctrinal
and other works, the devotional literature in the
Christian Library would alone have made the distri-
bution of the set immensely valuable to the Methodists and contributive to the preservation of Wesley's
religious ideals.

It is necessary to turn to the Rules of the Methodist

Societies and to the *Minutes* of the Conferences to see how far the Society organization was intended to regulate and systematize the devotional life of the Methodists. The *General Rules of the United Societies* set forth three things expected of all who continue in the societies: (1) Doing no harm; (2) doing good; (3) "attending upon all the ordinances of God." This latter was explained as follows: "Such are, the public worship of God; the ministry of the word, either read or expounded; the supper of the Lord; family and private prayer; searching the Scriptures; and fasting, or abstinence." To secure the carrying out of this, as well as the other rules, the societies were under strict oversight. The more mature Christians met in "bands"; and the third "direction" to the bands, issued in 1744, was:

"Constantly to attend on all the ordinances of God: in particular,—

"1. To be at church and at the Lord's table every week, and at every public meeting of the Bands.

"2. To attend the ministry of the word every morning, unless distance, business, or sickness prevent.

"3. To use private prayer every day; and family prayer, if you are at the head of a family.

"4. To read the Scriptures, and meditate therein, at every vacant hour. And,—

"5. To observe, as days of fasting and abstinence, all Fridays in the year." [31]

More particular directions were given to the preachers, with the injunction that they should not only observe them themselves, but "enforce the use of them on all other persons." These directions, in the form of questions, were printed in the *Large Minutes* (1763). They stressed early rising and morning devotions, which Wesley believed conducive to both physical and spiritual health. Then the "means of grace" were set forth.

They are either Instituted or Prudential:—

"I. The Instituted are,

"(1) Prayer; private, family, public; consisting of deprecation, petition, intercession, and thanksgiving. Do you use each of these? Do you use private prayer every morning and evening? If you can, at five in the evening; and the hour before or after morning preaching [usually five or six o'clock]? Do you forecast daily, wherever you are, how to secure these hours? Do you avow it everywhere? Do you ask everywhere, 'Have you family prayer?' Do you retire at five o'clock?

"(2) Searching the Scriptures by,

"(i) Reading: Constantly, some part of every day; regularly, all the Bible in order; carefully, with the Notes; seriously, with prayer before and after; fruitfully, immediately practising what you learn there?

"(ii) Meditating: at set times? by any rule?

"(iii) Hearing: Every morning? Carefully; with prayer before, at, after; immediately putting in practice? Have you a New Testament always about you?

"(3) The Lord's supper: Do you use this at every opportunity? with solemn prayer before; with earnest and deliberate self-devotion?

"(4) Fasting: How do you fast every Friday?

"(5) Christian conference: Are you convinced how important and how difficult it is to 'order your conversation right?' Is it 'always in grace? seasoned with salt? meet to minister grace to the hearers?' Do not you converse too long at a time? Is not an hour commonly enough? Would it not be well always to have a determinate end in view; and to pray before and after it?

"II. Prudential Means we may use as common Christians, as Methodists, as Preachers, or as Assistants.

"(1) As common Christians. What particular rules have you in order to grow in grace? What arts of holy living?" [32]

Other "prudential means" are concerned with society meetings and the like and not particularly with "arts of holy living."

Before concluding this sketch of Wesley's devotional regulations, a word should be said about services peculiar to the Methodists. In the Conference *Minutes* of 1744-1748, preserved in John Bennet's and Wesley's copies,[33] there are calendars of "Watch-Nights, Intercession-Days, Love-Feasts and Letter-Days." In Bennet's Minutes for 1745, for example, the list is as follows:

Watch-Nights.	Inter-Days	Love-Feasts.	Letter-Days.
Aug. 2	Sept. 6	Aug. 18	Aug. 13
Aug. 28	Oct. 3	Sept. 15	Sept. 10
Sept. 27	Nov. 8	Oct. 13	Oct. 8
Nov. 1	Dec. 6	Nov. 17	Nov. 12
Nov. 30		Dec. 15	Dec. 10
Dec. 27			

This series of special days, about one a week, was in
addition to the regular class and band meetings, the
Friday fasts, the morning services, where held, and
the Sunday meetings. The "letter days" call for
little explanation. Early in the history of the Methodist Societies, a special session of the class meetings
was set aside for the reading of letters detailing individual experiences, the progress of the revival, and
the like. The Intercession days, the Love-feasts, and
the Watch nights were perhaps originally modeled
on Moravian services. The first were days set aside
for prayer services for special objects, the conversion
of friends, the ongoing of the work of God. The
others were more peculiarly Methodist meetings.

Wesley's explanation of his love feasts is as follows:
"In order to increase in them [members of the bands]
a grateful sense of all his mercies, I desired that, one
evening in a quarter, all the men in a band, on a second, all the women, would meet; and on a third, both
men and women together; that we might together
'eat bread,' as the ancient Christians did, 'with glad-
ness and singleness of heart.' At these love feasts (so
we termed them, retaining the name, as well as the
thing, which was in use from the beginning) our
food is only a little plain cake and water. But we
seldom return from them without being fed, not only
with the 'meat which perisheth,' but with 'that which
endureth to everlasting life.' " [34] Eating bread and
drinking water together, the members spoke of their
spiritual life, their trials and triumphs, their hopes
and fears. Later, all members of the classes, not

merely the "select bands," were permitted to join in this observance.

The watch nights were outgrowths of a practice which seems to have sprung up spontaneously at Kingswood. A number of people frequently met at the school and spent the greater part of the night in prayer, praise, and thanksgiving. "Some advised me," wrote Wesley, "to put an end to this; but, upon weighing the thing thoroughly, and comparing it with the practice of the ancient Christians, I could see no cause to forbid it. Rather, I believed it might be made of more general use. So I sent them word, I designed to watch with them on the Friday nearest the full moon, that we might have light thither and back again. I gave public notice of this the Sunday before, and, withal, that I intended to preach; desiring they, and they only, would meet me there, who could do it without prejudice to their business or families. On Friday abundance of people came, began preaching between eight and nine and we continued till a little beyond the noon of night, singing, praying, and praising God." [35]

This was the general plan for later watch nights. "We have often found a peculiar blessing at these seasons," wrote Wesley. "There is generally a deep awe upon the congregation, perhaps in some measure owing to the silence of the night, particularly in singing the hymn, with which we commonly conclude:

> Harken to the solemn voice,
> The awful midnight cry!
> Waiting souls, rejoice, rejoice,
> And feel the Bridegroom nigh." [36]

To an objecting clergyman, Wesley's reply was: "Sir, did you never see the word 'Vigil' in your Common-Prayer Book? Do you know what it means? If not, permit me to tell you, that it was customary with the ancient Christians to spend whole nights in prayer; and that these nights were termed *Vigilian,* or Vigils. Therefore for spending a part of some nights in this manner, in public and solemn prayer, we have not only the authority of our own national Church, but of the universal Church, in the earliest ages." [37]

Thus did Wesley invoke the authority of the Primitive Church for methods he thought useful in promoting and guiding the devotional life of his followers. In all, his aim was to deepen the individual's sense of the love of God; but this could not be done without the use of means. "Why are we not more holy?" was one of the questions in the *Large Minutes.* The answer was "Chiefly because we are enthusiasts; looking for the end, without using the means." To the eighteenth century this answer was more meaningful than it is to the reader to-day. Enthusiasm was, in their minds, associated with those sectaries of the Commonwealth who claimed to possess the Holy Spirit, who despised the Church and its ordinances and the slower and more prosaic methods which historic Christianity had ordained for the nurture of the spiritual life. If the Methodist talked of being "filled with the Spirit," he did not mean—or, at least, Wesley did not intend for him to mean—anything that precluded the sober and time-honored means of grace.

CHAPTER X

WESLEY'S DOCTRINE OF THE CHURCH

IF Wesley strove to preserve discipline and method in religion, he also sought to keep his followers in the stream of Church life. In any discussion of Wesley's beliefs about the Church one must reckon with a confusion that is partly owing to the dust of controversy and partly to a failure to distinguish carefully Wesley's essential ideas. The student of Wesley will do well to have in mind the various forms which the corporate fellowship of Christians has taken in the West. Usually these are distinguished as episcopal, presbyterian, independent, and the like; but such definitions rest upon matters of organization rather than upon any deep-lying social differences. The sociological divisions which have been made familiar to Western readers through the writings of Ernst Troeltsch offer a better basis for the study of Wesley's great experiment.[1]

Troeltsch recognized three great types "of the sociological development of Christian thought:" the Church, the sect, and mysticism. It is with the first two that one has to do in considering Wesley, for he early repudiated mysticism. The Church-type, to characterize very briefly Troeltsch's idea, attempts universality and uniformity. Its essence is its objective, institutional character, and it makes place in the institution for various degrees of capacity and maturity. "The Church is the great educator of the nations." To an extent, the Church compromises with the social order in which it exists. The sect-type, on the other hand, aspires to "direct personal fellowship between the members of the group" and seeks for "personal inward perfection." The sects are voluntary groups and small in comparison with the larger and supposedly universal institutions of the Church-type. Troeltsch believed that both types stem back into the New Testament; but the Church-type emphasizes grace, while the sect-type tends to exalt the Law, as, for example, the Sermon on the Mount.

However much of a caricature of Troeltsch's elaborate discussion the above paragraph may be, perhaps it makes plain that there is a vital distinction between the two types of institutional expression. There is, of course, no thought of prejudgment by the use of the terms, "church" and "sect." While the latter name rose partly as a term of reproach, those groups which may be called sects, to distinguish the sociological type to which they belong, are granted by most liberal Christians to-day the right to be considered Christian churches as truly as any other. The nomenclature is only for the sake of preserving the distinctions between the ideals and structure of the two groups.

No one will deny that Wesley began as a High Churchman devoted to the Church of England. His father and mother were both of the same persuasion, and his brothers remained much the same throughout

their lives. High Churchmanship, in the eighteenth-
century sense, let it be said again, was not a matter
of ritualism. In 1755, when the question of separation from the Church of England was being hotly
debated, Charles Wesley set forth his High Church
views in the following lines:

> Yet, while I warmly for her faith contend,
> Shall I her blots and blemishes defend?
> Inventions added in a fatal hour,
> Human appendages of pomp and power
> Whatever shines in outward grandeur great,
> I give it up—a creature of the State!
> Let others for the shape and colour fight,
> Of garments short or long, or black or white;
> Or, fairly matched, in furious battle join
> For and against the sponsors and the sign;
> Copes, hoods, and surplices the Church miscall,
> And fiercely run their heads against the wall;
> Far different care is mine; o'er earth to see
> Diffused her true essential piety.[2]

The Churchmanship of the Wesleys in Oxford was
the Churchmanship of the early eighteenth century,
consisting of devotion to the Church, high ideas of
passive obedience and the like, to which they added
the ordering of their lives by what they conceived to
have been the customs of the Early Church, especially
in the observance of fasts and in ascetic practices.

In Oxford, Wesley had been led to prize the *Apostolic Constitutions* as of the highest antiquity and
authority. During part of his sojourn in America,
Wesley was studying the *Constitutions* and was much
influenced by them until he decided that they were of
later date than he had thought. But a study of these

Constitutions of the fourth century reveal much which either directly influenced Wesley or was congruent with his beliefs at this time. According to the *Constitutions,* there were to be daily services, morning and evening, and fasting on Wednesdays and Fridays. The eucharist is spoken of as an "unbloody sacrifice," and baptism is the "laver of regeneration." Marriage of the clergy, while not forbidden, was restricted; and among those whom the clergy were forbidden to marry were servants and widows, a prohibition which may partly explain Charles' violent opposition to John's proposed marriage to Grace Murray and his actual marriage with Mrs. Vazeille. The threefold order of the ministry was taught, and it was expressly stated that presbyters were not permitted to ordain deacons, deaconesses or readers, not even singers or porters. All ordination was restricted to bishops.

In the *Ecclesiastical* or *Apostolical Canons,* which he also studied at this time, there are other points of belief which coincide with his position in Oxford and, largely, in America. Trine immersion is enjoined; the marriage of unmarried clergy forbidden; and the three orders uncompromisingly proclaimed.

On the question of apostolic succession, Wesley at this time, held high views. It is unnecessary to illustrate this, since the fact is generally admitted. But it may be worth while to state more fully Wesley's position on the Lord's Supper and on baptism during this earlier period. In 1725, Wesley wrote his mother that he had always supposed "that when I communicated worthily, *i.e.,* with faith and humility, and thankfulness, my preceding sins were *ipso facto* forgiven me." To this his mother agreed, although her answer would indicate that she is thinking of repentance and the state of mind of the communicant rather than of communication itself.[3] In Wesley's *Forms of Prayer* (1733), the prayer for Sunday evening thanks God "for so often feeding my soul and body with thy most precious body and blood, those pledges of love, and sure conveyances of strength and comfort."[4] The prayer for the communicant is that he may approach the altar with gifts of "humility, faith, hope, love, and all those holy dispositions which become the solemn remembrance of a crucified Saviour." The Lord's Supper was a real means of grace, but the emphasis is placed upon the disposition of the communicant in his solemn remembrance of the Lord's death.

On his voyage to America, Wesley was reading Brevint, probably, as his editor says, the preface concerning the Christian "Sacrament and Sacrifice,"[5] which the Wesleys later reprinted. "At the holy table," wrote Brevint, "the people meet to worship God, and God is present to meet and bless His people." The Sacrament is a memorial, a sign of present graces, a means of grace, a pledge of future glory, a commemorative sacrifice, a sacrifice of ourselves and our goods. Brevint's position, which Wesley so far accepted as later to reprint it as a preface to *Hymns on the Lord's Supper*,[6] may be seen from a few short excerpts.

The Lord's Supper "is not a bare memorial only, but may actually convey as many blessings to me, as it brings curses on the profane receiver. Indeed, in

239

what manner this is done I know not; it is enough for me to admire." "This Victim having been offered up in the fulness of times, and in the midst of the world, which is Christ's great temple, and having been thence carried up to heaven, which is His sanctuary, from thence spreads salvation all around, as the burnt-offering did its smoke. And thus His body and blood have everywhere, but especially at this Sacrament, a true and real presence. . . . This great and holy mystery communicates to us the death of our blessed Lord, both as offering Himself to God, and as giving Himself to man. As He offered Himself to God, it enters me into that mystical body for which He died, and which is dead with Christ; yea, it sets me on the very shoulders of that eternal Priest, while He offers up Himself and intercedes for His spiritual Israel. And by this means it conveys to me the communion of His sufferings, which leads to a communion in all His graces and glories. As He offers Himself to man, the holy Sacrament is, after the Sacrifice for sin, the true sacrifice of peace-offerings, and the table purposely set to receive those mercies that are sent down from His altar." "Nevertheless, this sacrifice, which by a real oblation was not to be offered more than once, is by a devout and thankful commemoration to be offered up every day. . . . And thus do we every day offer unto God the meritorious sufferings of our Lord, as the only sure ground whereon God may give, and we obtain, the blessings we pray for. . . . To men it is a sacred table, where God's minister is ordered to represent from God his Master the passion of His dear Son, as still fresh, and still powerful for their eternal salvation. And to God it is an altar, whereon men mystically present to Him the same sacrifice, as still bleeding and sueing for mercy."

These lengthy quotations are necessary, since there is no doubt that they represent John Wesley's views before 1738. In the same way, numerous references attest his belief in baptismal regeneration. Here again, views expressed by another set forth clearly what he seems himself to have believed. In this instance the "other" was his father. In 1700, Samuel Wesley wrote a "Short Treatise on Baptism," and John published it with some abridgment.[7] Its general tenor is clear from a few quotations. The benefits received from baptism are "the washing away the guilt of original sin, by the application of the merits of Christ's death"; entering into covenant with God; admission into the Church. "By baptism, we who are 'by nature children of wrath,' are made the children of God. And this regeneration which our Church in so many places ascribes to baptism is more than barely being admitted into the Church, though commonly connected therewith. . . . By water, then, as a means, the water of baptism, we are regenerated or born again; whence it is also called by the Apostle, 'the washing of baptism.' Our Church therefore ascribes no greater virtue to baptism than Christ himself has done. Nor does she ascribe it to the outward washing, but to the inward grace, which, added thereto, makes it a sacrament. Herein a principle of grace is infused, which will not be wholly taken away, unless we quench the Holy Spirit of God by long-continued wickedness." The treatise further defends effusion as a mode—although the quantity of water used was said not to be material—and the baptism of infants.

This is high doctrine, indeed; but his doctrines, overstrained and highflying as some of them were, must not be allowed to cloud the essential beauty of his piety nor of his conception of the Church. Perhaps nowhere in his writings is there a phrase which more aptly sets forth his ideal of the Church than that which occurs in his *Forms of Prayer,* where he speaks of the Church as the "Catholic seminary of divine love." [8] The Church is a guide and support and, in a true sense, brings men into the presence of Christ.

It has been assumed by some writers on Methodism that the conviction which Wesley arrived at, about 1738, concerning salvation by faith, and his own heightened experience of the love of God changed his High Church views and made him a liberal Churchman, if not a Dissenter at heart. Nothing could be further from the truth. Five months after the Aldersgate experience, John and Charles Wesley had an interview with the Bishop of London, Edmund Gibson; and in that interview the Wesleys contended for the rebaptizing of those who had received Dissenters' baptism and were dissatisfied with it. The Bishop disapproved, having no liking for rebaptism and believing Dissenters' baptism valid. The next month Charles called again on the Bishop and somewhat incensed that prelate by insisting on approval for rebaptism of a woman who had been baptized by a Dissenter.[9] December 30, 1745, seven and a half years after Aldersgate, Wesley wrote to his brother-in-law,

Wesley Hall, concerning the Church and ministry: "We believe it would not be right for us to administer either baptism or the Lord's supper unless we had a commission so to do from those bishops whom we apprehend to be in succession from the Apostles. . . . We believe that the threefold order of ministers . . . is not only authorized by its apostolical institution, but also by the written Word." [10] Three weeks after writing this letter, Wesley read the book which changed his opinions concerning the nature of the ministry in the Primitive Church; but the point to be noticed here is that changed views of immediate communion with God or of faith did not compel new conceptions of the Church and ministry. The most that can be said is that increased emphasis upon faith tended to soften Wesley's zeal for institutional requirements, and association with non-Churchmen weakened his exclusiveness.

In many parishes, Methodists were excluded from the communion table. In others, the Methodists scrupled to receive the sacraments at the hands of men whom they believed ungodly. Some of the preachers insisted that they should have the right to administer the sacraments as well as to preach. The question of separation from the Church was becoming acute. In the Conference of 1744, the question, "Do we separate from the Church?" was answered: "We do not. We hold communion therewith for conscience sake, by constantly attending both the word preached, and the sacraments administered therein." But already Wesley was forced to face the possibility that, after his death, the Methodists might secede from the Church. "We are persuaded," runs the answer to Question 12, "the body of our hearers will even after our death remain in the Church, unless they be thrust out. We believe notwithstanding either that they will be thrust out, or that they will leaven the whole Church. We do, and will do, all we can to prevent those consequences which are supposed likely to happen after our death. But we cannot with good conscience neglect the present opportunity of saving souls while we live, for fear of consequences which may possibly or probably happen after we are dead." [11]

Already, by 1745, Wesley was defining schism as causeless breach, rupture, or division within the Church; and he declared the Methodists were no more guilty of this than they were of murder. [12] This definition of schism helped Wesley, not only in defending the Methodists from the accusations of their enemies, but also for discussion of the legality of separation. He could not say that separation was illegal, if he regarded schism, not as the sin of leaving the Church, but as raising needless divisions within the Church.

By 1755, the situation was tense. Charles was in a state of excitement that vented itself in letters to all and sundry. He confided to a close friend that he was doubtful of his brother. The preachers, he feared, would overpersuade John. [13] Already Charles and John were disputing whether ordination meant separation. John said, "No"; Charles, "Yes." The preachers were, indeed, pressing Wesley hard; and, in September, 1755, he wrote to the Rev. Samuel Walker that

244

some of the arguments put forth he could not answer. The arguments were, that the preachers could not confine themselves to the Liturgy, and that there were several things in the Book of Common Prayer which seemed contrary to Scripture. Besides, the laws of the Church were in part papistical. Finally, many of the ministers of the Established Church were not sent of God, and their doctrines were subversive to the gospel. Wesley confessed that he could not at that time answer to his own satisfaction, and that his decision to remain in the Church rested on no good premises—a terrible condition for a logician. But he insisted that the essence of the Church to him was not in her orders and laws but in her doctrines and worship.[14]

It is not necessary to follow the controversy over separation, which recurred again and again; for the present it is enough to note that Wesley was arriving at a definition of the Church. Already, in his *Earnest Appeal,* he had said that the Church is visibly joined "by assembling together to hear His word and partake of His supper." And Wesley interpreted the XIXth Article of Faith as defining the visible Church of England by three essentials: (1) living faith; (2) preaching, and consequently hearing the pure word of God; (3) a due administration of the sacraments, "the ordinary means whereby God increaseth faith." [15] According to Wesley, the Church visible is defined not by Catholic but by Protestant standards. The Church is to promote faith, but its essentials are doctrine and worship. But Wesley's growing tolerance was too much even for a strict adherence to the demand for "pure" doctrine or for unsullied worship. In his old age, he admitted that he could not defend the Article altogether. To do so would be to declare the Church of Rome not even a part of the Catholic Church. "Whoever they are that have 'one Spirit, one hope, one Lord, one faith, one God and Father of all,' I can easily bear with their holding wrong opinions, yea, and superstitious modes of worship. Nor would I, on these accounts, scruple still to include them within the pale of the catholic Church; neither would I have any objection to receive them, if they desired it, as members of the Church of England." [16] As early as 1755, Wesley declared that he who has no assurance that his sins are forgiven may have "a kind or degree of faith which distinguishes him not only from a devil but also from an heathen"; and he added that, on this faith, he might "admit him to the Lord's Supper." [17] The Church was distinguished by doctrine and worship, but the terms were inclusive, not exclusive.

Wesley did not intend that his Methodist societies should be taken for a church. When Troeltsch wrote that Methodism "belonged essentially to the sect-type and not to the church-type, in spite of its earnest desire to remain inside the Established Church," [18] he was thinking of the Methodist Societies and not of Wesley's own ideal for them. Canon Overton once wrote: "It is a purely modern notion that the Wesleyan movement ever was, or ever was intended to be, except by Wesley—a Church movement." [19] But Overton's exception is just the point: Wesley did intend his movement to be a *Church movement.* Unless his repeated statements, repeated for fifty years, are to be set down as sentimental maunderings, the conclusion is not to be avoided that he wished his societies to be societies *within* the Church. He came to prefer the simplicity of Methodist meetings to the drawlings of clerks and the unedifying sermons of unawakened clergymen; but he insisted that Methodist services were purposely designed *not* to be worship, as that term is understood technically. The Methodist service was worship, "but not such as supersedes the Church Service; it presupposes public prayer, like the sermons at the University. If it were designed to be instead of the Church Service, it would be essentially defective; for it seldom has the four grand parts of public prayer, deprecation, petition, intercession, and thanksgiving." [20] Tyerman thought Wesley was wrong in insisting on short prayers in Methodist services, but he understood that Wesley required this because the services did not supersede but presupposed the public prayer of the Church.

No one supposes that Wesley contemplated the existence of two types of church organization, the church-type and the sect-type, as sociological institutions, and deliberately set about their combination. But, in the face of the evidence, it seems impossible to avoid the conclusion that Wesley did deliberately seek to combine the qualities of an individualistic, intense religious piety, best attainable at its highest in a voluntary society, with those qualities characteristic of the Church. That this did not endure in England after Wesley's death, was doubtless inevitable; but its failure should not obscure the Founder's dream.

That this was Wesley's ideal was shown plainly in the setting up of the Methodist Church in America. Whatever may be said of his ordinations, this much is sure: Wesley deliberately inaugurated a Church in America. Unquestionably the American Methodists departed from Wesley's wishes in this respect, but he intended to provide for the continuation of Church life for those who could no longer enjoy this under the English Establishment. His purpose was plainly expressed in his certificate to Dr. Coke. He would take care of those who wished "to continue under my care, and still adhere to the doctrines and discipline of the Church of England" and who "are greatly distressed for want of ministers to administer the sacraments of baptism and the Lord's supper, according to the usage of the said Church." [21] In other words, since the mark of union with a Church, according to Wesley, is unity of doctrine and worship, he was providing for just that. To accomplish this further, Wesley issued what he called an "edition" of the Prayer Book, abridged and renamed "Sunday Service." Just as in England he had tried to retain his followers as members of a religious society within the Church, so in America he designed the continuance of Church life according to the doctrines and worship of the Church of England, although not in dependence upon English bishops, and with such changes in Articles and Liturgy as seemed necessary in view of American conditions.

Wesley's belief in the Church is evidenced also by his continued belief in the importance of the sacraments. In one who insisted so much that the visible

Church is a company of faithful men, and who believed so heartily in regeneration, the retention of infant baptism is, at first thought, inconsistent. But Wesley never believed baptism a mere ceremony. He noted that faith was given to some of his converts when he baptized them; and he had regard for that "inward grace, which is supposed by our Church to be given with and through that sign to all infants." [22] His father's tract which was quoted to illustrate Wesley's views on baptism before 1738, was published by Wesley in 1756; and there is no indication that Wesley then disagreed with it. Indeed, the tract was printed without any note that it was a reprint of his father's treatise. There is some indication that Wesley modified his views in later years. In Sermon XXXIX, he declared it to be certain that "our Church" supposes all baptized in infancy to be at the same time born again. "Nor is it an objection of any weight against this," he added, "that we cannot comprehend how this work can be wrought in infants. For neither can we comprehend how it is wrought in a person of mature years." Sugden thinks that his further statement may indicate some hesitation: "Whatever be the case with infants, it is sure all of riper years who are baptized are not at the same time born again." [23] In Wesley's *Sunday Service,* which he prepared for the American Church, the service is abridged, and there are two significant omissions. In the minister's closing exhortation to thankful prayer, he is to say: "Seeing now, dearly beloved brethren, that this Child is grafted into the body of Christ's Church," instead of "regenerate and grafted" as the Prayer Book has it.

Also in the Thanksgiving prayer, "that it hath pleased thee to regenerate this infant with thy Holy Spirit, to receive him for thine own child by adoption" has been changed to read: "that it hath pleased thee to receive this Infant for thine own Child by adoption." But the change was not thorough, for Wesley retained the prayers "to sanctify water to the mystical washing away of sin," and "that he may receive remission of his sins by spiritual regeneration." Wesley wavered as to baptismal regeneration, but he continued to regard the sacrament of baptism as a conferring of grace.

Whatever Wesley's views on baptism, his interests were not centered there. Baptism was a rite already performed so far as most of his hearers were concerned. The Lord's Supper was on a different footing. There is the less need for details here, since Dr. Rattenbury has an excellent exposition of Wesley's views accessible to readers in *Wesley's Legacy to the World*.[24] It is necessary only to make clear the general nature of Wesley's views throughout his evangelical ministry.

To understand Wesley's high conception of the Lord's Supper one must keep in mind his discussion of the means of grace in his sermon on that subject, which is included in the Standard Sermons.[25] There are, says Wesley, means which are ordained of God as the usual channels of His grace. These means Wesley understood to be "outward signs, words, or actions, ordained of God, and appointed for this end, to be the ordinary channels whereby He might convey to man, preventing, justifying, or sanctifying grace." The words which he uses are from the Prayer Book. The chief of these means are prayer, searching the Scriptures, receiving the Lord's Supper; but their value depends upon their subservience to the end of religion. "Use all means as means .... not for their own sake, but in order to the renewal of your soul in righteousness and true holiness." There is in them no intrinsic power whatsoever. In this spirit one should partake of the Lord's Supper, for in this "ye openly exhibit the same by these visible signs, before God and angels, and men; ye manifest your solemn remembrance of His death, till He cometh in the clouds of heaven." Eating of that bread and drinking of that cup are "the outward, visible means whereby God conveys into our souls all that spiritual grace, that righteousness, and peace, and joy in the Holy Ghost, which were purchased by the body of Christ once broken, and the blood of Christ once shed for us."

In 1745, John and Charles Wesley published their *Hymns on the Lord's Supper,* signing themselves "Presbyters of the Church of England" and prefixing as a preface extracts from Dr. Brevint on "The Christian Sacrament and Sacrifice." [26] Thus the book which John Wesley read on his way to America was reprinted with hymns arranged under the various divisions of the Preface. The communicant was to expect the presence of Christ at the sacrament:

> In Thy ordinance appear,
> Come and meet Thy followers here.
>
> Sinner, with awe draw near,
> And find thy Saviour here.

The Lord's Supper is the supreme rite in which the recipient may expect the grace of God:

> Fasting He doth, and hearing bless,
> And prayer can much avail,
> Good vessels all to draw the grace
> Out of salvation's well.
>
> But none like this mysterious rite
> Which dying mercy gave,
> Can draw forth all His promised might
> And all His will to save.

Certainly the manner of this conveying of grace is mysterious, but the Wesleys reject any suggestion of materialism in the sacrament:

> These the virtue did convey,
> Yet still remains the same.
>
> Who shall say how bread and wine
> God into man conveys!

In a real sense, the Lord's Supper is a showing forth of Christ's death, not only to men, but to God.

> Father, let the sinner go,
> The Lamb did once atone,
> Lo! we to Thy justice show
> The passion of Thy Son.

And in this sense the Eucharist is a sacrifice, a commemorative sacrifice.

> The death Thou never canst repeat,
> Once offer'd up to die no more.

Yet may we celebrate below,
     And daily thus Thine offering show
          Exposed before Thy Father's eyes;
In this tremendous mystery
     Present Thee bleeding on a tree,
          Our everlasting Sacrifice.

But not only is the sacrament a commemorative sacrifice before God, but it is a sacrifice of man himself and of all that he has.

Take my soul and body's powers,
     Take my memory, mind, and will,
All my goods, and all my hours,
     All I know, and all I feel,
All I think, and speak, and do;
     Take my heart—but make it new.

These quotations will give some idea of the Wesleys' hymns for the Lord's Supper. It should be plain from these that the doctrine was not Roman but evangelical, in the best sense of the word, and true to the highest type of Anglican piety. Wesley makes several claims for the sacrament. In the first place, it is commanded. It is also, as the Reformers thought, a preaching of the gospel. But the sacrament is a real means of grace; the recipient is to take it in faith that the Lord will fulfil his promises and confer upon the true worshiper "that righteousness, and peace, and joy in the Holy Ghost, which were purchased by the body of Christ once broken, and the blood of Christ once shed for us." [27]

Thinking of the Lord's Supper as at the heart of Christian worship, Wesley also regarded it as peculiarly fitted for those who can truly say, "the remembrance of our sins is grievous unto us." "In latter times," he wrote, "many have affirmed that the Lord's Supper is not a converting, but a confirming ordinance. And among us it has been diligently taught that none but those who are converted, who have received the Holy Ghost, who are believers in the full sense, ought to communicate. But experience shows the gross falsehood of that assertion that the Lord's Supper is not a converting ordinance. Ye are the witnesses. For many now present know, the very beginning of your conversion to God (perhaps, in some, the first deep conviction) was wrought at the Lord's Supper." [28] Or, as he put it again: "no fitness is required at the time of communicating, but a sense of our state, of our utter sinfulness and helplessness."

These hymns were published in 1745, and the statements just quoted were made in 1740. That essentially these opinions were retained by Wesley throughout his ministry is evident from his publishing in 1788 a sermon on "The Duty of Constant Communion" [29] which he had written for his pupils in Oxford in 1733. In this sermon he declares the Lord's Supper to entail as benefits: "the forgiveness of our past sins, the present strengthening and refreshing of our souls." And he lays upon sinners especially the necessity of coming to the Communion: "what surer way have we of procuring pardon from him, than the showing forth the Lord's death; and beseeching him, for the sake of his Son's sufferings, to blot out all our sins?" By practice and precept, Wesley urged his people to attend the Lord's Supper. In 1764, in the midst of his work, he advised the societies at Bristol to lose no opportunities of receiving the sacrament. All who neglected it suffered loss; most of them had become "dead as stones." [30]   Three years before he died, he wrote to one of his preachers concerning a young man who neglected this sacrament, that, "if he obstinately persists in that neglect, you can't give him any more tickets for our society." [31]   "The Church and the Sacraments" was not a rallying cry but an expression of Wesley's unwavering devotion to the visible symbols and means of the ever-present and ever-active grace of God.

It is evident, then, that to Wesley the *esse* of a visible Church is the possession of doctrines and sacraments: for a visible Church is a congregation of faithful men, "in the which the pure Word of God is preached, and the Sacraments duly administered according to Christ's ordinance in all those things that of necessity are requisite to the same." Because of this definition, Wesley contended, until his death, that he had not separated from the Church of England: he held to what he considered to be the essentials of Anglican doctrine; and he worshiped, whenever possible, in communion with the Church of England. Although he had not in everything obeyed the bishops, he had remained in communion with the Church and he held her doctrines. Whether such a definition and such a defense are in themselves defensible is not now the question. Undoubtedly Wesley so believed.

But while Wesley believed the *esse* of the Church to be doctrine and worship, of which the sacrament of the Lord's Supper was a central part, he did not despise the outward government of the Church. This belonged to the *bene esse* of the Church, and even after he had become convinced that there was no one form of church government required in Scripture, he yet retained his belief in the wisdom and expediency of the government of the Church of England.

Wesley had not come easily by his change in belief concerning church government. As late as 1745, as has been seen, he held to his High Church views that three orders of the ministry were required by Scripture and by the practice and teaching of the Primitive Church. With more ingenuity than reason, he had defended his preaching throughout the kingdom on the ground that he had, in ordination, received "an indelible character" which gave him power to preach and to administer the sacraments without regard to parish boundaries. The Moravians were novel and unprimitive in their church discipline, it seemed to him, because their bishops were "mere shadows," and were so named only to please those who lay stress upon the "Threefold Order." The Moravian ordination seemed, to him, evidence that they looked upon episcopal ordination as nothing. These objections Wesley listed, in a letter to the church at Herrnhut, as among those things "which seem not agreeable to the gospel of Christ." [32]

Such firmly held opinions, which were agreeable to him by reason of his High Church upbringing, were little affected by his belief that conscious fellowship with God is the privilege of all Christians or by his own experience in Aldersgate Street. But the opinions could not hold against what he took to be cogent argument. The Man of Reason was as real as the Churchman or the Saint in Wesley. In 1746, he read Chancellor King's book on the constitution of the Primitive Church and was thereby convinced that bishops and presbyters, or elders, are of the same order "and consequently have the same right to ordain." This is, of course, a direct denial of the claim that episcopal government wherein the bishops alone can ordain is by divine right. This view was confirmed to Wesley by reading Stillingfleet's *Irenicon*. Of the latter he wrote, in 1756: "I think he has unanswerably proved that neither Christ nor His Apostles prescribed any particular form of Church government, and that the plea for the divine right of Episcopacy was never heard of in the primitive Church." [33]

Such a position may be thought by modern readers to have been a greater innovation in the eighteenth century than it really was. Nineteenth-century controversies have tended to slur over the fact that many of the great names of the English Church in the sixteenth and seventeenth centuries, to say nothing of the eighteenth, can be cited for this very doctrine concerning episcopacy. For this matter, no less than St. Thomas Aquinas in the thirteenth century can be quoted for the view that the episcopate is not a distinct order; and with him agreed most of the schoolmen.[34] It was Archbishop Ussher who answered Charles the First's question as to whether presbyters in the Ancient Church ordained, by saying: "I can shew your Majesty more, even where Presbyters alone successively ordained Bishops." [35]

The Archbishop's reference was to the presbyters of Alexandria, according to Jerome's account—a classic reference for this matter. In the eighteenth century, after Queen Anne, the bishop "retained much of the former respect, but it was not quite of the kind it had been when the belief in episcopacy as a divinely appointed constitution remained comparatively unimpaired." [36] Archbishop Manning thought that the Revolution of 1688 "greatly weakened in the Anglican Church the hold of episcopacy as a divine institution." And a writer who died in 1770 testified that "in my younger days, to deny the divine succession of bishops was rank atheism."

It may be well to look more closely at some statements of Stillingfleet and King in the books which so much influenced Wesley that he threw over a doctrine he had held from his youth and adopted the one to which he was faithful for the remainder of his life. The whole design of Stillingfleet's book, according to his own statement, was "to prove that the form of church government is a mere matter of prudence, regulated by the word of God." [37] He thinks a great proof of this is, that "after episcopal government was settled in the church, yet ordination by presbyters was looked upon as valid." [38] King says that a presbyter is "a person in holy orders, having thereby an inherent right to perform the whole office of a bishop; but being possessed of no place or parish, not actually discharging it, without the permission and consent of the bishop of a place or parish." [39] These views are based upon the assumption that bishops in the Primitive Church were presbyters in charge of a church, and that there were as many bishops as churches. Indeed, King likens the relations of bishops and presbyters in the Primitive Church to that existing in the Church of England between rectors and curates. Both have the authority of the Church to the full ministry of the Church, but jurisdiction in a particular place lies in the bishop.[40]

Here is a distinction between spiritual power and jurisdiction. Into the first, according to King, the deacon and the presbyter, or bishop, using presbyter and bishop to mean the same "order," are inducted by ordination, "the grant of a peculiar commission and power, which remains indelible in the person to whom it is committed, and can never be obliterated or rased out, except the person himself cause it by his heresy, apostacy, or most extremely gross and scandalous impiety." "Now this sort of ordination," adds King, "was conferred only upon deacons and presbyters, or on deacons and bishops, presbyters and bishops being here to be considered as all one, as ministers of the church universal." [41] The question is not now whether King was correct but what he taught in the book which convinced John Wesley that bishops and presbyters are of the same order.

The convictions which had come to him through Lord King's book, later confirmed by reading Stillingfleet, Wesley held for thirty-eight years before he acted upon them. In 1784 he set apart Richard Whatcoat and Thomas Vasey as elders and Dr. Thomas Coke as superintendent for the American Methodists, events concerning the meaning of which reams of good paper and no little ink have been expended. Later, he ordained several other men, most of them for Scotland, but at least three for England, one of these latter being Alexander Mather, who was also "set apart" as superintendent. If Wesley had not set apart Coke, and later Mather, as superintendents, there would be no question as to what he had done. It would be accepted that he had acted upon his belief that presbyters have the right to ordain, that he had, as Whatcoat said of his own case, "formed a presbyter" and ordained his preachers deacons and presbyters. But what was he doing when he "set apart" Coke as superintendent?

For the High Churchman of the present day, the answer is easy. Wesley, in his enthusiasm—or in his senility—violated a fundamental law and attempted to confer a higher order of ministry than he himself possessed. There is no more succinct statement of this view than Charles Wesley's doggerel:

> Wesley his hands on Coke hath laid,
> But who laid hands on him?

Others, reacting from such a view, have contended that Wesley meant nothing in particular and everything in general by thus setting apart a superintendent. He was merely appointing Coke to look after the American Methodists in place of Wesley himself. Or, the answer is expanded by saying that Wesley meant nothing by any of his ordinations. He had come to the conclusion that ordination is merely official appointment. But before deciding on any explanation of Wesley's conduct, the student of Methodism should recall certain facts concerning Wesley's attitude and intentions.

In the first place, Wesley's sole aim, kept constantly before his mind, if we are to believe his own words, was "to promote, so far as I am able, vital, practical religion; and by the grace of God to beget, preserve and increase the life of God in the souls of men." [42] This he said in 1756, and this he continued to say until his death, his depreciators themselves being judges. In the name of his high purpose, he had violated the customs, if not the laws, of the Church of England; and he had expressly said that he would violate them further, if necessary for the gospel's sake.

This intention of Wesley was aided, in so far as matters of government were concerned, by his belief that no form of church polity was ordained of God or provable by Scripture as the sole, valid mode. His conclusions, ratified by much modern scholarship, were those of his instructors, Bishop Stillingfleet and Chancellor King, that, in the Primitive Church, there were different forms of government, and the rule determining polity was that of prudence.

But it must be remembered also that Wesley had a predilection, fostered by his training and by all his sentimental associations, for the Church of England. In 1785, he wrote that he was as firmly attached to the Church of England as ever.[43]   In 1756, he declared "the Episcopal form of Church government to be both scriptural and apostolical." "I mean," he added, "well agreeing with the practice and writings of the Apostles. But that it is prescribed in Scripture I do not believe." [44]   A quarter of a century later, he reiterated that he preferred episcopal ordination to any other, "where it can be had." This is understandable not as a prejudice but as Wesley's conviction growing out of his high respect for the ministry of the Church. That he could ever have thought the setting apart of a ministry by the Church of no importance is an impossible conclusion for any remembering his high estimate of the sacraments and of the ministry of the Word. Again, let it be repeated, that to him, the sacraments were not magical; there was in them no *opus operatum*. But they were real means of grace, and the Christian or the seeker after God neglected them at the peril of his soul. But these sacraments could be administered only by authorized ministers of the visible Church.

Once more, one must reckon with Wesley's belief in the church-type of Christianity. As much as he was devoted to his societies as voluntary associations for the promotion of holiness, he never for one moment thought of substituting a loose, edifying, disciplinary institution for the Church with its ministry and its sacraments. True, he was not bound by a narrow ecclesiasticism. He once employed a layman to help distribute the cup, but he defended his action by appeal to the Early Church. And he believed that the divine commission was more important than any visible calling by the Church. But he was too much the practical Englishman, as well as too much the son of a great tradition, to envisage an amorphous Christianity long enduring without the visible Church. This is the explanation of his famous "Korah" sermon, preached in 1789, which many have taken as a

recantation of his ordinations.[45] What Wesley was
actually doing was to denounce those preachers who
had taken upon themselves the authority to administer
the sacraments simply because they had the authority
to preach. Lay-preaching was allowed by Wesley
because he thought it a necessity and agreeable to the
principle of the Church; but lay-administration of
the sacraments he did not so consider, and he would
have none of it. This was not ecclesiasticism but a
sense of the value of institutions which it was part
of his mission to bring over from the older world into
the new. If his followers have at any time imagined
that he was but a preacher of a spiritual Christianity
without institutional ties or social duties, without corporate worship or the means of grace efficacious to
the believing soul, the fault is not Wesley's. He repeated his fundamental doctrines often enough.

Wesley was a practical administrator, one of the
greatest executive minds of his century. His own experience had taught him what his close acquaintance
with the Anglican Church would have given him
otherwise: an appreciation for the jurisdictional side
of the Church. His constant criticism of the English bishops was that their superintendency was not
effective for practical godliness. Modern analogies
must not be allowed to warp Wesley's idea here.
Present-day churches, especially in America, have
more and more separated certain phases of administration, after the fashion of business, into the hands of
"boards"; but no such analogy will help to the understanding of Wesley's mind. In the eighteenth century, the spiritual work of the Church was not so

divorced from administration. What he would have said about modern church organization is not to the point here, nor is it perhaps a subject for meditation by the pious. The parish priest had certain administrative work to do, and the English bishop, in addition to his "spiritual" duties of confirmation and ordination, had large executive and administrative tasks. The idea of administration as part of the work of the ministry was perfectly familiar to Wesley by tradition and temperament, and this work was connected in his mind, not with semi-clerical postions, but with the ministry of the Church.

Remembering then Wesley's primary purpose, his conviction that government is of the *bene esse* but not of the *esse* of the Church, his predilection for episcopal polity, and his deep sense both of the importance of the spiritual and of the administrative work of the ministry, one may contemplate what actually happened in 1784.

Wesley knew the American people and what was going on in America better than most people in England knew them. His own experience in Georgia had given point to his warning to Lord Dartmouth and to Lord North, in 1775, that the Americans were not to be trifled with and that they were devoted to liberty. In England, he had for years been forced to withstand the importunities of his preachers for ordination, and he knew that the Americans, with less patience and with more excuse, were clamoring for a ministry competent to administer the sacraments. All this he set forth in the letter to the American Methodists which he sent with Coke and his helpers.

He had explained the necessity of the case to the Bishop of London, asking his help. But the bishop "peremptorily refused," and other bishops agreed, saying they had nothing to do with America. "Then," said Wesley, "I saw my way clear, and was fully convinced what it was my duty to do."

In Drew's *Life of Coke,* it is said, and in quotation evidently from Coke himself, that Wesley conferred privately with the Doctor in 1784, telling him of the plan to settle a Church in America. Drew (or Coke?) declared that Wesley, "keeping his eye upon the conduct of the primitive churches in the ages of unadulterated Christianity, had much admired the mode of ordaining bishops which the church of Alexandria had practiced. That to preserve its purity, that church would never suffer the interference of a foreign bishop in any of their ordinations; but that the presbyters of that venerable apostolic church, on the death of a bishop, exercised the right of ordaining another from their own body, by the laying on of hands . . . and finally, that being himself a presbyter, he wished Dr. Coke to accept ordination from his hands, and to proceed in that character to the continent of America, to superintend the societies in the United States." Did Wesley suggest all this to Coke in that first interview? [46]

There is no need at this late date to discuss the character of Dr. Coke. He was a great missionary, fearless and apostolic in his ministry; but he was a man who wanted to be a bishop. That he later suggested union with the newly formed Protestant Episcopal Church in America proves nothing. Wesley might have doubted the wisdom of such a union, but it was consonant with his own intention. But Coke also offered, towards the end of his life, to return to the Church of England, if he were made a bishop in India. Moreover, in the letter which he wrote Wesley in August, 1784, it looks as if Wesley had first suggested that Coke go to America and ordain the preachers there by virtue of the authority which Coke already had, that of a presbyter of the Church of England, the same status as Wesley's own. This seems probable from Coke's urgent tone to Wesley. He may "want all the influence in America" which Wesley can give. He goes on to urge his claims for trust and to suggest even the details, the house in which the ordination could take place. "I shall entreat you to ponder these things," he ends.[47]

To say that Coke did not truly interpret Wesley's meaning in the first conversation in February, 1784, is not to say that Coke lied. Wesley did keep his eyes on the Primitive Church, and he did admire the example of the venerable, apostolic church of Alexandria in ordaining bishops by the hands of presbyters. It is highly probable that, as Coke said, Wesley gave him Lord King's book to study and several months to decide. But the conference had afterward appointed Coke, Whatcoat, and Vasey to America, although they disagreed with any proposal to ordain them. The matter is not certain. Wesley himself brought it up at the Conference, and Pawson thought that Wesley's mind was made up. Nevertheless, Coke's letter looks as if a little urging were yet necessary before Wesley took the step.

However this may be, on the second of September, Wesley "set apart as a superintendent, by the imposition of my hands, and prayer, (being assisted by other ordained ministers,) Thomas Coke, doctor of civil law, a presbyter of the Church of England." Tyerman's judgment is well known: "Wesley meant the ceremony to be a mere formality likely to recommend his delegate to the favour of the Methodists in America: Coke, in his ambition, wished, and intended it to be considered as an ordination to a bishopric." [48] That Coke so intended is undeniable. In America, he asserted as much in his sermon at the ordination of Asbury to be superintendent. Wesley disavowed any responsibility for what Coke said, and Henry Moore declares that Wesley had solemnly warned Coke not to use the title of bishop. But what had Wesley meant to do?

The words, "set apart," have been taken as support for Tyerman's view; but Wesley's Diary would seem to deprive this of force. His entries for the days in question are:

"Sept. 1. 4 prayed, Ordained R. Whatcoat and T. Vasey.
"Sept. 2. 4 prayed, Ordained Dr. Coke!" [49]

Whatever he chose to say in public, in his Diary he said simply that he had "ordained." Nor do the terms which he used give much information; for he liked his own nomenclature. In Acts xx. 28 he had translated "bishops" as "overseers." In his certificates for Whatcoat and Vasey and in the *Sunday Service* for America, he changed "presbyters" to "elders." There is no reason to think he may not have done likewise with "bishop," simply substituting "superintendent." The word was well known: it was used for Lutheran bishops, and Thomas Jackson quotes a work of 1698 by an English Churchman who prefers the same term.[50] Moreover, "superintendent" expressed Wesley's preference as against a diocesan episcopate, for which he thought there was no scriptural authority and little practical justification.

Contemporaries seem to have thought that Wesley meant to ordain a bishop. This was Charles' broken-hearted conclusion. Certainly Coke and Asbury thought so. But no better testimony can be adduced than that of Henry Moore, whom Wesley later ordained a presbyter for England. Moore says roundly, that Wesley, "being peculiarly attached to every rite of the Church of England, he afterwards ordained Dr. Coke a superintendent. . . ." And Moore explains Wesley's feelings about the word "bishop" in thorough consonance with what is otherwise known of Wesley's attitude: "But the association in his mind, between the assumed title, and the display connected with it in the later ages of the church, was too strong. He could not, at that moment, separate the plain, laborious Bishops of the American Societies, where there is no legal establishment, from the dignified Prelates of the mighty Empire of Great Britain. That our brethren who are in that office, are true Scriptural Bishops," added Moore, "I have no doubt at all; nor do I wish that the title should be relinquished, as it is grown into use, and is known, by every one in the United States, to designate men distinguished only by their simplicity and abundant labours."[51] Moore was with

Wesley when the latter wrote to Asbury rebuking him for using the title, bishop, and there is no reason to doubt that Wesley expressed himself at this time concerning his reasons.

To Charles' accusations, John entered no denial of the fact. He contented himself with denying any intention to separate and by declaring that he believed himself a scriptural *episcopos*. It is hard to believe that Emory's conclusion is not right, that, if Wesley had not intended to make Coke a superintendent, in the sense of an *episcopos,* he would have said so. And it is hard to avoid Emory's other arguments.[52] Wesley wrote to Asbury that he, Wesley, was "father of the whole family," and "in a measure, provide for you all." Asbury was an elder brother; Wesley was the father.

Did Wesley then intend to make Coke a bishop? Yes, in Wesley's meaning of the word. He did not intend to convey any sacerdotal powers. But he never intended that in any ordination, for he did not thus think of the ministry. Nor did he intend to confer upon Coke any ministerial power of ordination, whatever Coke thought. That power Coke already had, according to Wesley's theory, by virtue of his ordination as a presbyter of the Church of England. But in ordaining Coke he intended to do something, and something different from that which he did for Whatcoat and Vasey.

What that something was it is impossible to discover unless one is willing to take Wesley at his word. He had said, and repeatedly said, that he considered bishop and presbyter to be of the same order. He could not have meant the same sacerdotal, sacramentarian status; for Wesley did not hold to that conception of the ministry. Coke was a presbyter after his ordination, as he was before, having the same spiritual functions, the power of administering the sacraments and of ordination. But by his ordination Wesley sought to set Dr. Coke apart as a scriptural and primitive bishop, according to Wesley's idea of that office; and he defined the function by his translation of the title, "superintendent." He conferred no new spiritual character but an administrative authority. There is nothing vague or amorphous in this, except as it is made so by sacramentarian notions or by modern analogies. It is doubtful whether Wesley used the words "order" and "office" to distinguish between spiritual and administrative functions; but if the words are used in this sense they describe what he meant. The distinction is as old as the first century, and Wesley was not ignorant of it.

Both spiritual and administrative functions were in the ministry, and, therefore, it was by ordination, solemn setting apart by prayer and laying on of hands (which Augustine said meant prayer), that Wesley gave to Coke, Whatcoat, and Vasey their respective orders and offices. As to their spiritual powers, the three were *pares*. A superintendent, in Wesley's sense, had no confirmation or ordination as his special privilege. But as to their administrative, jurisdictional function, Coke was *primus inter pares*. Wesley never forgot King's analogy. In his comment on Acts xx. 17, Wesley had written of the elders of Ephesus: "These are called *bishops* in the 28th verse, (rendered *overseers* in our translation.) Perhaps elders and bishops were then the same; or no otherwise different than are the rector of a parish and his curates." [53] And Wesley believed that presbyters have the power to ordain bishops, that is those who have the spiritual power of presbyters and the administrative authority of superintendents.

One of Wesley's dominant ideas was always the Church, which is visibly a congregation of faithful men, in which the pure word of God is preached and the sacraments duly administered. But there must be organization also; and, although no single polity is *de jure divino,* Wesley preferred the model of the Church of England. This model was to be shorn of the pomp of power, the ostentation of Anglican episcopacy. His ideal was that which Henry Moore expressed as the common understanding in America of Methodist bishops, "men distinguished only by their simplicity and abundant labours." Dean H. N. Bate characterized Methodist episcopacy as "Presbyterian in origin, tripartite in function, mon-episcopal in practice." [54] The first two express the facts, so far as Wesley is concerned. It is possible that Wesley might have agreed with the third.

But, in America, the Methodists must be in a Church. There is reason to think that he anticipated the breaking away in England also and tried to provide for it by ordaining Henry Moore and Mather as superintendents. But it was not the way for English Methodists. For America there could be no other path, and Wesley would not have his people tied to loose societies, however helpful, deprived of the sacraments and a settled church life. His models were in the Scriptures, the Primitive Church, the Church of England; but, more than anything else, he would have the spiritual life of his followers, engendered, cherished, fed within a Church to which everyone might belong who had a desire to flee from the wrath to come and to be saved from their sins, and to seek the company of the people of God to assist them in working out their salvation. His spiritual children must not be deprived of their Christian heritage, membership in a Church that is "a catholic seminary of divine love."

CHAPTER XI

INDIVIDUALISM AND EMOTION IN WESLEY'S RELIGION

THROUGH this study of Wesley's religion and theology attention has been called to the tension between two elements in his experience and thought. On the one side, are his predilection for clear and distinct ideas; his appreciation of the moral struggle; his belief in the values of a disciplined life; and his devotion to the Church and to the means of grace. On the other side, are the individualistic character of much of his religion; the place given to emotion in the religious life; and his recognition of variety and growth. It will be helpful at this point to look more closely at these latter elements in Wesley's teaching.

That Wesley's appeal was individualistic is too well known to need any further stress. Not that he differed in this from large sections of the Christian Church then and now, for there has always been a strongly individualistic tendency in Christianity. It is customary to refer to Wesley's individualism as an inheritance from seventeenth-century nonconformity; but this is an unjustifiable narrowing of his background. Wesley insisted that there had been in the Church throughout the centuries Christians who believed and practiced a "spiritual" faith. He wondered, indeed, if these were not mainly those who were called heretics by rich and powerful Christians, and he introduced strange names into his company: Montanus and Pelagius are spoken of in high terms. Wesley recognized the power of the Reformation and of the efforts of the earlier Puritans; but he thought the latter declined in spirituality when they came to power in the Commonwealth. For his own work, Wesley found the beginnings in William Law. Infidelity increased after the Restoration until about 1725, "when Mr. Law published his 'Practical Treatise on Christian Perfection,' and, not long after, his 'Serious Call to a Devout and Holy Life.' Here the seed was sown, which soon grew up, and spread to Oxford, London, Bristol, Leeds, York, and, within a few years, to the greatest part of England, Scotland, and Ireland." [1] In High Churchmen like William Law, as well as in the early Puritans, Wesley recognized a worthy type of personal religion.

In the conclusion of his sermon on "The Circumcision of the Heart," which Wesley preached at St. Mary's, Oxford, January 1, 1733, he quoted from "those children of God" who, "being dead, still speak to us." The paragraph is a mosaic of quotations, but the sum of all is that personal piety which is not confined to the classical mystics but belongs to the Church Universal. " 'Desire not to live but to praise His name,' " quoted Wesley; " 'let all your thoughts, words, and works tend to His glory. Set your heart firm on Him, and on other things only as they are in and from Him. Let your soul be filled with so entire a love of Him that you may love nothing but for His sake.' 'Have a pure intention of heart, a steadfast regard to His glory in all your actions.' 'Fix your eye upon the blessed hope of your calling, and make all the things of the world minister unto it.' For then, and not till then, is that 'mind in us which was also in Christ Jesus'; when, in every motion of our heart, in every word of our tongue, in every work of our hands, we 'pursue nothing but in relation to Him, and in subordination to His pleasure.' " [2]

Reference has been made in an earlier chapter to what has been taken as evidence of the painful self-centeredness of Wesley before his "conversion," that he went to America to save his own soul. In his letter to Dr. Burton, in October, 1735, Wesley wrote, that his "chief motive, to which all the rest are subordinate, is the hope of saving my own soul." His second motive was his belief that he could do "more good in America." But Wesley's motives never changed. In 1788, he wrote that "I have only one thing to do, to save my own soul and those that hear me." [3] Not only are the motives unchanged, but neither is their order. In 1788, as in 1735, Wesley sought to save his own soul *and* the souls of others.

The truth is that Wesley believed religion to be personal, and an individualistic religion must seek the salvation of individual souls. In these pages, it has been contended that Wesley thought the Church necessary and would have nothing of "solitary" religion; but one must keep in mind that there have always been those who have united devotion to the Church with a fine type of individualistic piety. There is no contradiction here. The High Churchman of 1735 preached an individualistic religion; Wesley the Methodist of 1788 did likewise. The Christian lives within the framework of the Church and in the societies which are included in it; but religion is the experience of the individual, and to the individual must appeal be made. This is why Wesley's sermons were so effectual; they appealed directly to men. When John Nelson, afterward one of Wesley's most useful preachers, first heard him, it seemed to the stonemason that the preacher was speaking to him alone.[4] "Call upon thy God," cried Wesley in a characteristic paragraph in one of his sermons, "till He make His 'goodness to pass before thee' . . . cry unto Him day and night, who 'while we were without strength, died for the ungodly,' until thou knowest in whom thou hast believed, and canst say, 'My Lord, and my God!' Remember, 'always to pray, and not to faint,' till thou also canst lift up thy hand unto heaven, and declare to Him that liveth forever and ever, 'Lord Thou knowest all things, Thou knowest that I love Thee.' "[5]

Wesley's appeal was for concrete, individual experience. Concerning the varieties of individual experience Wesley was continuously curious. He was always interested in the different ways by which men might come to the love of God and the different ways in which that love might manifest itself. The best known of his collections of such data is that of the autobiographies of his preachers which have been published more than once. But his letters also are a storehouse of materials, revealing as they do his inquiries into the minutiæ of individual experience.

On one side of his mind, Wesley distrusted dreams and visions and the more exotic type of experience, and he warned his followers against them. But he showed an unusual interest in such matters, even when he expressed cautious judgments about them. Indeed, his doctrine that God expresses himself in the most minute details of life, supporting not only the Universe but also looking after the least things concerning his children, made for a willingness to listen at least to any story, however improbable. Wesley certainly kept alive a sense of wonder, and this was no doubt responsible for many of the excesses among the early Methodists.

If religion is primarily a concrete, individual experience, there must be variability. Although Wesley warned against relying on uncommon experiences or seeking unusual ones, nevertheless he recognized what he called the "irreconcilable variability in the operations of the Holy Spirit on the souls of men." No one formula could cover them all. But Wesley tried to reduce this "irreconcilable variability," so far as he could, not to uniformity in detail, but within such limits as would protect a reasonable and an ethical faith. He would restrict the ambitions of his followers, therefore, to increase of love. They were in danger of forgetting that "love is the highest gift of God; humble, gentle, patient love; that all visions, revelations, manifestations, whatever, are little things compared to love; and that all the gifts above-mentioned are either the same with, or infinitely inferior to, it." "There is nothing higher in religion," he added; "there is, in effect, nothing else; if you look for anything but more love, you are looking wide of the mark, you are getting out of the royal way. . . . Settle it then in your heart, that from the moment God has saved you from all sin, you are to aim at nothing more, but more of that love described in the thirteenth of the Corinthians. You can go no higher than this, till you are carried into Abraham's Bosom." [6]

To this concrete, individual experience appeal is made for convincing evidence of the truth of religion.

> What we ourselves have felt and seen
>   With confidence we tell,
> And publish to the sons of men
>   The signs infallible.

But this experience involves the irrational side of man's nature, and Wesley thought of religion as rooted in this side of man's life. As early as 1726, he had seen "that giving even all my life to God (supposing it possible to do this, and go no farther) would profit me nothing, unless I gave my heart, yea, all my heart, to him." He saw that simplicity of intention, and purity of affection, that is, "one design in all we speak or do, and one desire ruling all our tempers," are indeed "the wings of the soul" by which it ascends to the mount of the Lord. He desired the mind of Christ, although he conceived religion (*circa* 1729) "as an uniform following of Christ, an entire inward and outward conformity to our Master." [7] In 1733, in the sermon on "The Circumcision of the Heart," Wesley defined religion in terms with which he agreed

278

nearly half a century later. Religion, which here is called the "circumcision of the heart," is "that habitual disposition of soul which, in the sacred writings, is termed holiness; and which directly implies, the being cleansed from sin, 'from all filthiness both of flesh and spirit'; and, by consequence, the being endued with these virtues which were in Christ Jesus; the being so 'renewed in the spirit of our mind,' as to be 'perfect as our Father in heaven is perfect.' " Later in the sermon he spoke of love toward God as "the one perfect good" which is to be the ultimate end of every Christian.[8] In a sermon which he preached at Savannah in 1736, Wesley was yet more explicit. The chief sense of the words, "though I bestow all my goods to feed the poor . . . . and have not love, it profiteth me nothing," he conceives to be nothing less than the following: "that whatsoever we do, and whatsoever we suffer, if we are not renewed in the spirit of our mind, by 'the love of God shed abroad in our hearts by the Holy Ghost given unto us,' we cannot enter into life eternal. None can enter there, unless in virtue of the covenant which God hath given unto man in the Son of his love." [9]

When Wesley, then, declared that the real root of religion is "in the hidden man of the heart," he was not making a new discovery; he was but developing an idea which had been in his preaching before 1738. It may be wearisome to repeat constantly that, after 1738, Wesley's change was mainly a change in emphasis, owing to his intense realization of that which he had previously preached; but it is necessary to make clear that Wesley did not, in 1738, suddenly

perceive the importance of "attitude," of the disposition of the heart, of love. But, undoubtedly, he
came to see more clearly the place of love in religion.
Love, he saw, drives out evil, is the motive of obedience to God and service to mankind.

To root religion in the irrational nature of man
was in accordance with the drift of the age. Shaftesbury had based his ethical theory on natural benevolence, although he had, of course, guarded his theory
by positing the necessity of social good and of a well-
balanced individual. The notion that goodness is
rooted in good nature was becoming popular; Fielding's highest praise seems to have been to say of a
man that he had a "benevolent heart." In this view,
which was developing during this period, it is true that
"conscience ceases to be a power that sits in judgment
on the ordinary self and inhibits its impulses. It
tends, so far as it is recognized at all, to become itself
an instinct and an emotion." [10] How did Wesley's
idea of religion as love fit into the growing romantic
tendency to exalt the instincts and emotions of man?

In the first place, it must be remembered that
Wesley thought of love, in the religious sense, as the
gift of God. Man in his natural state, unassisted by
the divine grace, is incapable of the love of God or
of his neighbor in any truly religious way. The love
of God is called out by the perception that God loves
us, and that perception is faith. Man sees that God
has, for Christ's sake, forgiven his sins and does
now love him; "we love Him because He first loved
us." Then is the love of God shed abroad in man's
heart by the Holy Spirit. Now this may seem a

gesture to theological necessity; but it is, in reality, a true expression of Wesley's belief that religious love is not a natural instinct, not simply the overflow of "natural benevolence," but a response to a perception, or an experience, of the love of God. There is here an objective reference which cannot be ignored if one is to understand Wesley's meaning.

Moreover, he sometimes equates love with holiness. This is because Wesley conceives of love as active good will and as the intention of man's innermost being. Nothing but God is the religious man's desire and goal; and this intention of the heart, supplemented by active good will, at once cleanses and energizes. As has been said, Wesley meant by love, not simply an emotion, but a "sentiment," a complex of emotions. Love is not mere feeling but the whole direction of life. The significance of "the love of God shed abroad" in the heart is stated clearly in Wesley's sermon on "Spiritual Worship": "Then it is that heaven is opened in the soul, that the proper heavenly state commences, while the love of God, as loving us, is shed abroad in the heart, instantly producing love to all mankind; general, pure benevolence, together with its genuine fruits, lowliness, meekness, patience, contentedness in every state; an entire, clear, full acquiescence in the whole will of God, enabling us to 'rejoice evermore, and in everything to give thanks.' " [11]

But there is undoubtedly a tone of feeling in love so defined. It may vary from the strange warming of the heart which was perhaps Wesley's own most emotional experience of religion, to the Beatific Vision which is the lot of the saints above:

> The flame of angelical love
> Is kindled at Jesus's face;
> And all the enjoyment above
> Consists in the rapturous gaze!

The religion of love, as preached by the Wesleys as well as by their followers, was oftentimes an intensely emotional religion. Joy and peace, as well as love, are the fruits of the Spirit; and men can feel these. But, in addition to these, the man who hears the gospel is subject to other emotions.

The sinner confronted with his lost estate was normally supposed to be stricken with the danger of his situation.[12] And there was further the melancholy of those who regarded life as a vale of tears. One of the first editions of the Methodist hymn book carried a hymn which for lugubriousness equals the best efforts of the "Graveyard" poets.

> Thou wretched man of sorrow,
>   Whose eye all day o'erflow,
> Indulge thy grief and borrow
>   The night for farther woe;
> In ceaseless lamentation
>   Thy solemn moments spend,
> And groan in expectation,
>   That pain with life shall end.
>
> Till then in fix'd despair
>   Of all relief I live,
> My utmost burden bear,
>   And now retire to grieve;

> To taste my only pleasure,
> In secret sighs complain,
> Augment my mournful measure
> And aggravate my pain.

This suggests that some of the Methodists enjoyed their sorrow; and, while these lines cannot be charged to John Wesley, it is well known that he had no little fondness for Young's "Night Thoughts," a poem marked by a melancholy approaching self-pity. Wesley believed, as he once wrote to one of his correspondents, that "it is a blessed thing to sorrow after a godly sort." [13] Such an attitude was fostered by the ascetic element in Wesley; his fear of worldliness caused him to forbid much that would have contributed to the merriment of his people. And there was in him something akin to melancholy also. In describing the religion of love, Wesley quoted Pope's lines:

> Eternal sunshine of the spotless mind;
> Each prayer accepted, and each wish resign'd;
> Desires composed, affections ever even,
> Tears that delight, and sighs that waft to heaven.

Nevertheless, John Wesley was not given to lowness of spirits, and one of his preachers asserted that Wesley tempted him to levity. Certainly, if Wesley could not at times escape the fashionable melancholy, normally he was for cheerfulness and joy. Of some of his brother's hymns, John Wesley wrote: "some still savor of that poisonous mysticism, with which we were both not a little tainted before we went to America. This gave a gloomy caste, first to his mind, and then to many of his verses. This made him fre-

quently describe religion as a melancholy thing. . . ." [14]
While it is impossible now to tell exactly which hymns
were written by John and which by Charles, it may
be inferred from the above that John Wesley preferred songs in which the joy of religion was set forth.
And certainly the Methodist hymnbook contained
many of the sort. On his birthday, the Methodist
could sing:

> Away with my fears!
> The glad morning appears
> When an heir of salvation was born!
> From Jehovah I came,
> For his glory I am,
> And to Him I with singing return.

At any time, Wesley's follower could sing of the fruits
of the Spirit:

> We who in Christ believe
> That He for us hath died,
> His unknown peace receive,
> And feel his blood applied:
> Exults for joy our rising soul,
> Disburden'd of her load,
> And swells unutterably full
> Of glory and of God.
>
> How happy are they,
> Who the Savior obey,
> And have laid up their treasures above,
> Tongue cannot express
> The sweet comfort and peace
> Of a soul in its earliest love.
>
> In the heavenly Lamb
> Thrice happy I am;
> My heart it doth dance at the sound of Thy name.

There is no question as to the intensity of the emotional reactions manifested in the Methodist meetings. The most violent occurred only during the first two years and largely in certain areas. Davenport thought that these manifestations were owing to the ignorant character of the people to whom the Methodists came in these areas and during these years.[15] At any rate, the "scenes" did not recur after that time under the preaching of the Wesleys themselves. One or two quotations will illustrate the more extreme type of experiences.

"As my mother bore me with great pain [wrote one], so did I feel great pain in my soul in being born of God. Indeed I thought the pains of death were upon me, and that my soul was then taking leave of the body. I thought I was going to Him whom I saw with strong faith standing ready to receive me. In this violent agony I continued about four hours; and then I began to feel the 'Spirit of God bearing witness with my spirit that I was born of God.' Because I was a child of God He 'sent forth the Spirit of His Son into me, crying, Abba, Father.' For that is the cry of every new-born soul. O mighty, powerful, happy change! I who had nothing but devils ready to drag me to hell, now found I had angels to guard me to my reconciled Father; and my Judge, who just before stood ready to condemn me, was now become my righteousness. But I cannot express what God hath done for my soul. . . . I loved. The Spirit cried strong in my heart. I trembled: I sang: I joined my voice with those that 'excel in strength.' "[16]

In these early meetings men and women were

struck down; and strong crying and tears, followed by shouts of joy, excited the wonder of some and the ribaldry of others. One such scene may serve for many which occurred in the years immediately succeeding 1738. In Baldwin Street, Bristol—the date is April, 1739—Wesley expounded the fourth chapter of Acts. "We then called upon God to confirm His word. Immediately one that stood by (to our no small surprise) cried out aloud, with the utmost vehemence, even as in the agonies of death. But we continued in prayer till 'a new song was put in her mouth, a thanksgiving unto our God.' Soon after, two other persons (well known in this place, as labouring to live in all good conscience towards all men) were seized with strong pain, and constrained to 'roar for the disquietness of their heart.' But it was not long before they likewise burst forth into praise to God their Saviour. The last who called upon God, as out of the belly of hell, was J[ohn] E[llis], a stranger in Bristol. And in a short space he also was overwhelmed with joy and love, knowing that God had healed his backslidings." [17]

Attention has been frequently called to the psychological conditions evoked by the Wesleys in the setting and conduct of their meetings. Interest was aroused by early morning meetings or by the spectacle of a clergyman in canonicals preaching on the street or in the fields. Sometimes the place was such as to affect the emotions, and the sight of a great crowd listening intently or joining lustily in song was itself moving. "I cannot say I have ever seen a more awful sight," wrote Wesley of such scenes, "than when on Rose-Green, or the top of Hannam Mount, some thousands of people were calmly joined together in solemn waiting upon God, while

> They stood, and under open air adored
> The God who made both air, earth, heaven, and sky.

And, whether they were listening to his word with attention as still as night, or were lifting up their voice in praise as the sound of many waters, many a time have I been constrained to say in my heart, 'How dreadful is this place! This' also 'is no other than the house of God! This is the gate of heaven.' " [18]

The hymns and the tunes to which they were sung also contributed to the psychological conditions. As Dimond says, "the mental condition desired in the congregation is akin to that induced by the romantic poet, who seeks to create in the minds of his readers 'that willing suspension of disbelief for the moment, which constitutes poetic faith.' " [19] In this condition, the crowd was suggestible to a high degree. There is evidence that the hymns created in many the surprise and interest which is necessary if the state of "poetic faith" is to be attained. The hymns also offered an opportunity of emotional expression for the congregation. In words which were usually understandable and with tunes sometimes taken from popular songs and at all times singable, the people could express their penitence, their resolutions, their fears, their sorrows, and their joys.

One must not forget, too, the often demonstrated power of the Christian story over the minds and hearts of men. The elemental drama of the life and

287

death of Jesus has for centuries been the most deeply affecting of all of mankind's stories. If Wesley, unlike Whitefield, did not make use of dramatic methods in his preaching, he presupposed always the saga of the Cross. And he and his brother reinforced the power of the sermon with their emphasis upon the sacraments, especially the Lord's Supper, ancient symbol of the broken body and of the shed blood. With hymns written for these dramatic observances, the Wesleys reinforced the emotional appeal of the symbol. In this manner they dramatized the Christian Year and the Christian life. The Wesleys published, for example, Hymns on the Lord's Supper, Hymns for the Nativity, Hymns for our Lord's Resurrection, Hymns for Ascension Day, Hymns on the Great Festivals, Hymns for New Year's Day, Hymns for Times of Trouble, Hymns of Petition and Thanksgiving, Funeral Hymns, Hymns for the Watchnight, Hymns of Intercession. And within these and other collections were hymns for every Christian mood.

There was another way in which Wesley uncovered the sources of deep feeling. He taught his followers to regard the disinherited with sympathy. In this there is no little of what the eighteenth century called "sensibility." Wesley advised Lady Maxwell of his doubt that anyone can have too much sensibility of human pain "unless it unfits one for duties of life," [20] and he wrote Hannah Ball that sensibility is not too great unless "it hurts the body or unfits you for some part of your duty." [21] This sensibility Wesley would increase by contact with the poor. He advised ladies of his acquaintance to visit the poor, overcoming their repugnance to "dirt and an hundred disgusting circumstances." [22] For this reason he advised carrying relief rather than sending it: so doing one comforted the poor and helped oneself, "as it is far more apt to soften our heart, and make us naturally care for each other." [23]

While Wesley devised some meritorious social plans, such as lending money to workmen so that they might buy their own tools, on the whole his approach was individualistic. He endeavored to create sympathy, to arouse a sense of brotherhood for all the poor children of God. If one reads Wesley's tract, "Thoughts upon Slavery," [24] the method by which he did this becomes evident. The Negroes are first described in their African home. Wesley had learned that the North American Indian was not the idyllic savage, but he yet believed that the Negro was. He quotes from a Frenchman's account of parts of Guinea: "Which way soever I turned my eyes, I beheld a perfect image of pure nature: an agreeable solitude, bounded on every side by a charming landscape; the rural situation of cottages in the midst of trees; the ease and quietness of the Negroes, reclined under the shade of the spreading foliage, with the simplicity of their dress and manner: The whole revived in my mind the idea of our first parents, and I seemed to contemplate the world in its primitive state." These Negroes were a reasonable, peaceable people, civil and courteous, practicing justice, mercy, and truth above the Europeans of the eighteenth century. But from this Eden on earth the Negroes were taken with every cruelty and sold in America. There, "banished from their country, from their friends and relations forever, from every comfort of life, they are reduced to a state scarce any way preferable to that of beasts of burden." In his terse way Wesley sketched a horrible picture of life in slavery. "In general, a few roots, not of the nicest kind, usually yams or potatoes, are their food; and two rags, that neither screen them from the heat of the day, nor the cold of the night, their covering." "The time they work in the West Indies is from day-break to noon, and from two o'clock till dark; during which time, they are attended by overseers, who, if they think them dilatory, or think anything not so well done as it should be, whip them most unmercifully, so that you may see their bodies long after wealed and scarred usually from the shoulders to the waist." "Did the Creator intend that the noblest creatures in the visible world should live such a life as this?

"Are these thy glorious work, Parent of Good?"

In the same way, Wesley pictured the horrors of war. In a sermon preached in 1775 for the benefit of the widows and orphans of the soldiers "who lately fell near Boston, in New England," Wesley painted with only a little stronger colors than in other denunciations of war, although here his zeal was fed by his Tory sentiments: "But who can describe the complicated misery which is contained in this [the fell monster, war]? Hark! the cannon's roar! A pitchy cloud covers the face of the sky. Noise, confusion, terror, reign over all! Dying groans are on every side. The bodies of men are pierced, torn, hewed in pieces; their blood is poured on the earth like water! Their souls take their flight into the eternal world; perhaps into everlasting misery. The ministers of grace turn away from the horrid scene; the ministers of vengeance triumph." "But which of these warriors all the while considered the wife of his youth, that is now left a disconsolate widow,—perhaps with none that careth for her; perhaps, deprived of her only comfort and support, and not having where to lay her head? Who considered his helpless children, now desolate orphans,—it may be crying for bread, while their mother has nothing left to give them but her sorrows and her tears?" [25]

Hogarth depicted the horrors of Gin Lane; Wesley described the houses of the distillers. These distillers were murderers "of His Majesty's subjects by wholesale, neither does their eye pity or spare." And what is their gain? "Is it not the blood of these men? Who then would envy their large estates and sumptuous palaces? A curse is in the midst of them: the curse of God cleaves to the stones, the timber, the furniture of them! The curse of God is in their gardens, their walks, their groves; a fire that burns to the nethermost hell! Blood, blood is there: the foundation, the floor, the walls, the roof, are stained with blood!" [26]

Wesley, with his constant journeying, demanded much of his horse as well as of himself; but he was careful to admonish his preachers to care for the beasts that bore them, even entering such advice into the *Minutes* of the Conference of 1765. There are not many passages in Wesley's writings about cruelty

291

to animals, although in several places he speculates about their souls, their state in the time of man's innocence, and the possibility of their moving up the Chain of Being in some future time. But in his Journal for 1756 he printed in full a long letter about kindness to animals which breathes the spirit of romantic sympathy. "Is it not unnatural and inhuman," asks the writer of the letter, "to put them to more pain than is necessary for the service of man? . . . May not the great law of equity, doing as we would be done to, be extended even to them? May we not suppose ourselves in their place, and thence determine what they may fairly expect from us? . . . If tenderness, mercy, and compassion to the brute creatures were impressed on the infant breast, and conducted into action according to its little power, would it not be confirmed in the human heart? And might not this early prepossession be for ever established there, and through a happy bias extend its benevolence to the whole creation? Does not experience show the sad effects of a contrary education? While children, instead of being taught benevolence to irrationals, are suffered to torment first poor little insects and then every helpless creature that comes in their way, can it be expected that, being thus inured to cruelty and oppression even in their tender years, they should relent when they come to age and be susceptible of compassion even to rationals? . . . I am persuaded you are not insensible of the pain given to every Christian, every humane heart, by those savage diversions, bull-baiting, cock-fighting, horse-racing, and hunting? Can any of these irrational and unnatural sports appear otherwise than cruel, unless through early prejudice or entire want of consideration and reflection? And if a man is void of these, does he deserve the name of man?" [27]

There is no question that Wesley approved the sentiments of this letter, but one would hesitate to say that he would have gone as far as the evangelical Cowper:

> I would not enter on my list of friends
> (Though graced with polish'd manners and fine sense,
> Yet wanting sensibility) the man
> Who needlessly sets foot upon a worm.

In his sermon before the "Humane Society," an organization to revive those apparently struck with sudden death, Wesley appealed to the sensibilities of both Christian and non-Christian. To those who did not believe in "that Revelation which breathes nothing but benevolence," he said: "Yet even to you I would address a few words; for, if you are not Christians, you are men. You too are susceptible of kind impressions: You have the feelings of humanity. Has not your heart too glowed at that noble sentiment; worthy the heart and the lips of the highest Christian,—

Homo sum: Humanus nihil a me alienum puto?
Have you not also sympathized with the afflicted? How many times have you been pained at human misery? When you have beheld a scene of deep distress, has not your soul melted within you?

> "And now and then a sigh you stole,
> And tears began to flow." [28]

To the Christian, Wesley plead that the language of their heart might be:

> Thy mind throughout my life be shown,
>   While list'ning to the wretches' cry,
> The widows and the orphans' groan,
>   On mercy's wings I swiftly fly,
> The poor and helpless to relieve,
> My life, my all, for them to give!

So much space has been given to the emotional basis of Wesley's humanitarianism because it has not always been understood that, in stirring the hearts of his hearers, he laid a deep foundation for the humanitarian passion of early Methodists and contributed to the reform movements of the nineteenth century. Giving to the people a release for their emotions in religion, Wesley also directed them to new objects for their sympathies: the poor, the slaves, the victims of predatory society, even the animals themselves. But in this Wesley avoided that evil which has been charged against some of the romantic tendencies of the period. Professor Babbitt quotes from Burke a cutting criticism: "The greatest crimes do not arise so much from a want of feeling for others as from an over-sensibility for ourselves and an over-indulgence to our own desires. . . . They [he refers to the French 'philosophes'] explode or render odious or contemptible that class of virtues which restrain the appetite. These are at least nine out of ten of the virtues. In the place of all this they substitute a virtue which they call humanity or benevolence. . . . When their disciples are thus left free and guided only by present feeling, they are no longer to be depended on for good or evil." [29]

Whatever may have been true of the "philosophes," Wesley cannot be charged with having reduced morality to present feeling. Throughout his life he had no patience with the doctrine that one is to do good only when feeling free to do it.[30] Wesley once remarked that his mother did not feel for others nearly so much as did his father, but she did ten times more; and he advised his correspondent to labor to do, leaving God to supply the feeling.[31] In the light of what has been said in previous chapters, there is no need to labor this point; but it should be kept in mind by all who attempt to estimate the emotional content of Wesley's teaching. After all, he had said that sensibility could not be too great *unless* it interfered with one's *duty*. Duty is the word which distinguishes Wesley from the natural romanticists: for duty with him implied a higher reference, the will of God. Wesley's grand motive for humanitarian work was the imitation of Christ.

There is no need to say anything further in regard to Wesley's doctrine of variability. Certainly he did not believe in or encourage a mechanical uniformity in the religious life. But contemporary attention was centered too much upon the unusual features in Methodism. The extraordinary scenes which accompanied the first Methodist meetings raised the old fears of popular tumult and forever associated Methodism, in the minds of many, with disorder and distraction. It is untrue to say that Wesley himself preferred the abnormal; but he was interested in it. It should not be surprising, then, that less-balanced minds should have welcomed the unusual in experience and have made the test of truth the measure of departure from the normal.

One of Wesley's early opponents declared a characteristic of an enthusiast to be a desire to wander and to travel in far countries.[32] When Wesley returned from America, one of his attractions for the crowds was that he had been in a strange and romantic land. He had gone there expecting to learn from the simple savage, but in this he had been disillusioned. Nevertheless, after his "conversion," he had started out for Herrnhut, the abode of the Moravians in Germany, "to see where the Christians live." But if Wesley was undeceived in America and in Germany, he still retained his illusions about other far-off places. As has been seen, he was quite willing to believe that Negroes dwelt in idyllic peace and innocence in Africa. But whatever may have been true of his successors in the Church of England and out of it, Wesley's romantic interest in far countries—he was continuously reading travel books—had little to do with his missionary interest. Except for America, he was not greatly concerned to establish missions. The main reason, of course, was that Wesley's practical sense forbade his undertaking any enterprise unless he was in condition adequately to support it. But he was also not much taken with the missionary accomplishments of the past. The Jesuits had, he thought, done everything but preach the gospel; and while he was convinced that savages could become Christians— the miners of Kingwood were near enough savages—

Wesley did little himself to establish missions beyond those set up among English colonists.

There was, indeed, a far-off ideal before Wesley's eyes. He desired always to re-establish primitive Christianity. He thought of his work as an attempt to set up a New Testament fellowship. Reverencing as he did the early Fathers of the Church as those nearest to the fountain-head, he kept before himself always the ideal—or what he thought to be the ideal—of the first decades. To his *First Appeal* he appended a poem, "Primitive Christianity," which is partly as follows:

> A little Church in every house,
> They joyfully conspired to raise
> Their ceaseless sacrifice of praise.
>
> O What an age of golden days!
> O what a choice, peculiar race!
> Wash'd in the Lamb's all-cleansing blood,
> Anointed Kings and priests to God.
>
> Where shall I wander now to find
> The successors they left behind?
> The faithful whom I seek in vain,
> Are 'minished from the sons of men.
> Ye different sects, who all declare,
> "Lo, here is Christ!" or, "Christ is there!"
> Your stronger proofs divinely give,
> And shew me where the Christians live.

And Wesley's was undoubtedly the exhortation of the poem:

> In them let all mankind behold
> How Christians lived in days of old.

In looking back over Wesley's teaching, his individualism, his insistence upon the varieties of Christian experience, upon the place of emotion in the religious life, his laying of an emotional basis for good deeds, and his setting up as an ideal the life of a far-off, partially understood, and much simpler day, it is easy to see that he was opening the way for an intensely individualistic, subjective, and emotional religion. He intended to do nothing of the sort. His own temperament and training, his own philosophic position and prejudices, all guarded him against the excesses of such a faith. He could no more reduce religion to feeling than to ceremony or dogma. He could not conceive of a religion of the "natural man." Fallen as he is, man must have the workings of divine grace and the constant discipline of a true imitation of Christ and the aid of the Church. The Bible, interpreted usually by the Fathers of the first three Christian centuries, and reason, as well as one's own experience and the experience of one's fellows, must all be called in. These protected Wesley from romantic excesses. He could go far in appreciation of feelings and diversities; but he could only go so far.

Not so with his followers. They lacked his training and prejudices; they also lacked his nature. Only constant effort kept the fanatics weeded out of the societies, and not always before they had done real hurt. Sometimes, indeed, Wesley, in his kindness—Charles called it credulity—allowed those to remain who were obviously not balanced, emotionally at least. And in frontier America, there was little Church tradition, little training in self-discipline, little of that experience which usually kept the Oxford scholar neatly within the bounds of common sense. The preacher who came with his stirring message of heart religion appealed to untutored men, and he called them to a religion of the spirit, not of forms and ceremonies and ordinances. The class-meetings did much to offset the pure romanticism of this early Methodism, and the ascetic tradition helped also. But, on the whole, the world has concluded that Methodism was a religion of feeling. But what the Founder of Methodism intended is another matter.

CHAPTER XII

JOHN WESLEY AND MODERN RELIGION

AT the conclusion of this study of Wesley's experience and theology there remains the direct question as to his relation to modern religion. How far did he influence the religion of the nineteenth and early twentieth centuries? And how far and in what way is his work pertinent to-day?

It is beyond disputing that Wesley contributed to the spread of a religion of feeling. An individualistic, emotional religion was inevitably the result of Methodist preaching under the circumstances of their work. In England, the classes to which the Methodists generally appealed were those who were strangers to that Chesterfieldian suppression of feelings which has always been practiced in certain circles. When the miners of Kingswood listened to the eloquence of the preacher, tears made white furrows down their blackened faces. Powerful fears and powerful joys produced scenes which marked Methodist meetings in America and gave to Wesley's followers the nickname of "noisy Methodists." The people of the frontiers had little warmth or color in their lives; dangers and privations left them little time or means for the enjoyment of any but the more primitive emotions. For them the camp meeting with its stirring preaching and singing was an escape from grim everyday realities.

In both England and America, the appeal of the Methodists to the individual was in perfect accord with the circumstances of the people. It was in the industrial North, not in the agricultural South, of England that the Methodists found their converts. In the towns springing up around the new industries of the early nineteenth century, the population was cut off from older institutions. The Church did little to care for these new areas of dense population, and the Methodists came to supply the lack. In America, the settlements were isolated by forests and streams from the stable institutions of an older society; and the strongly individualistic tone of American life made the Methodist message especially appealing. Certainly, it is in the conditions which, both in England and America, favored an emotional, individualistic religion that one must find reasons for the popularity and growth of the Methodists. This is not to forget the self-sacrificing work of the circuit riders in both countries nor the influence of a message which had left off much which common people neither understood nor desired. But the time was propitious: in literature, feeling was a dominant note; in politics, liberty was a slogan.

Historians of theology have long recognized that Wesley and Methodism, taken in its broadest sense, contributed to the breaking up of the old orthodoxy and of eighteenth-century rationalism. In this way, they were important factors in creating the modern age. Interpreters of our "religious situation" are likely to dwell upon the intellectual sources of contemporary religion.[1] If Christian experience is to the fore in large areas of Western Christendom, Schleiermacher is praised or condemned according to the predilection of the writer.[2] And the strong ethical interest of modern religion is traced back through Ritschl to Kant. There is no thought of denying the importance of these thinkers for theology. But an idea does not usually appear first in formal theology and then later in popular religion. The formulations of the theologians, if not derived at least partly from popular religion, are received by the people because of previous preparation by circumstances or the emphases of accepted leaders. Certainly, before the work of Schleiermacher had much influence in England and America, the Methodist Revival had prepared millions to minimize orthodoxy and to rely on inner experience rather than upon syllogisms. On the whole, Schleiermacher influenced the theologians; John Wesley, the preachers.

The contribution of the Methodists to the breakdown of the older orthodoxy and rationalism was in their emphasis upon a milder conception of God, upon Christian experience as taking precedence over dogmas, and in their stress upon feeling. While the Methodist preachers, unlike Wesley, were rather fond of hell in their preaching, they insisted upon the mercy of God offered to all and combatted the ideas of the Calvinists as too harsh to be true to the gospel picture. Frequently, they poured scorn upon the subtleties of the theologians and reduced the gospel to a simplicity that was bare indeed. And as they preached the necessity of conviction and conversion, of assurance, of "heartfelt" religion, the Methodists helped make the climate impossible for stringent orthodoxies or rationalistic appeals.

It is necessary to say more concerning one of the characteristics of much modern religion, the emphasis upon Christian experience. Schleiermacher gave this respectability in theology, and the idea of the priority of experience became central in much Christian thought in the nineteenth century. The results for theology were, as President McGiffert pointed out several years ago, to change theology from "a system of metaphysics, or an effort to explain the world of man and nature" to "a formulation of the truth given in the religious experience of the man who theologizes." Psychology and not philosophy became the characteristic Christian discipline. A religion which exalted experience was for many reasons acceptable in the nineteenth century. Traditional religious authorities were being called into question by natural science and the new historical criticism. When men were doubtful of the Bible as it had been understood by pre-nineteenth century piety, when their conceptions of the natural world were being dissolved by the new science, they turned gratefully to the inner witness.

> If e'er when faith had fallen asleep,
>   I heard a voice, "believe no more,"
>   And heard an ever-breaking shore
> That tumbled in the Godless deep,
>
> A warmth within the breast would melt
>   The freezing reason's colder part,
>   And like a man in wrath the heart
> Stood up and answered, "I have felt."

In a transition period, this appeal to experience undoubtedly saved Christian apologetics from becoming simply an echo of arguments which had long since
lost their meaning. It was natural that theology
should turn its attention to the analysis of this experience. Thus was opened up a fruitful field; and
much good work, some of it of enduring value, was
done in the study of the varieties of religious experience. At last, it seemed that religion could become a
science, or, at the least, the object of disinterested,
scientific investigation. If little could be known
directly about God, the soul of man could be examined in conversion, in faith, in love. It was also natural that interest should be aroused in directing religious experience; and hence arose the important work
of religious education. These modern preoccupa-
tions are rooted in the doctrine of Christian experience. One cannot be educated in religion who is
merely the passive recipient of uncontrollable grace.

So far as preparation for these developments of
modern religion is concerned, much must be attributed to the influence of Methodism. And it is not
accidental that the Methodist churches have gone far
in religious education, although their contributions to
the psychology of religion have not been so noteworthy. In some other ways, the influence of Methodism is discernible. It is tempting to find Wesley's
influence in the social gospel so characteristic of recent
years in England and America. Perhaps the widespread interest of Methodists in social reform is a
transfer of their belief in individual perfection to a
belief in the perfect society. But Wesley's influence

here is doubtless rather in the strongly ethical tone of his teaching.

Certainly, humanitarianism as a whole owes much to the Evangelical Movement. Not only Wesley but all those who rediscovered the poor and aroused pity for them are responsible for modern humanitarianism. And the Methodists did their part to promote benevolent feelings. However inadequate as a motive for social action, the broadening of the horizon of Christian people is one of the heartening achievements of modern religion.

Eighteenth-century Methodism's passion for perfection has not been so prominent in modern Methodist circles. However faulty and dangerous the movements, unquestionably the various types of Pentecostalism have been largely the witnesses of the abiding power of genuine desire for perfect obedience and a life given "wholly to God." Too often these have taken the forms of a "spiritualism"—in the older theological sense—divorced from ethical and churchly meanings. But this influence is yet active in numerous sects and cults which have great appeal among the masses.

In America, Methodism has aided also that extreme individualism which transformed the Church into a mere association distinguishable from other organizations only by its interest in religion. A passion for multiplying organizational machinery has become in many groups the only sign of corporate life. It is not accidental that the Methodists in America have led in the race to create the maximum number of boards and committees. The somewhat in-

volved machinery of Methodism from the beginning
gave a proper start for this, and the gibe that Methodism suffers from "wheels within wheels" has become
increasingly true. But, in the meantime, the Church
idea has been lost and its place taken by the notion of
Christianity as an individual possession and experience
which really needs, except for promotional purposes,
no corporate expression.

Along these lines must Wesley's influence in the
nineteenth century be traced: the mitigation of orthodoxy, the softening of older, mechanical, and
harsh conceptions of God and His relations to the
world; the exaltation of Christian experience; the
dominance of ethical interest; a marked humanitarianism; a lingering, if sporadic, interest in perfection; and a predilection for organization. But these
have prepared the way for exaggeration and for developments which have gone farther than the devout
ever dreamed. Indeed, the preaching of Methodists
and of Methodistic denominations prepared the way
for much which would not have been accepted widely
if the shibboleths of popular religion and of theology
had not often been the same. And these developments
have brought at last a storm of criticism which bids
fair to bring all that is called "modern religion" into
disrepute. This is not the place to review the whole
field upon which there is to-day so much marching
and countermarching that the main impression obtainable by the onlooker is simply that there is something vitally wrong with religion. The purpose here
is to consider only those attacks which are directed
at elements in modern faith which have relation, how-

ever remote, with Methodism. On the whole, the charges against religion to-day are that it is not religious, and that, such as it is, there is no efficient gearing with the problems of contemporary life.

That religion has in large part lost its vitality, and more especially in the areas where the cultural level is relatively high, needs no particular proving. Certainly there remains, in sections of Protestantism at least, little sense of the awfulness of God, of Otto's *mysterium tremendum*. If the God of Calvinism is dead, his place has been taken by an Indulgent Being who is surprisingly like a complacent American father.[3] The story of the prodigal son no longer astonishes by its portrayal of forgiveness. The modern reaction is: "What else could the father have done?" And the *a fortiori* argument once so popular against the Calvinistic conception of an angry God, that the Deity could not do what a good man would not do, has been changed to read that God does only what a good man does.

But more directly is attack being made against an overemphasis upon Christian experience. If we can learn about God only from our own experience, then God may be only an experience of man. And so He has become for many only a projection of man's ideals, social and individual. So far has this gone that a serious student of worship is compelled to begin with the question whether a modern man *can* worship.[4] All this has been helped by the domination of science, which has intrenched man and his experiences within the closed system of the natural order. If man can know God only through his own experiences and man is only a part of the natural order, then God becomes simply one factor, if one, in the Universe that man knows.

Religion, so conceived, loses its autonomy and becomes only a part of the cultural life of man. Indeed, the term is broadened to include all man's non-egoistic interests. In 1915, President McGiffert recognized this tendency in modern religion, when he commented on the influence of Schleiermacher: "one of the most notable things in the modern situation is the vast enlargement and enrichment of the idea of religion to which the emancipation from the old servitude has led. It is widely recognized to-day that whenever a man is interested in something else than the life of the mere senses, or is devoted to something else than his own selfish welfare, there is religion."[5]

If God has been humanized, and if religion has been reduced to a cultural phenomenon, the ethical side of religion has been exalted. Be religious in order to be good was the watchword of the Enlightenment; but modern religion has tended to say that morality *is* religion. And in compensation for the loss of God, man has deified his moral passion. Consequently, the very age that saw the attenuation of traditional religion saw the rise of an even deeper ethical interest. This was also a part of man's modern outlook. Since God, such as He is, is to be found in man's moral ideals, these ideals may be realized. Utopia is just around the corner. Therefore, in America especially, the emotional drive formerly directed toward God and canalized in love toward God and toward men because they are His children, was utilized for reform. But this very reform has run into strange waters. Whereas the western world seemed on its happy way to a promised land of motor cars and high wages, the debacle of the post-war period has left men hopeless as to the ultimate attainment of social perfection. So long as "progress" seemed always to win, it was enough if religion furnished the cheering section in our economic and political stadium. But progress fumbled, and the cheer leaders have been strangely quiet. With a somewhat sickening abruptness it has become evident that modern religion has little to say when the Chamber of Commerce fails.

In another way, there is disillusionment. So sure was everyone that the battle for religious tolerance had been won, that it has been difficult to persuade some that there is actually being fought out again the old struggle between man's conscience and the State. And it is hard to meet the logic of a State which claims to be the embodiment of man's national and racial ideals and demands the right to take its place in the pantheon of gods who are themselves simply the projections of man's ideals. It is true also that much of the demand that the Church shall be free to speak on every issue, political, economic, and moral, seems beside the point when one remembers that the Church has little or nothing to say.

The dilemma of modern Christianity is plain enough. Having reduced religion to the experience of the religious man, having refused to seek God except in consciousness, modern man has awakened to the fact that God has been lost in the Universe of which man is so small a part. And man, the magnificent conqueror of the nineteenth century, has been lost also. The war informed many people of a depth in human depravity which had been forgotten or ignored. This was followed by a popular literature which left no cupboard unopened. Whereas it had been the thing to look on the sunny side of the street, readers came to expect nothing less than incest and murder in their mildest novels. The list of evils from which people pray to be delivered in the Litany seemed to many a woefully inadequate account of human perversities. Especially was this true for those whom psychoanalysis taught to believe that the minds of clergymen and superannuated maiden aunts are sinks of iniquity. It was a bad time to talk of the evidences of Christian experience.

It has become, moreover, a bad time to talk of the possibility of "educating" men into the Kingdom of God. If human beings are as they have been pictured in popular literature and in popular "scientific" books for the last decade or so, then the doctrine of Calvin and Jonathan Edwards are understatements of mankind's predicament. And what is true of religious education is true also of the "social gospel." The prohibition debacle marked the end of an era in man's hope for social regeneration. Right or wrong, the prohibition crusade in America was the result of a great faith in man's betterment by social control; and its end was for many a terrible disillusionment. In the field of politics the same thing is to be seen. Religious writers tiring of smooth talk about a better world are saying openly that moral man lives always in an immoral society. It is a poor time for idealists and for the hope to build Jerusalem in England's fair and pleasant land.

It is perhaps unnecessary to say that many voices have been raised against the reduction of religion to human aspirations or to a corollary of modern optimism. In this country, notable efforts have been made to establish a "realistic theology" which will do justice to the hard facts of life without sacrificing all that has been gained by earlier emphasis upon Christian experience and moral effort.[6] But the major attacks which have been launched against modern religion have gone at the roots.

The most widely advertised of these is a reassertion of the transcendence of God. God is in heaven, man is upon earth. There can be no commerce between them save as God breaks through from beyond upon man's passivity. "All experience is itself relative. Wherever experience is taken as the starting point, the religious relationship from the very first is based upon something human and relative which cannot possibly represent the Absolute."[7] And man is evil; there is a positive something blocking the way between him and God which can only be removed by the Atonement of Christ. There is no room for earthbound man to seek assurance and comfort, save in his knowledge of his own sinfulness and of the revelation made in Christ. Certainly, there is little place here for a social ethic based upon the possibility of man's achieving a better world here and now. The return is to a more than Calvinistic conception of God yonder and man here, and to man's utter dependence upon the will of God, unconditioned, absolute.

There is also an attack being made upon modern religion from another quarter.[8] The subjectivism and optimism of religion is assailed by Catholic doctrine. Man has nothing to worship because he finds God only in himself. Against this is set the "objective" worship of Catholicism; man is made dependent upon the grace of God mediated through the Church. Authority is not in the religious consciousness but in the institution. Over against the anarchic character of present-day religion, Catholicism sets the unified authority of the Church which interprets and directs and mediates for man. Catholicism spends no time talking about bringing in the Kingdom of God by the natural efforts of men of good-will. Christianity is a supernatural life, and only those whose lives have been raised to the supernatural plane by the infusion of grace can hope to be lifted above the evils inherent in the natural man.

It would be useless to elaborate upon the importance of these two movements, which have been brought to attention in this country mainly by the followers of Karl Barth and by Anglo-Catholicism. Their attacks are against liberalism in religion, and the term takes in much more than the characteristics of modern religion which have been detailed here. But both strike at any religion which gives a primary place to Christian experience; and Barthianism seems to many to make ethical striving not indifferent but apparently useless for this world. Both correct tendencies in modern religion which most theologians now deplore; and it would seem that, unless there is amendment of these obvious fallacies, there must be a complete reorientation of the religious thought of this generation.

It has been the purpose of this study to determine, as accurately as possible, the facts concerning John Wesley's experience and theology. In the course of the study it has become apparent that in many ways his thought differed from that which has been popularly ascribed to him. Undoubtedly his influence in the nineteenth century was along lines coinciding with the Romantic interests manifested in so many fields in that century. But the full significance of Wesley cannot be understood by a study of those parts of his message which were most readily appreciated by his contemporaries or by his immediate followers. Every generation hears according to its predilections, and often the very assumptions which a prophet holds as primary are lost. This, the present writer ventures to think, is precisely what happened to John Wesley. The real Wesley, seen in the light of his full intention, has a word not only for a generation exulting in spiritual freedom and in the employment of their emotions in religious experience, but for a time that has seen the results of overemphasis upon these elements of religion.

Over against a humanistic religion it is entirely proper to set Wesley's religion of grace.[9] Religion, for Wesley, is God-given. This, it must be repeated, is not the note of one Christian system but of historic Christianity from the beginning. Religion is directed toward God, not as a natural law, not as a projection of man's ideals, not as the creation of his social "consciousness," but as objective *reality*. Only, it would be untrue to Wesley and to countless other Christian thinkers, to make God completely objective in the sense that man and the world are outside of him as a table is objective to the cabinet worker who makes it. In so far as eighteenth-century terminology made it possible, Wesley expressed his belief in a God who is both transcendent and immanent. Modern nervousness over "both-ands" ought not to make us forget that some things are both-and. Wesley's belief in God as objective Reality and his God-centered religion of grace did not commit him to a God who is "completely other," whose commerce with man is only by a breaking through from the beyond upon man's incapacity and passivity.

Wesley's opinion of the nature of man cannot be described simply by saying that he accepted the dogma of the Fall. It is truer to say that Wesley expressed his essential ideas of man through this doctrine, adapted and interpreted in the light of eighteenth-century philosophy, natural science, and psychology, as well as eighteenth-century theology. Whether Wesley would have believed in the dogma of the Fall of Man if he had lived in the nineteenth century no one knows, but for Wesley in the eighteenth century there was no other explanation possible to a religious man educated as he had been. But it is evident to all who read his writings that he was sure that the contemporary picture of man bore out the doctrine that man is evil. His own experiences and his observations of war and slavery were his evidences. There is a universe of difference between man as Wesley knew him in America and Europe and the "natural man" of Rousseau's rosy dreams. Yet the inference must not be pushed too far.

Wesley did not conceive of man as absolutely corrupted and helpless to the point that he can be saved only by the breaking through of the irresistible grace of God. If there were such a thing as a purely "natural man," this would be so. But there is no "natural man." All men have the preventing grace of God which enables them to co-operate with grace. Man is thus dependent upon God, but man is also dependent upon his own efforts; for no grace is effectual without the response of man. This is neither Calvinism nor Rousseauism. It is a realistic view of man's evil, individual and social, coupled with a belief that man can be rescued from his dire condition by the grace of God seconded by man's effort.

"The bias of nature is set the wrong way," said Wesley; and he did not mean that the universe is made wrong, but that things are out of joint. And what modern writer, psychoanalyzing his grandfather or viewing the iniquities of society, will say that he was in error? But something can be done about it besides waiting for the irresistible grace of God or of Economic Forces. In a little pamphlet directed against the teachings of Rousseau's *Emile*, Wesley states one thing that can be done. "Education," he wrote, "is designed to set it right. This, by the grace of God, is to turn the bias from self-will, pride, anger, revenge, and the love of the world, to resignation, lowliness, meekness, and the love of God.[10] Wesley's interest was primarily in the individual, and it may be said, once for all, that his educational methods were usually wrong; but his conception of the place of education for Christian living was right. Man, co-operating with the grace of God, can do something to change the bias.

But Wesley's realism in regard to man extended beyond a pessimistic opinion of man's bias toward evil. He did not expect that man's experience of conversion and of present salvation would necessarily produce a Christian life. Therefore, he included in the program of his societies a system of education and of discipline. For this he made use of the traditional exercises of the Christian Church, fasting, meditation, prayer, and constant good works, as well as the guidance of religious societies and classes. There is no claim that Wesley's *system* is one which could be adopted in all ages and times. It was freely charged in the middle of the last century by writers in the main sympathetic, that the structure of Methodism narrowed the life of its adherents, perpetuated a cramping and erroneous set of doctrines, and encouraged an uncontrolled emotionalism. Whether this is true or not is beside the point. What Wesley intended for a people, largely uneducated and cared for by no religious agency, and what may have come of his system are different things. But in a day when religion is rebuked for an unwarranted trust in a discredited human nature, Wesley stands out as a realistic leader who believed that the bias of human nature can only be changed by the grace of God plus discipline and education.

And this was to be carried on within a Church. In the middle of the nineteenth century, Isaac Taylor criticized the Methodists for the "sectarianism" of their organization. But Wesley did not intend for his followers to be organized into the close system of a sect, much less into an imitation of a modern business corporation. The Church was to furnish the broader outlook, while the societies within the Church provided intense discipline and training. If Methodists turned their societies into a "gathered" church, a sect for the converted, Wesley is not to blame. While he denied divine authority to any type of organization, he never conceived of Christianity without a Church. To him the ministry is a ministry sent of God but set apart by the Church, and the sacraments are means of grace. The true Church is always the invisible company of God's children, but the visible Church is necessary for a Christian's life here. There must be corporate life and worship within the "catholic seminary of divine love."

Wesley could not have shared the hope of the nineteenth century—and many of his followers—that God in His goodness is automatically bringing the world nearer and nearer to the Utopia of the Kingdom. A Tory, he did not share the growing enthusiasm of his age for social reform. The reason is largely that he was a Tory; but another reason is that he did not believe human nature sufficiently good for such large-scale experiments. Human nature must be changed first. True he would have nothing of the limitations of providence which were current in orthodox eighteenth-century theology. God is in everything, nature, history, and in the actions of the man who would respond to grace. He held to a belief in

God's personal providence that is impossible for this age; but he did not believe in inevitable progress. The individual or nation that sinneth shall die. Only changed men can bring a changed world. It was old-fashioned in the days of Rousseau and Cordorcet; it is new-fashioned now.

It is unnecessary to add to what has already been said about Wesley's ethical teaching. Man must go on striving; and so highly did Wesley value moral effort that he was sure that God would finally reject none who feared Him and worked righteousness. For the heathen this meant those who followed the light they had. But the true Christian lives a supernatural life: it is the life of God in the soul of man. And living so, there is no compromise with worldly orders or ideas. This gives the anachronistic tone to his teaching about money. Man's vocation is in the world, and so far as he can he lives in it; but he judges the world by Christian standards. In this Wesley recaptured, or rather carried over, the traditional autonomy of Christianity. There can be no surrender to the time-spirit: Christians in their outlook on life must be something more than mirrors of contemporary economic and political theories; in Wesley's own words, they must be "singular" or be damned.

Wesley was also, it must not be left unsaid, a son of the Enlightenment. The great movement which did so much to free Western men from the shackles of superstition did much also for the founder of Methodism. If the modern revolt against what is called liberalism means a return to unworthy ideas about God, to aristocratic doctrines of the elect, to a fanatical shutting up of the grace of God to those who can pronounce theological shibboleths or to those who belong to certain cults, then the world had better go on with liberalism. And Wesley is not a forerunner of any such crusade for obscurantism. If his heterodoxies have become orthodoxies, it is his spirit that counts. He conceived of the Christian life as extending through all the stages from little children to perfect men and women. Little children are little children, and adults are adults; but God is the Father of all, and the Church is the home for all who desire to flee from the wrath to come and to be saved from their sins and who desire the help of the people of God in working out their salvation.

Notable in Wesley's liberalism is his doctrine of Christian authority. If the nineteenth century—and some modern commentators—have erred in calling Wesley as a witness to the sole authority of Christian experience, so do they err who make Wesley a fundamentalist who would have nothing but the naked word of Scripture. He knew the Christian tradition and respected it; the early Fathers are the best interpreters of the Scriptures: but man's reason and experience must also be called in. We know little of God, according to Wesley, speaking of natural theology, save as we know him in the world about us: and all man's knowledge must be brought into play here. In terms of eighteenth-century thought, old-fashioned enough now, Wesley was contending that man must use all the channels open to human personality that by all means he may reach the ultimate authority —God.

For Wesley, then, God is God and not man; and man is a sinful creature living in an imperfect body, as his times—and ours—attest. Nor can education or social efforts alone suffice to bring order to his chaos and righteousness to his ways. But neither is the unassisted grace of God, mediated through sacraments or experienced in emotional moments, conversion or anything else, sufficient for the regeneration of man and his society. There must be constant moral struggle, the effort of man in education and discipline. The grace of God is given, but it must be accompanied by man's effort. And not alone; there is no such thing as "solitary religion." Man must have a corporate religious life, and the sacraments are means of grace, material accompaniments of God's continuous favor. In all there must be the free exercise of man's mind working on the material of tradition, of the world about him, and of his own experience.

But to say this and no more would be to repeat the error of the nineteenth century in another way. Wesley's religion was a personal experience of the love of God and of the love of man. In him lived again the spirit of the great mystics, not their ecstasies but their sense of the nearness and goodness of God. With him religion became once more a flaming fire, a passion for perfection which swept aside economic theories and ancient respectabilities. He was not in the genteel tradition, but in the way of the prophets. Entrenched social wrong and individual evil alike became the enemies of the Almighty. But he was also a prophet of the joyful heart. Again and again, John Wesley warned his followers that he was not responsible for the theology of Charles' hymns; but he kept on singing them. Religion is joy and peace, as well as righteousness. If God is a hidden God, He may be found, in part at least, in the experience of man; for religion is the life of God in the soul of man.

It is this combination of mystical experience with the ethical, the rational, and the institutional elements in religion which gives Wesley his place in the history of Christianity. Phrased in another way, it may be said that he joined the tendencies toward regulation and control, toward uniformity and universality, with the tendencies toward emotion, diversity, and freedom. And he did this without sacrificing either the doctrine of grace or the ethical interests of religion: "The earth brings forth no corn (as the soul no holiness)," he wrote, "without both the care and toil of man, and the benign influence of heaven." For our times, therefore, he is a prophet warning against the separation of God and man by minimizing the place of either. But above all he is a prophet calling men to repentance. The problems of our fathers have given place to the dilemmas of the modern world. But the ancient word lives on. And those who would make normative neither the traditions of past ages nor the latest findings of contemporaries, may well turn to one who stood at the beginning of our modern world, bringing with him old-world conceptions of Christianity and merging them with the intuitions of the newer time.

NOTES

THE basis of modern editions of the works of John Wesley is the third edition, edited by Thomas Jackson in 1831. Quotations from the works in these notes are from an 1872 reprint of this edition in 14 volumes. The pagination differs somewhat in different issues, but the references can be easily found. The standard edition of the *Journal* was edited by Nehemiah Curnock in 8 volumes, London, Epworth Press, 1909-16; of the first 53 sermons, the *Standard Sermons*, edited by Edward H. Sugden, 2 vols., London, Epworth Press, 1921; of the letters, *The Letters of John Wesley*, edited by John Telford, 8 vols., London, Epworth Press, 1931. *The Poetical Works of John and Charles Wesley*, collected and arranged by G. Osborn, 13 vols., London, Wesleyan Methodist Conference Office, 1868-72, are also frequently referred to in the notes. The bibliography of the Wesleys is by Green, second edition, London, Methodist Publishing House, 1906. The *Proceedings* of the Wesley Historical Society are indispensable aids to all students of Wesley.

CHAPTER I

1. For unfavorable criticism of Methodism as a social and political force, see especially the works of J. L. and B. Hammond, *e.g.*, *The Town Labourer*, 1760-1832, New York, Longmans, 1919. A more favorable view is taken by Elie Halévy, *History of the English People in 1815*, London, Unwin, 1924. Recent books which display a sound knowledge of the Wesleyan Movement and of English social and political history are: Wellman J. Warner, *The Wesleyan Movement in the Industrial Revolution*, London, Longmans, 1930; Maldwyn Hughes, *John Wesley and the Eighteenth Century*, New York,

John Wesley and Modern Religion

Abingdon, 1933; E. R. Taylor, *Methodism and Politics, 1791-1851*, Cambridge, University Press, 1935.

2. Herbert Heaton, art., "Industrial Revolution," *Encyclopaedia of the Social Sciences*.

3. See Maldwyn Hughes, *op. cit.*, chap. vi.

4. *Johnson's England*, Edited by A. S. Turberville, Oxford, Clarendon Press, 1933, vol. ii, p. 29.

5. Cf. William Allan Neilson, *Essentials of Poetry*, Boston and New York, Houghton Mifflin, c. 1912.

6. Robert M. Wernaer, *Romanticism and the Romantic School in Germany*, New York, Appleton, 1910, pp. 6-7.

7. Cf. Irving Babbitt's works, esp. *Rousseau and Romanticism*, Boston and New York, Houghton Mifflin, 1919. On the different definitions of Romanticism, see Paul Kaufman, "Defining Romanticism," *Modern Language Notes*, vol. 40 (1925), pp. 193-204; Arthur O. Lovejoy, "On the Discriminations of Romanticisms," *Proceedings of the Modern Language Association*, vol. 39 (1924), pp. 229-253. The most extensive bibliography of Romanticism is in Babbitt's *Rousseau and Romanticism*. A later, but much shorter, bibliography is appended to G. Ant. Borghese's art., "Romanticism," *Encyclopaedia of the Social Sciences*.

8. Alfred North Whitehead, *Science and the Modern World*, New York, Macmillan, 1927, p. 118.

9. E. A. Burtt, *The Metaphysical Foundations of Modern Physical Science*, London, Kegan Paul, 1925, p. 299.

10. See Chauncey Brewster Tinker's charming book by this title, Princeton, Princeton University Press, 1922. See also H. N. Fairchild, *The Noble Savage*, New York, Columbia University Press, 1928.

11. Arthur O. Lovejoy, "Optimism and Romanticism," *Publications of the Modern Language Association*, vol. 20 (1927), pp. 921-945.

12. J. H. Randall, Jr., *The Making of the Modern Mind*, Boston and New York, Houghton Mifflin, 1926, p. 391.

13. H. L. Stewart, "Theology and Romanticism," *Harvard Theological Review*, vol. 13 (1920), pp. 361-389.

14. Otto Pfleiderer, *The Philosophy of Religion on the Basis of Its History*, Eng. Trans., London, 1886-88, vol. i, p. 262.

15. John Baillie, *The Interpretation of Religion*, New York, Scribners, 1928, pt. ii, chap. iii.

16. A. C. McGiffert, *Protestant Thought before Kant*, New York, Scribners, 1915, p. 175. For suggestions as to the relations between Methodism and the Romantic Movement in Literature, see A. W. Harrison, "Romanticism in Religious Revivals," *Hibbert Journal*, July, 1933; F. Brompton Harvey, "Methodism and the Romantic Movement," *London Quarterly and Holborn Review*, July, 1934.

CHAPTER II

1. Norman Sykes, *Edmund Gibson, Bishop of London, 1669-1748*, Oxford, University Press, 1926, p. 5.

Notes

2. Sydney G. Dimond, *The Psychology of the Methodist Revival*, Oxford, University Press, 1926, p. 25.

3. *Johnson's England*, vol. i, p. i.

4. Matthew Tindal, *Christianity as Old as Creation* (first edition, London, 1730; the edition quoted was published in Newburgh, 1798), pp. 188-190

5. Arthur O. Lovejoy, "The Parallel of Deism and Classicism," *Modern Philology*, vol. 29 (1932), p. 3.

6. *The Art of Preaching: in Imitation of Horace's Art of Poetry*. London: Printed for R. Dodsley, at Tully's Head, in Pall Mall.

7. The classical account of the Religious Societies is Josiah Woodward, *Account of the Rise and Progress of the Religious Societies in the City of London*. The sixth edition of this work was published in 1744. For good accounts of the societies, see John S. Simon, *John Wesley and the Religious Societies*, London, Epworth Press, 1921, chap. i; J. Wickham Legg, *English Church Life from the Restoration to the Tractarian Movement*, London, Longmans, 1914, chap. ix.

8. Legg, *op. cit.*, p. 309.

9. *Ibid.*, p. 310.

10. *Ibid.*, pp. 295-296, 313.

11. J. H. Overton, *Life in the English Church*, 1660-1714, London, 1885, pp. 216-219; cf. Simon, *op. cit.*, p. 21.

12. Legg, *op. cit.*, p. 338. On devotional works in this period see below, chap. xi.

13. On Wesley's indebtedness to Jeremy Taylor, see Curnock's Introduction to the Standard Edition of the *Journal*, vol. i, p. 51, and Wesley's Preface to the first journal, vol. i, p. 83. Wesley was not introduced to Taylor, nor for that matter to Kempis and other devotional writers, by his mother, as has often been suggested. Curnock thought that the most likely person was a younger daughter of the Rev. Lionel Kirkham, rector of Stanton. (*Journal*, vol. i, pp. 15-16.)

14. Simon, *op. cit.*, p. 51.

15. *Ibid.*, p. 49.

16. Thomas Comber, *Christianity no Enthusiasm*, London, 1678, p. 88.

17. See G. M. Trevelyan, *England under Queen Anne: Blenheim*, London, Longmans, 1930, p. 52.

18. Legg, *op. cit.*, p. 383.

19. *Ibid*.

20. Samuel Wesley, *Poems on Several Occasions*, London, 1736, pp. 65-77.

21. Trevelyan, *op. cit.*, p. 70.

22. Robert Nelson, *Practice of True Devotion, in relation to the End, as well as the Means of Religion*, London, n.d., p. xx.

23. *Ibid.*, p. 26.

24. R. H. Tawney, *Religion and the Rise of Capitalism*, London, John Murray, 1926, p. 227.

25. On this phase of seventeenth-century English religious life, see Rufus M. Jones, *Studies in Mystical Religion*, London, Macmillan, 1909; and *Spiritual Reformers in the 16th and 17th Centuries*, London, Macmillan, 1914. On

the early Quakers, see William Braithwaite, *The Beginnings of Quakerism,* London, Macmillan, 1912. Margaret Lewis Bailey, *Milton and Jakob Boehme,* New York, Oxford University Press, 1914, attempts to trace the influence of Bœhme in England, particularly on Milton. I have tried to trace the doctrine of immediate inspiration in this period in my *Historical Backgrounds of Early Methodist Enthusiasm,* New York, Columbia University Press, 1931.
26. Lee, *op. cit.,* pp. 56-57, and the references given there.

CHAPTER III

THERE are numerous lives of John Wesley; but the classic work is still Luke Tyerman, *The Life and Times of John Wesley,* 3 vols., London, Harper & Brothers, 1870. The facts of Wesley's life and much related material have been brought together in the light of recent research in five volumes by the late Dr. John S. Simon: *John Wesley and the Religious Societies,* London, Epworth Press, 1921; *John Wesley and the Methodist Societies,* London, Epworth Press, 1923; *John Wesley and the Advance of Methodism,* London, Epworth Press, 1925; *John Wesley the Master Builder, London,* Epworth Press, 1927; *John Wesley, the Last Phase,* London, Epworth Press, 1934. The last volume was completed by Dr. Simon's son-in-law, Dr. A. W. Harrison. Among the shorter lives of Wesley may be mentioned John Telford, *Life of John Wesley,* London, new edition revised, Epworth Press, 1924 (first edition, 1886); W. H. Fitchett, *Wesley and His Century,* London, Smith Elder, 1906 (often reprinted, in this country by Cokesbury Press); W. H. Hutton, *John Wesley,* London, Macmillan, 1927 (in "Great Churchman" series); Umphrey Lee, *The Lord's Horseman,* New York, Appleton-Century, 1928; Arnold Lunn, *John Wesley,* Zondervan, 1929. Robert Southey's *The Life of John Wesley,* 2 vols., London, 1820, is still worth reading.

1. *Works,* vol. xiii, p. 272.
2. Hutton, *John Wesley,* p. 13.
3. *Letters,* vol. vi, p. 156.
4. *Works,* vol. viii, p. 227.
5. *Arminian Magazine,* vol. i (1778), p. 141.
6. Luke Tyerman, *The Life and Times of the Rev. Samuel Wesley, A.M.,* London, Simpkin, Marshall & Co., 1866, p. 439.
7. *Ibid.,* p. 339.
8. *Ibid.,* pp. 383, 387; see Legg, *English Church Life,* p. 35.
9. Tyerman, *op. cit.,* p. 127.

Notes

10. *Letters,* vol. viii, p. 269.

11. *Ibid.,* vol. i, p. 25.

12. For this and the following quotations, see *Journal,* vol. iii, pp. 33-39.

13. Tyerman, *Life and Times of the Rev. John Wesley,* vol. i, p. 23.

14. *Journal,* vol. i, p. 476.

15. Tyerman, *op. cit.,* vol. i, p. 18.

16. On Oxford in the eighteenth century see C. E. Mallet, *A History of the University of Oxford,* Oxford, University Press, vol. iii, 1927. Short, popular accounts of eighteenth-century university education are given in Preserved Smith, *A History of Modern Culture,* New York, Henry Holt, 1930, vol. ii, p. 414, and in *Johnson's England,* vol. ii, chap. xxii, "Education, Schools, and Universities," by C. E. Mallet.

17. *Journal,* vol. i, pp. 65-66. See the whole of Curnock's description of Wesley's first Oxford Diary in *Journal,* vol. i, pp. 36-70.

18. N. Amhurst, *Terrae-Filius: or, the Secret History of the University of Oxford; in Several Essays,* London, first edition, 1726. The quotations are from the third edition, 1754, pp. 102-104.

19. See references cited above, n. 16.

20. *Works,* vol. xiii, p. 460.

21. *Ibid.,* p. 462.

22. *Letters,* vol. i, pp. 39-40.

23. *Works,* vol. xiii, pp. 498-499.

24. Cf. F. M. Davenport, *Primitive Traits in Religious Revivals,* New York, Macmillan, 1905 (now published by Truth Seeker), p. 148.

CHAPTER IV

1. *Works,* vol. xi, p. 366.

2. *Ibid.,* vol. vii, p. 421.

3. *Ibid.,* vol. xi, pp. 366-367.

4. *Ibid.,* vol. xi, p. 367.

5. *The Works of the Reverend William Law,* London, Privately reprinted for G. Moreton, 1892-93, vol. iii, pp. 6, 98, 8, 7, 25.

6. See below, p. 120, and note.

7. *Works of the Reverend William Law,* vol. iii, p. 25.

8. Sermon xiii, *Standard Sermons,* vol. i, pp. 267-268, 276.

9. *Letters,* vol. iv, p. 299.

10. *Ibid.,* vol. i, p. 114.

11. Sermon ci, *Works,* vol. vii, p. 148.

12. *Ibid.,* vol. vii, p. 147.

13. *Apostolic Constitutions,* bk. viii, par. vi. The translations are those of the *Ante-Nicene Fathers.*

14. *Ibid.,* bk. ii, par. lxiii. On gold and costly apparel, see bk. i, par. iii.

15. *Letters,* vol. i, p. 217. Cf. letter to Mrs. Chapman, *Ibid.,* pp. 218-220.

16. *Ibid.,* vol. i, p. 113. On Wesley's asceticism in his later teaching, see below, chap. viii.

17. *Ibid.*, vol. i, pp. 119-120.

18. *Ibid.*, vol. i, p. 21.

19. This and the following quotation are from *Letters*, vol. i, p. 19.

20. *Ibid.*, vol. i, p. 20.

21. *Ibid.*, vol. i, p. 22.

22. *Ibid.*, vol. i, pp. 166-178.

23. *Journal*, vol. i, p. 419.

24. See below, chap. vii.

25. *Letters*, vol. i, p. 207.

26. Wesley's letter to Dr. Burton is in *Letters*, vol. i, pp. 188-191.

27. Maximin Piette, *La réaction wesleyénne dans l'évolution protestante*, Brussels, Albert Dewit, 1925, p. 426.

28. *Journal*, vol. i, p. 152.

29. *Ibid.*, vol. i, pp. 142-143.

30. Curnock's note to *Journal*, vol. i, p. 141; Piette, *op. cit.*, pp. 430-431.

31. *Journal*, vol. i, p. 328.

32. *Ibid.*, vol. i, pp. 328-329.

33. *Ibid.*, vol. i, p. 415.

34. The quotations are from a reprint of the Charleston Hymnbook made by Rev. G. Osborn in 1882. There are only two copies of the hymnbook known to be extant; one of these is in the New York Public Library, 42d Street and Fifth Avenue.

35. *Letters*, vol. i, pp. 218-220.

36. Preface to Haliburton's Life, which Wesley published in 1739. The quotation is given from *Works*, vol. xiv, p. 212.

37. *Epistle of Clement*, chap. xxxi.

38. *Ibid.*, chap. xxxii.

39. *Epistle of Ignatius to the Ephesians*, chap. xiv.

40. See note 36.

41. "Life of Haliburton," Wesley's *Works*, First Collected Edition, Bristol, 1771-1774, vol. x, pp. 295-296.

42. First Collected Edition of Wesley's *Works*, vol. viii, p. 239.

43. *Journal*, vol. i, p. 435.

44. *Ibid.*, vol. i, p. 417.

45. Hymn xx of "Psalms and Hymns for Wednesday and Friday" in the Charleston Hymnbook.

CHAPTER V

1. *Journal*, vol. i, p. 435.

2. *Ibid.*, vol. i, pp. 418-420.

3. *Ibid.*, vol. i, pp. 421-424.

4. *Ibid.*, vol. i, p. 440.

5. *The Journal of the Rev. Charles Wesley, A.M.*, London, Wesleyan Methodist Book Concern, n.d., entry for April 25, 1738, vol. i, p. 85.

6. John Wesley's *Journal*, vol. i, p. 455, entry for April 23, 1738.

7. Piette, *La réaction wesleyénne*, p. 445.

Notes

8. *Journal*, vol. i, p. 461.

9. *Ibid.*, vol. i, p. 462.

10. For a discussion of Wesley's translation of Böhler's Latin, see *Proceedings Wesley Historical Society*, vol. v, p. 25.

11. *Journal*, vol. i, pp. 470-471.

12. *Ibid.*, vol. i, p. 472.

13. *Ibid.*, vol. i, pp. 475-476.

14. Dimond, *Psychology of the Methodist Revival*, p. 78. Dimond's discussion of Wesley's "Religious Sentiment" in chap. iv is a penetrating psychological study of his conversion.

15. *Letters*, vol. i, p. 262.

16. *Journal*, vol. i, p. 476.

17. *Journal*, vol. i, pp. 125-126. The summary is in the third person, but there is no reason to doubt that it is Wesley's own condition here described. Both Curnock and Sugden so understand it.

18. Quoted by J. E. Rattenbury, *Wesley's Legacy to the World*, Nashville, Cokesbury, 1929, p. 77.

19. *Journal*, vol. i, p. 298.

20. *Letters*, vol. v, p. 16.

21. *Ibid.*, vol. iii, p. 320.

22. *Ibid.*, vol. vii, p. 319.

23. *The Works of the Rev. John Wesley, M.A.*, First Collected Edition, Bristol, 1771-1774, vol. i, "To the Reader."

24. These corrections are given in the Standard Edition of the *Journal*, *ad loc.*

25. George Croft Cell, *The Rediscovery of John Wesley*, New York, Holt, 1935, pp. 179-180. The statement that Wesley never allowed these corrections "to get into print at all nor is he responsible" for their publication, is the less understandable since two of Wesley's best-known biographers, Whitehead, 1793, and Tyerman, 1870, both explicitly refer to the appearance of these corrections in the errata to volume xxvi of the First Collected Edition. It is in perfect accord with Wesley's habits that he did not trouble to correct the edition of the first and second journals which was appearing in 1775. He had prepared his corrections for the Collected Edition, and, despite his printer, he got them into print and was responsible for their publication.

26. *Works*, vol. xiii, p. 307.

27. See *Works*, vol. vii, pp. 422-424.

28. *Ibid.*, vol. xiii, p. 307.

29. *Letters*, vol. v, p. 281.

30. *Ibid.*, vol. vii, p. 298.

31. Dimond, *op. cit.*, p. 100.

32. Piette describes the faith which Böhler urged upon Wesley as "l'amour de Dieu intensement perçu," *La réaction wesleyénne*, p. 445. Piette's discussion of Wesley's religious experience is very suggestive.

33. Eugene W. Lyman, *The Meaning and Truth of Religion*, New York, Scribners, 1933, pp. 144-145.

34. *Journal*, vol. viii, p. 127.
35. *Ibid.*, vol. v, p. 94.
36. *Letters*, vol. v, p. 147.
37. *Ibid.*, vol. vi, p. 39.
38. Sermon xxi, *Standard Sermons*, vol. i, pp. 430-431.
39. *Letters*, vol. v, p. 206.
40. *Ibid.*, vol. iv, pp. 344-345.
41. *Ibid.*, vol. ii, p. 120.
42. *Ibid.*, vol. iv, p. 103.
43. *Ibid.*, vol. vi, p. 44.
44. See below, chap. x, for fuller reference to the *Sunday Service*.
45. See T. H. Barratt, "The Place of the Lord's Supper in Early Methodism," *London Quarterly Review*, July, 1923.
46. F. Luke Wiseman, *Charles Wesley*, New York, Abingdon, 1932, p. 172.

CHAPTER VI

On Wesley's theology, the student should consult: H. B. Workman, "The Place of Methodism in the Catholic Church," introductory chapter in *A New History of Methodism*, 2 vols., London, Hodder & Stoughton, 1909; Maximin Piette, *La Réaction wesleyénne dans l'évolution protestante*; George Eayrs, *John Wesley: Christian Philosopher and Church Founder*, London, Epworth Press, 1926; Howard Watkins-Jones, *The Holy Spirit from Arminius to Wesley*, London, Epworth Press, 1929; J. Ernest Rattenbury, *Wesley's Legacy to the World*, Nashville, Cokesbury, 1929; R. Newton Flew, *The Idea of Perfection in Christian Theology*, Oxford, University Press, 1934. After this manuscript was completed, there came to hand a Heidelberg theological dissertation by Dr. Erich von Eicken, *Rechtfertigung und Heiligung bei Wesley dargestellt unter Vergleichung mit den Anschauungen Luthers und Luthertums*, 1934. I am glad to be able to cite this excellent monograph in support of a number of points in this and the following chapters.

1. See especially, C. C. J. Webb, *Religious Thought in the Oxford Movement*, London, S.P.C.K., 1928, p. 53. See also R. Newton Flew, "Methodism and the Catholic Tradition," in *Northern Catholicism, Centenary Studies in the Oxford and Parallel Movements*, ed. by N. P. Williams and Charles Harris, London, S.P.C.K., 1933.
2. Cf. Trevelyan, *Blenheim*, pp. 60-61.
3. *Works*, vol. x, pp. 350-351.

Notes

4. Sermon v, *Standard Sermons*, vol. i, p. 121. See *Letters*, vol. vi, p. 298; vol. iii, pp. 108-109.

5. *Works*, vol. vi, p. 198; cf. vol. viii, pp. 197-198.

6. Sermon lxvii, *Works*, vol. vi, p. 316.

7. Sermon xviii, *Standard Sermons*, vol. i, p. 364.

8. Sermon lxvii, *Works*, vol. vi, pp. 320-322.

9. *Works*, vol. viii, p. 465.

10. Whitehead, *Science and the Modern World*, chap. v.

11. *Works*, vol. x, pp. 361-363, his tract, "Thoughts upon God's Sovereignty."

12. See for idea of scale of being, Wesley, *A Survey of the Wisdom of God in the Creation; or, a Compendium of Natural Philosophy*, London, 1784, vol. iv, pp. 72-114.

13. Sermon lx, *Works*, vol. vi, p. 246.

14. Sermon lxvii, *Works*, vol. vii, pp. 222-223.

15. Sermon lx, vol. vi, p. 244. Cf. St. Thomas Aquinas, *Summa Theologica*, Part I, 2, q. I, art. 8; q. 5 ad 2; q. II, art. 2; Plotinus, *Enneads* I, 4 and 5; Aristotle, *Nichomachean Ethics*, x, 1176a. (I am indebted for these references to Professor Robert L. Calhoun of Yale.) Lactantius, *Divine Institutions*, iii, x, says that "the chief good of man is in religion only: for the other things, even those which are supposed to be peculiar to man, are found in the other animals also."

16. Sermon lx, *Works*, vol. vi, pp. 249-250. Wesley advances this as a "conjecture."

17. *Ibid.*, p. 243.

18. Sermon lvii, *Works*, vol. vi, p. 223.

19. Law's *Works*, vol. iii, p. 22.

20. Wesley's *Works*, vol. ix, p. 221. Wesley's treatise, "The Doctrine of Original Sin," is in *Works*, vol. ix, pp. 192-464. Sermon xxxviii, "Original Sin" (*Standard Sermons*, vol. ii, pp. 207-225); Sermon xxxix, "The New Birth" (*ibid.*, vol. ii, pp. 225-243); and Sermon lvii, "On the Fall of Man" (*Works*, vol. vi, pp. 215-224), should also be consulted for Wesley's views on the subject.

21. On man's loss of the power of intuitive knowledge by the Fall, see Sermon lxii, *Works*, vol. vi, p. 270; and on faith as intuition, see passage in "An Earnest Appeal," *Works*, vol. vii, pp. 13-15. Wesley's conception of faith will be discussed below, chap. vii.

22. *Works*, vol. x, pp. 470-471.

23. C. C. J. Webb, "The Nature of Religious Experience," *Hibbert Journal*, vol. xxxii (1933), pp. 18-19.

24. Sermon lxxxv, *Works*, vol. vi, p. 512.

25. Charles Hardwick, *A History of the Articles of Religion*, Philadelphia, Hooker, 1860, p. 201.

26. Tyerman, *The Life and Times of Samuel Wesley*, p. 145. Cf. Beveridge, *Ecclesia Anglicana Ecclesia Catholica; or, the Doctrine of the Church of England consonant to Scripture, Reason, and Fathers*, Second edition, revised, Oxford, at the University Press, 1846, p. 279. The whole of Bever-

idge's chapter on Article X (pp. 274-285) should be read. Dr. Eicken, *op. cit.*, sees that the doctrine of preventing grace is characteristic of Wesley's theology, and that it became increasingly important for him as Wesley grew older, causing him to modify some of the more extreme statements which he had made concerning man's total depravity.

27. The following quotations are from these two short tracts, *Works*, vol. x, pp. 457-480. See Dr. Eicken's short excursus on "Wesley and Arminianism." In listing the influences which moved Wesley to reject determinism, Eicken gives first place to the influence of Wesley's home, the atmosphere of which was that of Laudian Anglicanism. Only later did Wesley show any influence from the Remonstrant theologians. This seems to me correct.

28. Sermon xxxii, *Standard Sermons*, vol. ii, p. 96.

29. Sermon xxxv, *Standard Sermons*, vol. ii, p. 154.

30. *Letters*, vol. ii, p. 387.

31. *Works*, vol. x, p. 484.

32. *Letters*, vol. vii, p. 106. In his Preface to the "Epistles of the Apostolical Fathers," Wesley used yet stronger language: "The plain inference is, not only that they were not mistaken in their interpretation of the gospel of Christ; but that in all the necessary parts of it, they were so assisted by the Holy Ghost, as to be scarce capable of mistaking. Consequently, we are to look on their writings, though not of equal authority with the holy Scriptures, (because neither were the authors of them called in so extraordinary a way to the writing of them, nor endued with so large a portion of the blessed Spirit,) yet as worthy of a much greater respect than any composures which have been made since; however men have afterwards written with more art, and a greater stock of human learning, than is to be found not only in the following pieces, but even in the New Testament itself." (*Works*, vol. xiv, p. 225.) This was published in the first volume of the Christian Library, in 1749.

33. Lancelot Andrewes, *Responsio ad Apologiam Cardinalis Bellarmini*, Oxford, Parker, 1851, p. 233.

34. Herbert Thorndike, *The Theological Works*, Oxford, Parker, vol. ii, pt. ii, pp. 426-7. On the Nonjurors, see J. H. Overton, *The Nonjurors*, New York, Whittaker, 1903. For a short account of the Tractarians' interest in the early Fathers, see H. P. Liddon, *Life of E. B. Pusey*, London, Longmans, 1893-1897, vol. i, chap. xviii, "The Library of the Fathers." The exigencies of controversy with the Roman Catholics made it desirable to emphasize the Fathers of the undivided Church. The controversy with the Calvinists perhaps turned attention to the Fathers before Augustine.

35. *Letters*, vol. v, p. 364.

36. *Ibid.*, vol. iv, p. 368.

37. *Works*, vol. viii, pp. 10-15.

38. *Ibid.*

39. *Ibid.*, vol. vi, p. 339; cf. Sermon xviii, *Standard Sermons*, vol. i, p. 364: "we are to see the Creator in the glass of every creature."

40. *Letters*, vol. viii, p. 89.

41. *Letters*, vol. i, p. 172.

Notes

42. *Ibid.*, vol. ii, pp. 383-385.
43. *Ibid.*, vol. ii, p. 383.
44. *Ibid.*, vol. vi, p. 136.
45. *Ibid.*, vol. vi, p. 129.
46. *Ibid.*, vol. vii, p. 392. See *Journal*, vol. i, p. 415n.
47. Cf. letter to Ann Loxdale, June, 1781, *Letters*, vol. vii, p. 67.
48. See H. B. Workman, "The Place of Methodism in the Catholic Church," introductory chapter to *A New History of Methodism*.
49. *Letters*, vol. i, p. 274.
50. *Ibid.*, vol. ii, p. 120.
51. *Ibid.*, vol. ii, p. 387.
52. *Ibid.*, vol. ii, p. 290.
53. *Ibid.*, vol. v, p. 24.

CHAPTER VII

1. See *Letters*, vol. iv, p. 297; *Standard Sermons*, vol. i, p. 150; *Works*, vol. vii, p. 29.
2. *Letters*, vol. viii, p. 218.
3. *Works*, vol. viii, pp. 10, 47.
4. Sermon xv, *Standard Sermons*, vol. i, pp. 301 ff.
5. *Ibid.*
6. *Ibid.*, p. 312.
7. *Works*, vol. viii, p. 48.
8. *Letters*, vol. vii, p. 298. Cf. the statement of one of Wesley's often-quoted Fathers, Macarius: "So very various is the way of grace in them, and such variety is there in the manner after which it conducts the soul, refreshing it according to the will and pleasure of God." (Homily x.)
9. *Works*, vol. viii, p. 24.
10. J. Agar Beet, "The Methodist Revival," *London Quarterly Review*, January, 1920, pp. 54-69. But see H. B. Workman, *New History of Methodism*, vol. i, p. 54n.
11. George Croft Cell, *op. cit.*, p. 199. On p. 153, Professor Cell speaks of Luther as the only authority, besides the Scriptures, which Wesley ever acknowledged "for his own doctrine of faith."
12. *Letters*, vol. iii, p. 321.
13. *Ibid.*, vol. iv, pp. 173-174.
14. *Works*, vol. viii, p. 13.
15. *Ibid.*, vol. viii, p. 198.
16. "The Life of God in the Soul of Man," quoted from reprint in First Collected Edition of Wesley's Works, vol. viii, p. 301.
17. *Works* (third edition), vol. viii, p. 428.
18. *Ibid.*, vol. viii, p. 48.
19. Sermon xxxi, *Standard Sermons*, vol. ii, p. 81.
20. *Works*, vol. vii, pp. 256-263.
21. See Augustine, "On Rebuke and Grace," chap. 40; Westminster Confession of Faith, chap. xviii.

22. Sermon cxxxviii, *Works*, vol. vii, p. 492.

23. *Journal*, vol. i, p. 191.

24. *Ibid.*, vol. ii, pp. 13-14.

25. *Works*, vol. viii, p. 282.

26. *Letters*, vol. ii, p. 46.

27. Quoted by Sugden. *Standard Sermons*, vol. i, p. 82n., from Southey, *Life of Wesley*, vol. i, p. 295.

28. Quoted by James Moffatt, *Love in the New Testament*, New York, Richard R. Smith, 1930, p. 141.

29. Art., "Justification," in *Encyclopaedia of Religion and Ethics*.

30. *Letters*, vol. iii, p. 161.

31. Sermon x, *Standard Sermons*, vol. i, p. 208.

32. *Ibid.*, p. 208.

33. *Works*, vol. viii, p. 3.

34. C. C. J. Webb, *Religious Thought in the Oxford Movement*, pp. 91, 89. Cf. also Yngve Brilioth, *Evangelicalism and the Oxford Movement*, Oxford, University Press, 1934, p. 48. Dr. Eicken has a similar statement in which he attributes to Wesley the conception which characterized the Oxford Movement: "Die Frage ist eben, ob das Leben des Gläubigen sich mehr am Karfreitag oder an Osten und Pfingsten, am 'Christus für uns' oder am gegenwärtigen, sieghaften, allmächtigen 'Christus in uns' aufzurichten hat. Für Luther bleibt lebenslang der 'Christus für uns' im Vordergrunde des Interesses, für Wesley aber hinsichtlich des Wiedergeborenen 'der Christus in uns.' " (*Rechtfertigung und Heiligung bei Wesley*, p. 67.)

35. Sermon xix, *Standard Sermons*, vol. i, p. 390.

36. *Letters*, vol. i, pp. 63-65.

37. Quoted in *Ekstatische Konfessionen*, edited by Martin Buber, Leipzig, Insel Verlag, 1923, p. 33.

38. *Journal*, vol. v, p. 244; cf. *Letters*, vol. iii, p. 356.

39. *Works*, vol. viii, p. 361. The date given in the *Works*, 1740, is evidently a mistake. See Green, Bibliography, *ad loc.*

40. See *John Bennet's Copy of the Minutes of the Conferences of 1744, 1745, 1747 and 1748; with Wesley's Copy of Those for 1746*, published as Number I of the *Proceedings Wesley Historical Society*, London, 1896.

41. *Letters*, vol. ii, p. 227.

42. *Ibid.*, vol. ii, p. 46.

43. *Arminian Magazine* (1779), pp. 119-123.

44. *Journal*, vol. ii, p. 467.

45. *Ibid.*, vol. ii, p. 174.

46. George Bull, *Harmonica Apostolica*, Oxford, Parker, 1842.

47. *Letters*, vol. ii, p. 187.

48. *Works*, vol. viii, pp. 336-338.

49. David Benham, *Memoirs of James Hutton*, London, Hamilton, Adams, 1856, p. 112.

50. Fletcher wrote a "Vindication of the Minutes" in five letters, which is his *First Check to Antinomianism*. This has often been reprinted. The reference here is to Letter iv, 5.

Notes

51. *Letters*, vol. v, p. 275.
52. Fletcher, *First Check*, Letter iv, 5. Cf. St. Thomas, *Summa*, Part I, 2, q. 114, art. 3.
53. Fletcher, *Fourth Check*, Letter i.
54. *Letters*, vol. vi, pp. 202-203.
55. Sermon cvii, *Works*, vol. vii, pp. 204-205.

CHAPTER VIII

1. The best discussion of the doctrine of Christian Perfection in Western theology is R. Newton Flew, *The Idea of Perfection in Christian Theology;* chap. xviii deals with William Law and xix with Wesley. There is now also the study of Eicken, *Rechtfertigung und Heiligung bei Wesley.* Students should read also H. B. Workman, "The Place of Methodism in the Life and Thought of the Christian Church," in *The New History of Methodism.* Dr. Sugden has written an illuminating introduction to Sermon xxxv, *Standard Sermons*, vol. ii, pp. 147-150.
2. *Letters*, vol. iv, pp. 298-299. Cf. *Works*, vol. xi, p. 444.
3. "The ripe fruit of medieval Christianity as concentrated in the life of the Cloister," is Dr. Inge's description of the *Imitation* (*Christian Mysticism*, London, Methuen, 1925, p. 194).
4. *Standard Sermons*, vol. i, pp. 263-279.
5. *Ibid.*, pp. 277-278.
6. *Ibid.*, p. 277n.
7. *Ibid.*, pp. 269-270 and note. Cf. *Works*, vol. xi, pp. 384-385.
8. *Works*, vol. xi, p. 370. See *Journal*, vol. ii, p. 49 and note. In the *Journal*, the words of Gradin are expanded to include what Henry Moore said was a description of Gradin's own experience, not a general definition: *verbo, cor quod antea instar maris turbulenti agitabatur, in summa fuit requie, instar maris serenis et tranquili.* It is possible that only later did Wesley see that this described Gradin's own experience, but not necessarily the experience of every child of God. See *Journal*, vol. ii, p. 49 and note 3.
9. *The Poetical Works*, vol. i, pp. 197-204.
10. See Sugden's note, *Standard Sermons*, vol. i, p. 234. The word "adult" is inserted in the First Collected Edition, as also the warning.
11. These changes are to be found, *Works*, vol. xi, pp. 379-380; *Poetical Works*, vol. i, pp. 199-201. For further evidence of Wesley's change of views concerning the state of those born again, see *Standard Sermons*, vol. i, p. 285n.
12. *Standard Sermons*, vol. ii, p. 156.
13. Law, *Works*, vol. iii, p. 27.
14. Flew, *op. cit.*, pp. 340-341.
15. Wesley, *Works*, vol. xi, p. 419.
16. *Ibid.*, p. 442.
17. *Standard Sermons*, vol. ii, p. 156.
18. Minutes of the Conference of 1744, *Works*, vol. viii, p. 285.
19. On Charles Wesley's views, see Luke Wiseman, *Charles Wesley*, pp. 157 ff.

20. *Works*, vol. xi, p. 446.

21. Sermon cxx, dated Madeley, March 26, 1790, *Works*, vol. vii, p. 317.

22. *Works*, vol. viii, pp. 68-69.

23. *Works*, vol. viii, p. 279.

24. Cell, *Rediscovery of John Wesley*, p. 347.

25. *Works*, vol. xi, p. 417.

26. Sermon l, *Standard Sermons*, vol. ii, pp. 457-458.

27. Sermon xlvii, *Standard Sermons*, vol. ii, p. 389.

28. Art., *Southwestern Christian Advocate*, Feb. 19, 1935.

29. *Works*, vol. xi, p. 401.

30. *Ibid.*, vol. xi, p. 420.

31. Sermon xvii, *Standard Sermons*, vol. i, p. 343.

32. *Ibid.*, pp. 342-343.

33. *Ibid.*, pp. 343-344.

34. *Ibid.*, p. 337.

35. Sermon xix, *Standard Sermons*, vol. i, p. 390.

36. Sermon xxvi, *ibid.*, p. 542.

37. For a brief account of the Christian doctrine of vocation, see R. L. Calhoun, *God and the Common Life*, New York, Scribners, 1935, pp. 17-33.

38. John M. Mecklin, *The Story of American Dissent*, New York, Harcourt, Brace, 1934, p. 279.

39. Law's *Works*, vol. iv, p. 14.

40. *Letters*, vol. i, p. 113.

41. *Standard Sermons*, vol. ii, p. 280. The following quotations are from this sermon, pp. 281-292.

42. The General Rules are reprinted in all Books of Discipline of American Methodists, and in *Works*, vol. viii, pp. 269-271.

43. *Works*, vol. viii, p. 354.

44. *Ibid.*, vol. xi, p. 473.

45. *Letters*, vol. vii, p. 12.

46. *Ibid.*, vol. vi, p. 47.

47. *Works*, vol. xi, pp. 458-459.

48. *Ibid.*, vol. viii, p. 286; *Proceedings Wesley Historical Society*, no. i, p. 23.

49. *Ibid.*, vol. viii, pp. 323-324.

50. R. H. Tawney, *Religion and the Rise of Capitalism*, p. 248.

51. Sermon xliv, *Standard Sermons*, vol. ii, pp. 319-320.

52. Tawney, *op. cit.*, p. 191.

53. *Standard Sermons*, vol. ii, pp. 316-317. The following quotations are from this sermon, "The Use of Money," pp. 309-327.

54. Sermon li, *Standard Sermons*, vol. ii, pp. 476-477.

55. Cell, *op. cit.*, chap. xvi.

56. Sermon xxviii, *Standard Sermons*, vol. ii, p. 36.

57. Sermon cvi, *Works*, vol. vii, p. 199. Cf. Sugden, *Standard Sermons*, vol. i, p. 61n; *Letters*, vol. vi, pp. 272-273.

58. Sermon lxxxix, *Works*, vol. vii, p. 28.

59. *Ibid.*, p. 29.
60. *Works*, vol. xi, p. 430.

CHAPTER IX

1. *Works*, vol. viii, p. 348.
2. See description of Wesley by John Hampson, a preacher who left the connection, in *Memoirs of the late John Wesley*, Sunderland, 1791, vol. iii, pp. 167-168.
3. *Journal*, vol. i, p. 85.
4. Law, *Works*, vol. iv, p. 10.
5. "The Oxford Methodists, Being some account of a Society of Young Gentlemen in that City, so denominated," quoted by Simon, *John Wesley and the Religious Societies*, pp. 97, 98. Simon thinks this pamphlet was written by William Law.
6. Samuel Wesley, *Poems on Several Occasions*, pp. 109-110.
7. *Journal*, vol. i, p. 101. Cf. Simon, *op. cit.*, pp. 95-96.
8. Edwyn Bevan, *Hellenism and Christianity*, New York, Doran, 1922, p. 144.
9. *Letters*, vol. i, p. 219.
10. *Ibid.*, vol. i, p. 152.
11. *Ibid.*, vol. i, p. 158.
12. *Ibid.*, vol. i, p. 160.
13. *Ibid.*, vol. vi, p. 6.
14. *Ibid.*, vol. v, p. 28.
15. *Ibid.*, vol. iii, p. 152.
16. *Works*, vol. viii, p. 32.
17. *Journal*, vol. vi, p. 7.
18. *Ibid.*, vol. vi, p. 54.
19. The copy of *The Sunday Services of the Methodists in North America, with Other Occasional Services* (London, 1784) which I have used, does not have as a preface the letter in which he notices these changes. Instead there is prefaced Wesley's letter to Coke and Asbury of September 10, 1784. The other preface appears in later editions. I have not checked other copies of the first edition to see whether the copy which I have used is deficient or Green is mistaken. Nolan B. Harmon, Jr. (*The Rites and Ritual of Episcopal Methodism*, Nashville, Cokesbury, 1926, p. 41) thinks that the omission of the holy days from the *Sunday Services* "was doubtless in conformity to the heavy emphasis that the early Methodist put on the practice of Scriptural holiness in season and out of season."
20. *Letters*, vol. vii, p. 256.
21. Sermon xxii, *Standard Sermons*, vol. i, p. 467.
22. Sermon cxvi, *Works*, vol. vii, pp. 288-289.
23. *Journal*, vol. vi, p. 495n.
24. *Letters*, vol. vi, p. 44.
25. *Ibid.*, vol. iv, p. 100.
26. *Ibid.*, vol iv, p. 103.

27. *Ibid.*, vol. iv, p. 272.
28. *Ibid.*, vol. vi, p. 7.
29. Green, *Bibliography*, no. 74.
30. *Ibid.*, no. 173.
31. *Works*, vol. vii, p. 274.
32. *Ibid.*, vol. viii, pp. 322-323.
33. *Proceedings W. H. S.*, no. 1.
34. *Works*, vol. viii, pp. 258-259.
35. *Ibid.*, pp. 255-256.
36. *Journal*, vol. ii, p. 536.
37. *Letters*, vol. ii, p. 287.

CHAPTER X

1. Ernst Troeltsch, *The Social Teaching of the Christian Church*, New York, Macmillan, 1931. For summary of his three types see vol. ii, p. 993.
2. *Poetical Works*, vol. iii, pp. 57-58.
3. *Letters*, vol. i, pp. 118 ff.
4. *Works*, vol. xi, p. 207.
5. *Journal*, vol. i, p. 133n.
6. For Brevint's preface, see *Poetical Works*, vol. iii, pp. 185-214.
7. *Works*, vol. x, pp. 188-201.
8. *Works*, vol. x, p. 208.
9. *Journal*, p. 93n and Charles Wesley's *Journal* for Oct. 20, 1738, and Nov. 14, 1738.
10. *Journal*, vol. iii, pp. 229-230.
11. *Works*, vol. viii, pp. 280-281.
12. *Ibid.*, pp. 235 ff.
13. Quoted by Tyerman, *op. cit.*, vol. ii, p. 202.
14. *Letters*, vol. iii, pp. 144-147.
15. *Works*, vol. viii, p. 31.
16. Sermon lxxiv, *Works*, vol. vi, p. 397.
17. *Letters*, vol. iii, p. 138.
18. See Troeltsch, *op cit.*, vol. ii, pp. 721-724.
19. Quoted by Simon, *Advance of Methodism*, p. 151.
20. *Works*, vol. viii, pp. 321-322.
21. *Journal*, vol. vii, facsimile facing p. 16. On Wesley's purpose, see J. A. Faulkner, *Burning Questions in Historic Christianity*, New York, Abingdon, 1930, chap. xiii.
22. *Works*, vol. viii, p. 48.
23. Sermon xxxix, *Standard Sermons*, vol. ii, p. 238; see Sugden on baptism, vol. i, pp. 280-282.
24. J. Ernest Rattenbury, *Wesley's Legacy to the World*, pp. 176-195.
25. Sermon xii, *Standard Sermons*, vol. i, pp. 237-262.
26. *Poetical Works*, vol. iii.
27. Sermon xii, *Standard Sermons*, vol. i, p. 253.
28. *Journal*, vol. ii, pp. 361-362.

Notes

29. Sermon ci, *Works*, vol. vii, pp. 147-156.

30. *Letters*, vol. iv, p. 272.

31. *Ibid.*, vol. viii, p. 41.

32. *Letters*, vol. i, pp. 349-350.

33. *Ibid.*, vol. iii, p. 182.

34. *Summa Theologica*, suppl. q. xl, v. "It was pointed out long ago by Jerome and by several of the Greek fathers, that there is no passage in the New Testament which compels the assumption that the terms 'Episcopos' and 'Presbyter' are the names of two different offices." (B. H. Streeter, *The Primitive Church*, New York, Macmillan, 1929, p. 114.)

35. *Reliquiae Baxterianae: Or, Mr. Richard Baxter's Narrative of . . . . his Life and Times*, London, 1696, bk. i, p. 206.

36. Charles J. Abbey, *The English Church and its Bishops, 1700-1800*, London, Longmans, 1887, pp. 369-370 and notes.

37. Edward Stillingfleet, *The Irenicon, or Pacificator: being a Reconciler as to Church Differences*, Philadelphia, Sorin, 1842, p. 438. Stillingfleet (1635-1699) first published his *Irenicon* in 1659.

38. *Ibid.*, p. 402.

39. Peter (Lord) King, *An Enquiry into the Constitution, Discipline, Unity, and Worship of the Primitive Church*, New York, 1841, p. 61. King (1669-1734) published his *Enquiry* in 1691.

40. *Ibid.*, p. 65.

41. *Ibid.*, p. 85.

42. *Letters*, vol. iii, p. 192.

43. *Letters*, vol. vii, p. 262.

44. *Ibid.*, vol. iii, p. 182.

45. Sermon cxv, *Works*, vol. vii, pp. 273-281. See John S. Simon, "Wesley's Ordinations," *Proceedings W. H. S.*, ix. 7, pp. 145-154.

46. Samuel Drew, *The Life of the Rev. Thomas Coke, LL.D.*, New York, 1818, p. 64.

47. Tyerman, *Life of John Wesley*, vol. iii, p. 429.

48. *Ibid.*, vol. iii, p. 434.

49. *Journal*, vol. vii, p. 15, Diary entry for Thursday, Sept. 2, 1784.

50. Thomas Jackson, *Life of Charles Wesley*, London, Wesleyan Conference office, 1841, vol. ii, p. 386. St. Thomas also uses the word "superintendent" (*Summa Theologica*, part II, 2, q. clxxxi, art. vi). He quotes Augustine, the relevant passage being *si velimus, latine "superintendere" possumus dicere.* (*De Civitate Dei*, xix, 19.) On origin of office of bishop as overseer of practical, including the financial, affairs of church, see Hans Lietzmann, *Geschichte der Alten Kirche*, Berlin and Leipzig, Verlag, Walter D. Gruyter, 1932, p. 148.

51. Henry Moore, *The Life of the Rev. John Wesley*, vol. ii, pp. 193, 203.

52. On all this, see John Emory, *A Defence of "Our Fathers," and of the Original Organization of the Methodist Episcopal Church*, New York, 1856.

53. Wesley, *Explanatory Notes upon the New Testament*, ad loc.

54. *Episcopacy, Ancient and Modern*, edited by Claude Jenkins and K. D. MacKenzie, London, S.P.C.K., 1930, p. 368.

CHAPTER XI

1. Sermon lxviii, *Works*, vol. vi, pp. 325-337.
2. Sermon xiii, *Standard Sermons*, vol. i, p. 279.
3. *Letters*, vol. viii, p. 63.
4. *Wesley's Veterans*, ed. by John Telford, London, n. d., vol. iii, p. 11.
5. Sermon ii, *Standard Sermons*, vol. i, pp. 66-67.
6. *Works*, vol. xi, p. 430.
7. *Ibid.*, vol. xi, pp. 366-367.
8. Sermon xiii, *Standard Sermons*, vol. i, pp. 263-279.
9. Sermon cxxxix, *Works*, vol. vii, p. 497.
10. Irving Babbitt, *Rousseau and Romanticism*, pp. 130-131.
11. Sermon lxxvii, *Works*, vol. vi, p. 430.
12. It is easy to overstate the place of fear as a motive in the Wesleyan Revival, especially so far as Wesley himself is concerned. After studying Methodist conversions, Dimond concludes that "the essential root of the emotional element in almost all the cases under review is the fear of loss to the essential self consequent upon a suddenly acquired sense of the reality and holiness of God, and the moral law by which their lives are at once judged and condemned." (Dimond, *Psychology of the Methodist Revival*, p. 201.)
13. *Letters*, vol. v, p. 320.
14. See F. Luke Wiseman, *Charles Wesley*, pp. 181-182.
15. Davenport, *Primitive Traits in Religious Revivals*, pp. 163-166.
16. *Journal*, vol. i, pp. 110-111.
17. *Ibid.*, vol. iii, p. 180.
18. *Works*, vol. viii, p. 112.
19. Dimond, *op. cit.*, p. 117; on the subject of this and the following paragraph, see Dimond's discussion, pp. 116-124.
20. *Letters*, vol. viii, p. 83.
21. *Ibid.*, vol. v, p. 320.
22. *Ibid.*, vol. vi, pp. 206-207.
23. *Journal*, vol. iv, p. 422.
24. *Works*, vol. xi, pp. 59-79.
25. Sermon cxxx, *Works*, vol. vii, pp. 404-405.
26. Sermon l, *Works*, vol. vi, p. 129.
27. *Journal*, vol. iv, p. 176.
28. Sermon xcix, *Works*, vol. vii, p. 137.
29. Babbitt, *op. cit.*, p. 143.
30. Cf. Wesley's attitude toward reception of the Lord's Supper:

> And shall I let Him go?
> If now I do not *feel*
> The streams of living water flow,
> Shall I forsake the well?

. . . .

Notes

His will is good and just:
Shall I His will withstand?
If Jesus bids me lick the dust,
I bow at His command.
　　　　—*Poetical Works*, vol. iii, pp. 276-277.

31. *Letters*, vol. vi, p. 18.

32. George Lavington, Bishop of Exeter, *The Enthusiasm of the Methodists and Papists compar'd*, London, 1749-1751, pt. i, p. 26.

CHAPTER XII

1. See, for example, the two excellent books by Professor Van Dusen, *The Plain Man Seeks for God*, New York, Scribners, 1932; and *God and These Times*, New York, Scribners, 1934.

2. For Schleiermacher, see W. B. Selbie, *Schleiermacher*, New York, Dutton, 1913.

3. In his review of Edwin Lewis, *Christian Manifesto*, New York, Abingdon, 1934, Bishop Francis J. McConnell recalls somebody's gibe that in our day the preaching of a divine fatherhood has become the preaching of the divine grandfatherhood—with all the suggestion of a grandfather's doddering inability to mark sharp distinctions between right and wrong and to treat them differently. (*Religion in Life*, vol. iii, no. 4, p. 616.)

4. Bernard C. Meland, *A Modern Man's Worship*, New York, Harper, 1934.

5. McGiffert, *op. cit.*, pp. 78-79.

6. A helpful book is Walter Marshall Horton, *Realistic Theology*, New York, Harper, 1934. His references to contemporary literature will introduce the reader to most of the material relevant for an understanding of the present situation in English and American theology. On contemporary theology, see E. E. Aubrey, *Present Theological Tendencies*, New York, Harper, 1936.

7. Adolph Keller, *Karl Barth and Christian Unity*, New York, Macmillan, 1933, p. 22. In spite of the number of works interpreting Barthianism, the student should read *Der Römerbrief*, of which there is now a good English translation. (Karl Barth, *The Epistle to the Romans*, Trans., Hoskyns, London, Oxford, 1933); and Emil Brunner, *The Mediator*, New York, Macmillan, 1934.

8. A short account of the Catholic movements in England and elsewhere are given in *Northern Catholicism, Centenary Studies in the Oxford and Parallel Movements*. See also *Essays Catholic and Critical*, ed. by E. G. Selwyn, New York, Macmillan, 1936.

9. It is the excellency of Professor Cells' work, *The Rediscovery of John Wesley*, that he emphasizes this.

10. "Thoughts on Educating Children," *Works*, xiii, pp. 474-477.

INDEX

Addison, Joseph, hymn of, 95-96

Aldersgate Street, Wesley's experience in, 13, 178; effect on his High Church views, 242-243; effect on his views of church government, 256; interpretation of, 89-90; later interpretation of, 99-103; significance of, 103-104

Alexandria, Church of, 258, 266

America, Wesley's gains in, 81, 82, 83; observations on experiences in, 76-77, 84, 103-104

American Revolution, 36

Amusements, 201-202

Andrewes, Lancelot, bishop, 133

Anglo-Catholicism, 312

Annesley, Samuel, 43

Antinomianism, 101, 188

Apostolic Canons, 217, 238

Apostolic Constitutions, 64-65, 78-79, 217, 237, 238

Apostolic Fathers, 79

Apostolic succession, 29-30, 238, 243

Aquinas, Thomas, 257

Arminian Magazine, 41

Arminianism, 120-121

Articles of Religion, for American Methodists, 171

Asbury, Francis, 268

Ascension Day, hymns for, 288

Asceticism, of Oxford Club, 65-66; Wesley's, 198-204, 217-218

Assembly of Divines, 126

Assurance, doctrine of, 135-138, 210; Augustine on, 155; Böhler on, 155-156; "full assurance of faith," 182-183, 192-193; Jeremy Taylor on, 67; those without, 210, 246; Wesley on, 148-149, 156-158; Westminster Confession on, 155

Atonement, 148-149, 159, 190

Atterbury, Francis, bishop, 42

Augustine, 103, 126, 155, 217

Austin, John, 227

Authority in religion, 130-143, 319

Babbitt, Irving, 294

Ball, Hannah, 288

Baptism, *Apostolic Constitutions* on, 38; Dissenters', 242; Jer. Taylor on, 66-67; trine immersion, 238; Wesley on, 61, 248, 250; Samuel Wesley on, 241-242

Baptismal regeneration, Wesley's early views on, 241; later views on, 249-250; Samuel Wesley on, 241-242

Barth, Karl, 312

343

Index

Fall of man, 121; and bodily perfection, 186; effect on brutes, 119

Familists, 36

Fasting, 201, 220, 221, 222-223, 229, 230, 238, 316

Fathers, Ante-Nicene, 132-133, 139; as authorities, 131-133, 143, 298; primitive, 39, 64, 132

Feeling, *see* Emotion

Fenelon, archbishop of Cambrai, 145

Festivals, hymns on the Great, 288

Fielding, Henry, 280

Fletcher, John, 169-170

Fleury, Claude, 64

Flew, R. Newton, 185

Francis of Assisi, 105, 208

Francke, A. H., 80

Freedom, 122-123

French Prophets, 36, 37

French Revolution, 6, 7

General Rules of the United Societies, 229

Georgia, 69-72

German hymns, 82

Ghosts, 37-38, 47-48, 112-113; *see* Old Jeffrey

Gibson, Edmund, bishop, 242

God, doctrine of, 114-118, 307, 311, 313-314

Good works, 68-69, 218-219, 316; *see also* Salvation

Goodloe, Robert W., 191-192

Grace, Anglican doctrine of, 126-127; catholic conception of, 126-127; conveyed by sacraments, 250-251; empowering, 125; irresistible, 124, 127; preventing, 124-126; Protestant ethic of, 190; salvation by, 160-161; Wesley's religion of, 160-161, 313-314

Gradin, Arvid, 182, 183, 192

"Graveyard" poets, 282

Green, John Richard, 18

Grotius, 118

Guyon, Madame, 224

Hale, Lord Chief Justice, 226

Haliburton, James, 79-80, 85, 150

Hall, Joseph, bishop, 226

Hall, Wesley, 243

Hallam, Henry, 27, 30

Happiness, and religion, 63, 182

Hartley, David, 128-129

Hayward, Dr., 198

Heiler, Friedrich, 106

Hickes, George, 223, 227-228

High Church, party in Church of England, 27-32; patristic learning of, 133

High Churchmanship, 27-32, 237; John Wesley's, 12-13, 40-41, 79, 82, 133, 216-217, 236-243, 256; Samuel Wesley's, 40-43, 64

347

Index

Index